MAD MAX AND PHILOSOPHY

The Blackwell Philosophy and Pop Culture Series
Series editor: William Irwin

A spoonful of sugar helps the medicine go down, and a healthy helping of popular culture clears the cobwebs from Kant. Philosophy has had a public relations problem for a few centuries now. This series aims to change that, showing that philosophy is relevant to your life—and not just for answering the big questions like "To be or not to be?" but for answering the little questions: "To watch or not to watch *South Park*?" Thinking deeply about TV, movies, and music doesn't make you a "complete idiot." In fact, it might make you a philosopher, someone who believes the unexamined life is not worth living and the unexamined cartoon is not worth watching.

For the full list of titles in the series, see www.andphilosophy.com.

MAD MAX AND PHILOSOPHY THINKING THROUGH THE WASTELAND

Edited by

Matthew P. Meyer and David Koepsell

WILEY Blackwell

Published by John Wiley & Sons, Inc., Hoboken, New Jersey.
Published simultaneously in Canada.

For general information on our other products and services or for technical support, please contact our Customer Care Department within the United States at (800) 762-2974, outside the United States at (317) 572-3993 or fax (317) 572-4002.

Wiley also publishes its books in a variety of electronic formats. Some content that appears in print may not be available in electronic formats. For more information about Wiley products, visit our web site at www.wiley.com.

Library of Congress Cataloging-in-Publication Data

Names: Meyer, Matthew P., editor. | Koepsell, David R. (David Richard), editor.
Title: Mad Max and philosophy : thinking through the Wasteland / edited by Matthew P. Meyer, David Koepsell.
Description: First edition. | Hoboken : Wiley, 2024. | Series: The Blackwell philosophy and pop culture series | Includes index.
Identifiers: LCCN 2023021906 (print) | LCCN 2023021907 (ebook) | ISBN 9781119870487 (hardback) | ISBN 9781119870494 (adobe pdf) | ISBN 9781119870500 (epub)
Subjects: LCSH: Mad Max (Motion picture : 1979) | Motion pictures–Philosophy. | Popular culture–Philosophy.
Classification: LCC PN1997.M2534 M33 2023 (print) | LCC PN1997.M2534 (ebook) | DDC 791.43/72–dc23/eng/20230523
LC record available at https://lccn.loc.gov/2023021906
LC ebook record available at https://lccn.loc.gov/2023021907

Cover images: © James O'Neil/Getty Images; © chaluk/Getty Images
Cover design: Wiley

Set in 10.5/13pt SabonLTStd by Straive, Pondicherry, India
SKY10069892_031824

Contents

Notes on Contributors

Lance Belluomini did his graduate work in philosophy at the University of California, Berkeley; San Francisco State University; and the University of Nebraska-Lincoln. He's recently published essays on *Tenet* and *The Mandalorian* in *The Palgrave Handbook of Popular Culture as Philosophy*. He's also contributed chapters to a variety of Wiley-Blackwell volumes such as *Inception*, *The Ultimate Star Wars*, *Indiana Jones*, and *Star Wars and Philosophy Strikes Back*. Clearly, the film *Mad Max: Fury Road* has had an influence on Lance. For instance, when rushing to get somewhere, he exclaims, "Fang it!" When unimpressed, he shouts, "Mediocre!"

Kiki Berk is an associate professor of philosophy at Southern New Hampshire University. She received her Ph.D. in philosophy from the VU University Amsterdam in 2010. Her research focuses on the philosophy of death and the philosophy of the meaning in life, especially in the works of Simone de Beauvoir and Jean-Paul Sartre. In her free time, she wanders the Wasteland in search of her better self.

Daniel Conway is a professor of philosophy and humanities, an affiliate professor of film studies and religious studies, and a courtesy professor in the School of Law and the Bush School of Government and Public Service at Texas A&M University. He has lectured and published widely on topics in post-Kantian European philosophy, political theory, aesthetics (especially literature and film), American philosophy, and genocide studies. He hopes that he is awaited, shiny and chrome, in Valhalla.

Laura T. Di Summa is an assistant professor of philosophy at William Paterson University. She has published extensively on film, visual arts, and criticism. She is the co-editor with Noël Carroll and Shawn Loht of *The Palgrave Handbook for the Philosophy of Film and Motion Pictures* and the author of *A Philosophy of Fashion Through Film*. After modeling her biking style on *Mad Max* and further refining it while pushing her son's stroller, she is now considering investing in a War Rig.

Ian J. Drake teaches in the Political Science and Law Department at Montclair State University. He obtained his Ph.D. in American history from the University of Maryland and his law degree from the University of Richmond. His teaching interests include the American judiciary and legal system; the U.S. Supreme Court and constitutional history; the history and contemporary study of law and society, broadly construed; and political theory.

David H. Gordon is an assistant teaching professor of philosophy at Loyola University Maryland in Baltimore, where he specializes in the history of philosophy, environmental philosophy, and the interdisciplinary study of science and religion. He has toiled long and hard in Socratic poverty, working as a mechanic and carpenter, as well as on fishing boats in Alaska. He can also turn a mean baseball bat on his lathe. When he's not asking why there is something rather than nothing, he wonders why Johnny the Boy didn't just throw the hacksaw at the cigarette lighter.

Jacob M. Held is a burnt out, desolate man. He wanders the Wasteland of academia, this blighted place, learning to live again. In the meantime, he is a professor of philosophy and assistant provost for academic assessment and general education at the University of Central Arkansas. He specializes in political and legal philosophy and nineteenth-century German philosophy, and he dabbles in medieval philosophy and the philosophy of religion. He has written many essays at the intersection of philosophy and popular culture and edited several volumes, including *Wonder Woman and Philosophy* (Wiley Blackwell, 2017), *Stephen King and Philosophy* (Rowman and Littlefield, 2016), and *Dr. Seuss and Philosophy* (Rowman and Littlefield, 2011).

Thanayi Jackson is an American historian. Born and raised in San José, California, she spent most of her days trying to escape capitalism as a disciple of Rock before a Griot banished her to History where, after a great odyssey through the University of Maryland, she assumed the identity of semi-mild-mannered professor. Jackson is a contributing author to *Black Panther and Philosophy* and has held positions at San José State University, Berea College, and, currently, Cal Poly San Luis Obispo. A fangirl of the Reconstruction period, her work examines transitions from slavery to freedom and all things Black Power. Jackson is a lifelong student of punx, drunx, freaks, geeks, revolutionary jocks and hippies, hip hop intellectuals, and heavy metal queens. As a result, she abides by a punk rock pedagogy whereby anything can be learned, everything can be deconstructed, and nothing can be lost.

Clint Jones earned his Ph.D. in social and political philosophy from the University of Kentucky and currently teaches full-time at Capital University in Ohio. In addition to numerous contributions to pop culture and philosophy titles, he has published articles and book chapters on utopianism, environmental philosophy, and critical theory. His recent published books include *Apocalyptic Ecology in the Graphic Novel* (McFarland); *Stranger, Creature, Thing, Other* (Cornerstone Press); and a forthcoming edited volume, *Contemporary Cowboys: Reimagining an American Archetype in Popular Culture* from Lexington Books. Though it is a mistake to hope, Clint nevertheless hopes his work will help you enjoy your *Mad Max* experience more fully—but he's just a doctor, not a fortuneteller.

Justin Kitchen teaches philosophy at San Francisco State University and California State University, Northridge. His work centers around virtue ethics and virtue epistemology; it draws often from Stoic philosophy and Indian Buddhism. As a fallback career, he has also been considering joining a zealous adrenaline-fueled war party in search of guzzolene.

David Koepsell has been teaching philosophy for 28 years at such places as the University at Buffalo, the Technical University of Delft, and now Texas A&M. He has authored and edited a dozen books and over 50 journal articles, chapters, and reports and has lectured around the world. Long a fan, he has used pop culture in his courses and research for as long as he has been teaching. Recently, he started the CinePhils podcast with fellow philosopher Rob Luzecky, which is about films and philosophy. He thinks his life would be complete if only he had the last of the V8 Interceptors, with Phase 4 heads, 600 horsepower through the wheels!

Karen Joan Kohoutek is an independent scholar who has published about weird fiction and cult films in various journals and literary websites, with recent works on *Black Panther* and Robert E. Howard and Doris Wishman's film oddity *Nude on the Moon*. She has also published a novella, *The Jack-o-Lantern Box*, and the reference book *Ici Repose: A Guide to St. Louis Cemetery No. 2, Square 3*, about the historic New Orleans cemetery, through Skull and Book Press. In her personal life, she is an Aunty and, at the same time, just a raggedy woman.

Leigh Kellmann Kolb is an associate professor of English at East Central College in Missouri. Her writing has appeared in publications including *Sons of Anarchy and Philosophy*, *Philosophy and Breaking Bad*, *Twin Peaks and Philosophy*, *Amy Schumer and Philosophy*, *The Handmaid's Tale and Philosophy*, *The Women of David Lynch: A Collection of Essays*, and *Better Living Through TV*. She's also written for *Vulture* and *Bitch Magazine* and serves as a screener and juror for film festivals. She shows *Mad Max: Fury Road* to her Composition II students at the end of each semester so they can take with them the pleasure of critically analyzing pop culture in hopes that they will help save—not kill—the world.

Andrew Kuzma is a bioethicist at Advocate Aurora Health Care in Milwaukee. He earned his Ph.D. at Marquette University. His research interests include moral distress, narrative ethics, the role of community in cultivating virtue, and Citadel-era conceptions of shiny and chrome. With his feral child, Madeleine, and the Imperator Lisa, he wanders the Wasteland as a man reduced to a single instinct: write.

Greg Littmann roared down the scorching asphalt in his battered white Toyota, with Wasteland bandits in close pursuit. He was tortured by the memories of the world that had been and was gone forever, a world in which he had been an associate professor of philosophy at SIUE. Once he had published on evolutionary epistemology, the philosophy of logic, and the philosophy of professional philosophy, among other subjects. He also had written numerous chapters for books relating philosophy to popular culture for the general public, including volumes on *Big Bang Theory*, *Black Mirror*, *Doctor Who*, *Game of Thrones*, *Star Trek*, and *Star Wars*. But now there was only the road, and the eternal hunt for food and fuel, and the human predators. He could see in the rear-view mirror that they were closing in, howling. The 18-wheeler loomed out of the red dust dead ahead, coming right at him. It was covered in metal spikes and leather-clad warriors. Screaming, Greg instinctively threw up his arms to protect his face. The ancient Greek philosopher Socrates believed that the only genuine harm that can befall a person is for them to become morally worse. If that's true, Greg was just fine.

Matthew P. Meyer is an associate professor of philosophy at the University of Wisconsin, Eau Claire. His main areas of study are existentialism, phenomenology, and psychoanalysis. He has written a study entitled *Archery and the Human Condition in Lacan, the Greeks, and Nietzsche: The Bow with the Greatest Tension* (Lexington, 2019) and has published articles and chapters on Nietzsche and film. He has also published in several Blackwell *Philosophy and Pop Culture* series books, on Sartre (and *The Office*), Nietzsche (and *House of Cards*), aesthetics (and *Westworld*), and Beauvoir (and *The Good Place*). Like Max, he's afraid he's beginning to enjoy that rat circus out there.

Edwardo Pérez, after being a pianist accompanying Ton Ton's saxophone, escaped Bartertown, seeking refuge with The Tribe Who Left. Years later, Edwardo found himself teaching rhetoric and critical theory as a professor of English at Tarrant County College in Hurst, Texas—where Edwardo also writes speculative fiction and contributes awesome chapters on popular culture and philosophy. Inspired by Savannah Nix, Edwardo continues to search for knowledge of the pre-apocalyptic world, when "those what had gone before had the knowing and the doing of things beyond our reckoning … even beyond our dreaming."

Jacob Quick is a lecturer and Ph.D. candidate in the Institute of Philosophy at KU Leuven. His doctoral research focuses on Simone Weil, Jacques Derrida, and animal ethics. When he's not reading, writing, or teaching philosophy, you can find him McFeasting in the halls of Valhalla.

Aeon J. Skoble is the Bruce and Patricia Bartlett Chair in Free Speech and Expression at Bridgewater State University, where he is also a professor of philosophy and co-coordinator of the program in philosophy, politics, and economics. He is the author of *Deleting the State: An Argument About Government* (Open Court, 2008) and

The Essential Robert Nozick (Fraser Institute, 2020); the editor of *Reading Rasmussen and Den Uyl: Critical Essays on Norms of Liberty* (Lexington Books, 2008); and co-editor of *Political Philosophy: Essential Selections* (Prentice-Hall, 1999) and *Reality, Reason, and Rights* (Lexington Books, 2011). In addition, he writes widely on the intersection of philosophy and popular culture, having co-editing *The Simpsons and Philosophy* (Open Court, 2000), *Woody Allen and Philosophy* (Open Court, 2004), *The Philosophy of TV Noir* (University Press of Kentucky, 2008), and *The Philosophy of Michael Mann* (University Press of Kentucky, 2014), and he has been a contributor to 14 other books on film and television. He would like to thank Lord Humungus for Helpful contributions to this essay.

Anthony Petros Spanakos is a professor of political science and law at Montclair State University. He is the co-editor of the *Conceptualising Comparative Politics* book series (Routledge) and has written extensively on Latin American politics, foreign policy, and popular culture and political theory. He was recently in a very changed Australia where quarantine rules suggested new possible directions for future *Mad Max* movies!

Joshua L. Tepley is a Professor of Philosophy at Saint Anselm College in Manchester, New Hampshire. He has a B.A. in Philosophy from Bucknell University and a Ph.D. in Philosophy from the University of Notre Dame. His current research interests include free will, personal identity, ontology (the study of being), and the intersection between philosophy and science fiction. He really hopes that he never needs, or becomes, a Bloodbag.

Paul Thomas is a project associate in the Inequality and Human Development Programme at the National Institute of Advanced Studies, India. He loves dissecting movies to bring out philosophical understandings from them. Being a first-time contributor to Wiley's *Philosophy and Pop Culture* series, he thoroughly enjoyed writing the essay just like how Max finds happiness in dealing with his unexpected encounters in the Wasteland.

Introduction: Doing Philosophy in the Wasteland

The *Mad Max* movies put the audience on the edge: on the edge of apocalypse, on the edge of social breakdown, on the edge of morality, on the edge of our seats. Throughout the franchise, we see Max, and many other characters, lose ties to what could be considered a "normal" life. All of this begins "just a few years from now." But despite Max's insistence that he has been reduced to the instinct to survive, deep down he is still attracted to "righteous causes."

As Max himself says in the opening dialogue of *Fury Road*: "I am the one who runs from the living and the dead." In some ways Max's journeys across the Wasteland are like doing philosophy: frustrating, difficult, often painful, but eventually enlightening. Both "hunted" and "haunted," Max is driven to extreme situations in which he wishes he didn't have a choice—in every movie he essentially evades the role of savior before assuming it. Maybe the haunting is a good sign in any case. It means Max still has a conscience—or most of one. Thus, Max as quasi-hero invites us to think about what we would do in this post-apocalyptic world of "fire and blood." What politics could we build? What ethics could we salvage for parts? The external conditions are abysmal. What about the internal ones?

Max's story echoes heroes and anti-heroes across the ages, recapitulating the paths taken by great adventurers as well as thinkers. An innocent, lawful inception, the loss of love and family, the search for meaning in a world gone mad, and the discovery of embers of humanity in the desert. The Wasteland is not just a place, as T. S. Eliot's poem of the same name makes clear, it exists among us and within us. It is a place ripe for self-discovery and for musing about the nature of humanity, for finding our essence, for discovering our souls.

Max's setting also invites us to think about what living would be like with all the comforts of modern western life stripped away.

In that way, many themes in the films provide useful contrasts to our own lives and lifestyles. In the essays that follow, we will see the stripped-down world of Max analyzed according to its politics, heroics, ethics, aesthetics, and more. We will see conventional views of these ideas tested—and we will consider whether these new ways of thinking apply to our own world.

As stark and dire as the world of Mad Max is, George Miller always strikes a chord of hope, which is how we close this project, in the hopes it enriches your enjoyment of the films, as well as of philosophy. We hope that you enjoy reading the book and that you too find the Wasteland an apt place for philosophizing.

Acknowledgments

While Max appears "alone" in the beginnings of the films, we realize pretty quickly that, for better or worse, he is not. Neither were we alone in the creation of this volume. First, we want to thank all of our contributing authors for their excellent ideas, fabulous writing full of wonderful insights, and patience in assembling this volume. Like Max's journeys, the creation of this volume led to new places we didn't expect. We'd like to thank Bill Irwin, the *Blackwell Philosophy and Pop Culture Series* editor, for his encouragement to put forward the volume, his advice and guidance, and for generally shepherding us through every step of the Wasteland. We'd also like to thank Will Croft and Charlie Hamlyn and the whole publishing team at Wiley Blackwell for turning this mad idea into a reality.

Matt would like to thank David for agreeing to co-edit and assemble this book together. Oddly, we both had the idea to assemble this volume for the first time almost immediately after seeing *Fury Road*, but it was only upon realizing that was not the last installment that we, along with Bill, realized that it would be a valuable contribution to the *Philosophy and Pop Culture Series*. Many thanks to David for his amazing ideas for essays and for his invaluable editing work throughout the assembly of the volume. Matt would also like to thank his family, Jill and Charlie, for putting up with moments of editing "insanity."

David would like to thank his family: Vanessa and the kids, Ame and Alex, as always, for putting up with his madness and his obsessions, including with popular culture and philosophy, as well as his parents who introduced him to film and film criticism at an early age. He is indebted to Matt for helping to marshal the resources and channel his procrastination into a final work of which we can all be proud.

Part I

POLITICS AFTER THE POX-ECLIPSE: ANARCHY, STATE, AND DYSTOPIA

Post-apocalyptic Anarchism in *Mad Max*

Aeon J. Skoble

In George Miller's 1979 film *Mad Max*, we are introduced to a post-apocalyptic dystopia in which official law enforcement is weak and predatory gangs are powerful. In three sequels, the breakdown of traditional social order is made even more explicit, and the protagonist's struggle, first for revenge and then later for justice, more difficult. Is this "anarchy"? Does anarchy entail violence, or is peaceful anarchism possible? What are the results of social breakdown? Is this portrayal of a lawless world realistic? This essay will explore the meanings of concepts such as *anarchy*, *government*, *society*, and *order* by looking at the social backdrop of this film franchise.

Anarchy and Apocalypse

Of course, a world of marauding biker gangs and violent warlords is exactly what people tend to imagine when they think of anarchy. Anarchy is associated with chaos and disorder, whereas words like *society* and *government* are associated with order. But just as the presence of a government is no guarantee of a functional and just social order, the absence of government shouldn't be taken to imply their lack.

To begin with, it's worth noting that the word *anarchy* doesn't even mean "no government" or "no order." It means "no rulers." The root word *archon*, for "ruler," is the same as in the word *monarchy*. So, modified by the *mono-* prefix, it means "one ruler" and modified by

Mad Max and Philosophy: Thinking Through the Wasteland, First Edition.
Edited by Matthew P. Meyer and David Koepsell.
© 2024 John Wiley & Sons, Inc. Published 2024 by John Wiley & Sons, Inc.

the negating *a-/an-* prefix, it means "no rulers." To equate "no rulers" with "no government" or "no order" is to beg an important question about the nature of social order and the extent to which it can be achieved without coercive authority imposed from the top down. The world Mad Max lives in offers us some useful touchpoints for thinking about this, but also, as we'll see, some less-than-useful ones.

We're never told explicitly what apocalyptic events happened, but context clues and scattered bits of dialogue imply wars for scarce resources, which of course are now more scarce. It's never explained why this would lead to the complete collapse of the social order. In the first film, it hasn't completely vanished. Max Rockatansky (played by Mel Gibson in the first three films and Tom Hardy in the fourth) is a police officer, of course, so there's some organized law enforcement apparatus. But, as the film depicts, their authority is often flouted and the biker gang that drives the plot seems to act with impunity, terrorizing people at will. So the police department seems like a vestigial force, greatly attenuated but still trying to protect innocents from the gangs. The vestiges of the court system that we see in the film are similarly attenuated and essentially toothless. Part of the problem seems to be that the structures in place for rights-protection are so remote and vestigial as to be insufficient for deterring the biker gangs and other outlaws. In this respect, *Mad Max* resembles a "Western" film where, even though there's technically a legal authority, it is either physically remote or else too weak to adequately respond to criminality. For example, in the 1993 Western *Tombstone,* there's a sheriff and a marshal, but the criminal gang "the Cowboys" acts with impunity, as if they need not worry themselves about law enforcement. Similarly, the "Nightrider" gang can roam freely and act as predators. What little police enforcement still exists can't pose a significant threat to them. Once Max becomes a vigilante, he *is* able to dispatch the gang, as his willingness to match their level of savagery permits strategies that might previously have been unavailable. With his family having been murdered and his revenge taken, Max himself is no longer part of the vestigial law enforcement apparatus, taking to the road as a loner.

Roaming the Wasteland

In the sequel films, we see Max on his aimless roaming, and his encounters with other pockets of people show an even further detachment from the old civilization he left behind. In the first film, there are towns and cities, people are still conducting commerce, and while there seem to be fewer people around, the ones who are there seem relatively healthy. Times are tough but recognizable. In each sequel film, this is less and less the case. Max is roaming not on the outskirts of a city, but through a literal Wasteland, and the few concentrations of people are exclusively either straggling bands of survivors or predatory gangs. There's evidence of environmental spoilage, but it's possible to grow food in some places, and while gasoline is scarce, there's obviously still enough to power all the cars, trucks, and motorcycles everyone uses. So it never becomes any more clear what exactly is the extent of the "apocalypse" or *why* it led to a breakdown of the social order. The explanation we might extract from Westerns, that in a frontier setting, authority structures are so removed as to be inefficacious, doesn't seem like it would explain what we see in these films.[1] In 1981's *The Road Warrior*, a small refinery has been converted to a tiny walled settlement and is besieged by a violent gang led by the mutant Humungus (Kjell Nilsson). The residents of the settlement hope to escape "to the coast" but we have no indication of whether that would be more hospitable—after all, the setting of the original film is near the coast. In 1985's *Mad Max Beyond Thunderdome*, Max encounters a town of sorts, governed by the despotic Aunty Entity (Tina Turner), but its governance is capricious and in some ways medieval, a regression from the Australia Max would have grown up in. He also encounters a colony of orphaned children, whom he helps find a way to Sydney, which we learn has been destroyed. In 2015's *Mad Max: Fury Road*, Max encounters a community ruled by mutant warlord Immortan Joe (Hugh Keays-Byrne). Neighboring "communities" are also ruled by warlords.

It's never explained how any of these situations might have emerged. As far as post-apocalyptic action films are concerned, that's not necessarily a bad thing. Cinematically, it can be sufficient that the protagonist find themselves in an outlandish and barbarous world because the drama derives from the protagonist's reactions to the situation. We don't need to know the origins of the founding of Bartertown, for instance; we just need to see how it operates and what dilemmas and challenges it poses for Max. However, what is acceptable or even advantageous to leave out of a movie is not acceptable for drawing philosophical conclusions. If I made a movie about a peaceful and prosperous society with a wise and benevolent monarch King Bob, it might be an excellent movie, but it would be a mistake to infer from it that "monarchy must be a desirable political system, because look

how great King Bob is." Similarly, one can be a fan of the *Mad Max*
series without concluding that "anarchism must be bad because it
would be terrible if we had violent mutant warlords." While the question of how Immortan Joe's Citadel came to be is unimportant cinematically, it's worth thinking about how realistic it is *if* we're trying to
think about political philosophy.

Not All Government Is Good Government

One reason not to take these scenarios as examples of anarchism is
that they seem less like examples of "no rulers" than they are examples of "bad rulers." Immortan Joe and Aunty Entity are in fact rulers.
They have power over their territories and the people in them. The
people they rule acquiesce to (even if not always enthusiastically
endorse) this control. That makes them rulers. Noting that they're not
the sorts of rulers we would expect to see in liberal democracies
doesn't make them not rulers. While it seems true that the Australia
Mad Max is roaming around in no longer has central, continent-wide
governance, it's also true that small, localized pockets of governance
have emerged, such as Bartertown and the Citadel and Bullet Farm.
That's importantly *not* the same thing as anarchism. To define *anarchism* as "the lack of the kind of government I like and am familiar
with" won't do. We can disapprove of Immortan Joe's rule while noting that he is in fact the ruler of the Citadel. That's not any different
from disapproving of Hitler while noting that he was in fact the ruler
of Nazi Germany.

Anarchism and Voluntarism

What would it actually look like to have no rulers? It would have to
mean that organized systems of production and trade would be voluntary. People can work together for their mutual benefit and common interest. They can even adopt rules for adjudicating disputes and
establishing boundaries for both conduct and physical space allocation. None of these features of social living *require* their imposition by
coercive authority, though of course that's the manner in which
we're most familiar with them. The seventeenth-century philosopher
Thomas Hobbes argued, however, that we wouldn't be able to sustain
such a system of voluntary cooperative order because each person is

a potential predator, and our fear and distrust leads us to regard each other as enemies, rendering social cooperation impossible.[2] This was why he argued for absolute monarchy as a "solution" to this problem, and this has been the underlying justification for coercive authority—if sometimes only tacitly—ever since.[3] On Hobbes's view, it makes perfect sense that Lord Humungus would attract and lead vicious predatory thugs to live by raiding others. Everyone in the gang is in sufficient fear of the Humungus's power as to motivate them to cooperate with gang activity and focus on common goals. That's exactly how Hobbes understood the sovereign: if everyone is in sufficient fear of the sovereign's power, only then can they be trusted to refrain from predatory behavior toward one another. For Hobbes, then, anarchism is bad not because we might get rulers like Immortan Joe, but because having no rulers at all is *worse* than having rulers like Immortan Joe.

There's not really good evidence for this, it turns out. The history of rulers offers far more examples of tyranny and enslavement than it does of egalitarian democracy. In contrast, there's abundant evidence of organically emerging orders based on mutual gain and benefit. It's just that we don't tend to classify those as "governance." We tend to conflate "governance" with "ruling," since the most obvious examples (good and bad) of the former come from the latter. But they're conceptually distinct. The evolution of international merchant law in the Middle Ages and the evolution of the common law in English villages are but two of the many examples of social order that arises from and is based on mutual benefit. This sort of "governance" is created by people's voluntary compliance.[4] Voluntary and mutually beneficial social orders are, contrary to Hobbes's assertion, more stable than oppressive orders, which invite both rebellion and invasion precisely because people are less likely to acquiesce to such orders when alternatives are available. That's not to say a tyrant may not have an iron grip on power for some particular timespan. Immortan Joe seems to be pretty secure in his reign, though of course it's a rebellion by some of his subjects that precipitates the plot of the movie, and when Imperator Furiosa (Charlize Theron) returns triumphant, the folks in the Citadel are perfectly happy to have her be in charge of the water. On the other hand, there's no cause for rebellion against an institution that provides mutual benefit.

The classic contrast between the worldview of Hobbes and that of seventeenth-century philosopher John Locke is based on (among other things) the idea that people can recognize the mutually advantageous nature of treating others as equals and cooperating with them for shared goals, though even for Locke, there is a reason for having *some* kind of ruler.[5] If we didn't have one, he argued, we might find it "inconvenient" to not have things like an impartial forum for dispute resolution. So—by consent—we authorize rulers who can provide things like this. This is far closer to an ideal of voluntary social order than what we see in Hobbes, and includes a right of rebellion against abusive sovereigns.

We can also see historical evidence of institutions for impartial dispute resolution that are *not* based on a ruler's prerogative, but rather emerge from people's voluntary agreement.[6] Consider firms like the American Arbitration Association. Parties in conflict agree to have their dispute settled by this firm rather than go to court. How would a firm such as this thrive? If it were known to be biased, people wouldn't agree to go there. But if they have a reputation for fair processes, people will be attracted to them. Impartial dispute resolution is one of the things Locke argues would be lacking in anarchism, thus necessitating some kind of sovereign power. But note that courts run by the sovereign need not be unbiased. For one thing, they're likely to be biased in the sovereign's favor, but beyond that, we have ample evidence of state-run courts being tainted with racism, or gender or class bias. A private arbitration firm with a reputation like that would not stay in business long. Also, the procedures can be unfair in other ways than overt bias. The titular Thunderdome of the third film isn't "biased" in the ways we normally think of bias, but at the same time, trial by combat doesn't seem like a particularly *fair* dispute resolution procedure. The American Arbitration Association, on the other hand, like similar firms, offers a much more reasonable mediation system. This is an example from the twentieth century, but similar institutions can be found as far back as the Middle Ages.

Is This Anarchy?

When people think of *Mad Max*–type scenarios as "why anarchism would be bad," it seems to be a matter of conflating "government" and "good government." The liberal democracy of Australia had effective policing, equality among citizens, a prosperous economy, rights protection, and courts of law. So if all of that gets replaced by War Boy raids rather than commerce, biker gangs who don't fear the police, and "two men enter, one man leaves" dispute resolution, we can all agree that *that's* bad. But it's unclear why we should think that's what anarchism is.[7] Anarchism isn't what you have when *this particular government* goes away; it's what you have when the *idea of rulers* goes away. In post-apocalyptic Australia, a reasonably decent government has degenerated into the worst-case scenario of bad government: small pockets of tyrannical warlords who wield power for the sake of their own advantage, without regard for any conception of equality or rights or consent. While we're not shown this explicitly, one can see how gangs like the Nightrider's from the first film could evolve into something like the army of the Humungus or the War Boys of the Citadel. That's the social evolution of a *political* arrangement: a very primitive one, to be sure, based on power and fear rather than a conception of the common good, but a political one nonetheless. That's in contrast with, not an example of, voluntary communities of consent-based social order. People think that the world of Mad Max is one of anarchy because the social order has broken down, but the lack of social order isn't what produces anarchy; it's what produces tyrannical warlords. The inefficacy of the police in the first film seems like it's the reason for predatory gangs, but of course the real world has many examples of predatory gangs. And the thinning of the police department shouldn't entail "now the Nightrider gang can take over"—there'd be nothing stopping anyone else from challenging that gang's authority. In the movie, that only describes a handful of individuals, though in later films we see it's gang versus gang. That's how we get the political evolution of the Citadel, the Bullet Farm, and Gas Town.

It Doesn't Have to Be Humungus

Taking Locke's conception of "inconveniences" as a model, anarchism would be undesirable if it meant we had no way of protecting ourselves from predators or adjudicating disputes. But interestingly, two things are observable empirically. First, even when we have a sovereign power, we are still liable to be preyed upon, sometimes because the ruler's protection is remote and inefficient (as in the 1979 film) and other times because the ruling power is itself predatory (as in the 2015 film); and we likewise can fail to have fair and unbiased dispute resolution (as in the 1985 film, or, say, more realistic situations such as depicted in *To Kill a Mockingbird*[8]). Second, mechanisms for protecting ourselves against predators, and institutions of reasonable dispute resolution, can arise and have arisen outside of political authorities, as people voluntarily cooperate for mutual advantage. So the post-apocalyptic world of Mad Max is not really an instructive example of "why anarchism would be bad" after all, despite it making for exciting and interesting filmmaking.

Notes

1 For an analysis of social order in Westerns and in perhaps surprisingly similar Samurai films, see my "Order Without Law: The Magnificent Seven, East and West," in McMahon and Csaki eds., *The Philosophy of the Western* (Lexington: University Press of Kentucky, 2010).

2 See Thomas Hobbes, *Leviathan* (London: Penguin 1951 [1651]).

3 For an analysis of this, see my *Deleting the State: An Argument About Government* (New York: Open Court, 2008). See also Michael Huemer, *The Problem of Political Authority* (Chicago: Palgrave Macmillan, 2013).

4 Classic sources for analyzing these phenomena include Harold Berman, *Law and Revolution* (Cambridge, MA: Harvard University Press, 1983), and Friedrich Hayek, *Law, Legislation, and Liberty* (Chicago: University of Chicago Press, 1973). More recently, see Gary Chartier, *Anarchy and Legal Order* (Cambridge: Cambridge University Press, 2013), and Edward Stringham, ed., *Anarchy and the Law* (Oakland, CA: Independent Institute, 2007).

5 See John Locke, *Two Treatises of Government* (Cambridge: Cambridge University Press, 1967 [1690]).

6 See Robert Axelrod, *The Evolution of Cooperation* (New York: Basic Books, 1984).

7 Sources as varied as *Christianity Today* (https://www.christianitytoday.com/ct/2015/may-web-only/mad-max-fury-road.html) and *Jacobin Magazine* (https://www.jacobinmag.com/2021/02/mad-max-capitalism) make this inference. The columnist for *Inquisitr* makes explicit these common assumptions(https://www.inquisitr.com/2382225/five-ways-mad-max-movie-franchise-destroys-anarchy-bliss/).

8 The 1960 novel by Harper Lee and the 1962 film by Robert Mulligan, in which an all-white jury in the Jim Crow South convicts a black man, despite compelling evidence that he could not have committed the crime, due to racial bias.

2

Even on the Road, Violence Is Not the Same as Power

Anthony Petros Spanakos and Ian J. Drake

The *Mad Max* movies depict a dystopian world in which people hope and struggle to live until, and perhaps past, tomorrow. There are roads and encampments, but few provide more than temporary, uncertain havens, and even the more developed towns like Bartertown are marked by insecurity and instability. Lives are "solitary, poor, nasty, brutish, and short"[1] because of the constant threat of arbitrary acts of violence, often committed in enclaves ruled by warlords or on the open road. In most contexts, there is no disinterested third party to adjudicate between the competing claims of, say, a biker and a road warrior, and so daily life is an unending state of "warre ... of every man against every man."[2] As the quotes suggest, the situation appears inspired by the works of the great British philosopher Thomas Hobbes (1588–1679) who argued that outside of an organized state, there are no morals, no possibility of justice or injustice. Rather, the state of nature leads to a struggle unto war in which, driven by needs and desires but bound by nothing, the person (or group) who can inflict the deadliest violence dominates. But that dominion can never be stable because even the greatest warrior sleeps and is thus vulnerable. Hobbes argued that the only way to escape this situation of perpetual danger was to recognize a sovereign to whom all consenting people ceded their natural liberty in exchange for security.

The *Mad Max* movies seem to depict such a world where people are in a vicious Hobbesian state of nature. But then why does the physically imposing Lord Humungus (*Road Warrior*) need the title "Lord" if his power comes from his violent capabilities? Why is there a Toadie

Mad Max and Philosophy: Thinking Through the Wasteland, First Edition.
Edited by Matthew P. Meyer and David Koepsell.
© 2024 John Wiley & Sons, Inc. Published 2024 by John Wiley & Sons, Inc.

to announce him? Why does Immortan Joe in *Fury Road* need rituals of releasing water and stories of Valhalla to motivate the War Boys when they go into battle and, eventually, turn kamakrazee? Niccolò Machiavelli (1469–1527) claimed that although fear was fundamental to stable and effective rule, it did not guarantee legitimacy.[3] Max Weber (1864–1920) famously distinguished power and authority, arguing that power involved force but authority assumed the legitimacy to make decisions and, if necessary, coerce others.[4] And contemporary philosopher Byung Chul Han (b. 1959) has argued that the use of violence is an effort to exercise power without mediation and is proof that the one lacks sufficient power to project his or her will on the other.[5] As we'll see, though *Mad Max* films seem Hobbesian, Han's understanding of power, obedience, and ritual turn out to be more fundamental.

"Only Those Mobile Enough to Scavenge, Brutal Enough to Pillage Survived"

The aesthetics of the *Mad Max* movies do not sanitize violence. The Road is open, there are no constraints, vehicles are all open to attack, and speed is fundamental for any type of security. There is little time to prepare for the next assault; security can only be considered temporary. There is no state, no order. The descent into such a state of nature is complete by the time of the second film, *The Road Warrior*. There is no police force in the desert. Instead, as the introductory narration makes clear, postnuclear war conditions have resulted in the abolition of civil society. "Men began to feed on men. On the roads, it was a white-line nightmare. Only those mobile enough to scavenge, brutal enough to pillage survived." This sounds like a reference to Hobbes's declaration that *homo homini lupus,* "man is a wolf to man."[6] As the narrator confirms, Max's nomadic life in the Wasteland results from the loss of legitimate governing authority and its supporting institutions. The idea of a protective state is a memory, or perhaps a myth, that is retained among the old and nostalgic. The threat of violence appears the sole claim that can be made upon another and, indeed, Max's freedom is secured by his ability to resist and deploy violence.

There is no place for shelter on the road or in the desert, and there is nothing to stop organized gangs from exercising violence on anyone who travels on a road that they control. The individuals who organize into communities to resist (in *Road Warrior*, for example) are more like victims than a proper community. Even more established polities like Bartertown in *Thunderdome* and the Citadel in *Fury Road* are dominated by savage violence. In the former, entertainment comes from watching gladiators battle, and in the latter people drug themselves, go kamakrazee, and then race toward death in a state of madness. There are, it seems, no constraints. The road on which Max and Furiosa's vehicles travel has no guardrails—a clear metaphor for a life that is constantly in danger.

Why "Lord" Humungus Has Epithets

Hobbes's infamous state of nature presents a frightening scenario in which rational but appetite-driven individuals realize that the absence of government causes insecurity so intense that they agree to transfer their freedom to a single, absolute sovereign who is capable of delivering security.[7] The Hobbesian account of the state of nature misses something critical, though: naked violence exists only when there are no constraints upon violence. The verb *nake*, which has fallen out of use (so much so that spell-check relentlessly places a red squiggly line below it) means to strip away. In order to think about a state of nature, we must try to imagine a time period before there was a political order which is, at least in part, maintained by a police force/militia/ professional military, judicial system, and so on. That is, to think of violence as naked requires stripping away the political system, the body that regulates violence legitimately.[8]

The *Mad Max* movies do not *begin* with a state of nature. Rather, Max Rockatansky is introduced as a police officer whose wife and child are murdered by a marauding biker gang. Prior to his family's murder, Max decides to leave the Main Force Patrol. He tenders his resignation to his commanding officer, Fifi, who tries to persuade Max to remain on the Force. Fifi tells Max he is "a winner" who is "on the top shelf." Fifi promises Max that, although people no longer "believe in heroes," Max and Fifi will "give 'em back their heroes." Max smiles wryly and claims he will no longer "go for that crap." When Fifi continues to beg Max to remain on the Force, Max protests that he is starting to enjoy "that rat circus out there" and believes that his "bronze badge" is the only thing the makes him "one of the good guys."

After his family's murder, Max leaves the Force to exact revenge on the murderers. The police force is the most basic institution of the state that maintains civic order. Yet, in Max's society the decay is so acute that the police cannot prevent the activities of the gangs, and only by leaving the force is Max able to attain some form of justice. As a representative of the crumbling "sovereign," the police force can no longer offer security. As a cop, Max knows this better than anyone else, and he responds personally in order to achieve the justice that the sovereign and its institutions cannot provide. After killing the men who murdered his family, Max becomes a wanderer in the Australian desert, voluntarily joining the Hobbesian state of nature into which civil society has descended.

The spectacular displays of brutality in the *Mad Max* films make it easy to forget there was once a political order, but that past has not been extinguished from memory and myth. More important, governance in *Mad Max* assumes categories and concepts of authority and ritual that demonstrate that rule is never sustained by violence alone. When there is a governing state, most people follow most rules— formal and informal—most of the time and do so without threat of violence as a motivating factor. When a police officer pulls over a car and orders the driver to produce proof of identity, the driver complies because the police officer is armed and can deploy deadly force. Compliance is usually the result of either fearing a ticket for disregarding the police officer's demands or simply following the law and doing what is right or, at least, expected. In either case, the driver complies because of the *authority* of the police officer. The police officers are authorized to enforce the law, including assigning tickets when the law is broken. They are authorized to do so by the state. So even though the police officer could ensure compliance by drawing a weapon and threatening the use of force, this is rarely necessary.[9] In contrast, consider the scenario in which late at night in a dark alley a private individual demands your wallet. Surely, violence motivates you to offer your wallet, but the mugger has no authority.

Max Weber draws an important distinction between power and authority.[10] According to his famous definition, a state is the organ that monopolizes the legitimate use of coercion in a given territory. *Power*, for Weber, assumes coercion, implied or explicit, while *authority* assumes legitimacy, that, in some way, people give the right to do X to some person or body. Hannah Arendt suggested something similar, though with different language. Seeking to rescue power from Machiavellian-style politics and return to a classical idea, Arendt insisted that power is the result of people, freely, acting in concert. Violence could compel action, but it could never have the positive, constructive, and ethical character of power.[11] As we'll see, Byung-Chul Han builds on both descriptions to offer a more complete reading of power.[12]

Lord Humungus's appearance (*Road Warrior*) gives a sense of *naked* violence. Other than a metal helmet and sparse leather, Humungus is indeed naked (he also has no body hair). Humungus stands out among his gang because of his size and power. In hand-to-hand combat, those certainly matter. But they cannot be enough, especially since much violence is exercised with weapons and while driving a vehicle. Humungus may have risen to rule over the others because he is the fiercest warrior, but, over time, might that not change? Perhaps the insane Wez might be more dangerous? Moreover, if Wez is insane, would he be obedient because Humungus is stronger? That assumes rationality. So there must be more to Humungus's power than threat of violence.

The Toadie announces Humungus as "Lord Humungus, the Warrior of the Wasteland, the Ayatollah of Rock and Rolla." These titles and epithets suggest that there is indeed something beyond physical power—however drawn from violent capabilities—that established and maintains Humungus's leadership. Why is Toadie's speech, or Toadie for that matter, necessary? Surely, Humungus and his gang, like the ancient Athenians, believe that "that the powerful exact what they can, and the weak accede to what they must."[13] Toadie's speech aims to intimidate and offer a chance for surrender, to reduce the relatively low risk of harm to Humungus's gang. But part of that intimidation derives from the titles that bear witness to the "lordship" of Humungus. He is the singular Warrior of the Wasteland, the Ayatollah (breath of God) of Rock and Rolla. While the timorous might not consider these titles representative of rightful rule (that is, political legitimacy), the titles suggest power that exceeds the realm of naked violence, that his dominion over the land is recognized by his gang and ought to be similarly recognized by others.

According to Han, power is most in evidence when it is not exercised. Power is the extension of the self into the other, when we are able to get you to do what we wish and have you believe that you are doing what *you* want to do in the first place. "Without the use of any violence, the holder of power takes his place in the *soul* of the other."[14] Under such conditions the person "follows" the holder of power "out of freedom."[15] Han argues that a terrifying power mediates itself through our consumption, desires, social media, and other forms, leading us to do what the power holder wants, voluntarily.[16] Power "turns into violence" when there is no mediation, as in a Hobbesian state of nature.[17] Han argues that "what makes power more effective is not coercion but the automatism of habit.... *Power shines in its own absence.*"[18] That is, if we habitualize the decisions *others* want us to make, power has succeeded in concealing itself. If Toadie can cow others through the titles Humungus bares, the latter's power is far greater than if compliance comes only after a display of violence.

Having a Toadie and Going Kamakrazee

According to Han, rituals, myths, habits, and language are essential for conditioning the subject of power to internalize the desires of the more powerful. For example, Japanese norms of honor, loyalty, patriotism, and traditions such as *seppuku* no doubt led many kamikazes to believe their suicide missions were voluntarily chosen. Rituals are important, according to Han, because of how they slow time and allow people to reflect on time itself.[19] Social media encourages us to experience time as a rush of indistinguishable moments, always fleeting, contributing to our anxiety. We perceive time as moving too quickly, but the issue, for Han, is one of mediation. "Time is lacking a rhythm that would provide order, and thus it falls out of step."[20] Rituals slow time; the names we give acts and the beliefs that undergird those acts contribute to a sense of order. Accepting an order produced by a power holder—internalizing its assumptions about duty, honor, and justice—delivers a stable form of obedience. Power is thus most effective when it is invisible. When order requires the regular, or increasingly intense, deployment of violence, order is less stable. The power over the person is weaker.

The road in the *Mad Max* films seems to be a place where violence rules instead of order. So time races with no purpose, and nothing can assign meaning. But there is more to the road, the encampments, and societies in *Mad Max* than this initial glance suggests.

We may also wonder why the gang needs a Toadie. If a gang succeeds from violence alone, it hardly needs a member who is not a fighter. If food, water, gasoline, and other desired goods are scarce, a gang should have as few people as necessary to ensure success in raiding. Unlike a city, it need not have a diversity of people performing specialized labor. A monarch or city will need a mouthpiece, bard, poet, or philosopher to compose songs of valor honoring previous leaders of a dynasty, reminding citizens that a good death is dying for the *patria,* and that justice is what conforms with the vision of the regime. That is, the sovereign needs such people not because they are useful in a pitched battle but because they can contribute to the internalization of the leader's will within the souls of citizens. The citizen who has committed epic tales to memory is likely to think his desire to die in battle for the *polis* is his own will, not that of the regime. Toadie's role and rhetoric, while appearing minor, is important in demonstrating an awareness of the need for legitimacy.

This can also be seen in *Fury Road* where Max escapes a deviant city and the road offers a better, though still dangerous, environment. The mythic construction of the leader has developed considerably from Humugus to Immortan Joe. The latter is also fierce and strong but, as is evident early in the film, his control over his people comes from mythic-symbolic acts. Immortan Joe releases water in massive abundance to the raptured delight of his people, who, living in an oppressive polity in a state of scarcity, see the act as providential. His warriors, the "half-lives," believe a myth that going to battle will bring them to Valhalla. Before going into a potentially deadly battle, they take some form of drug and go Kamakrazee. They literally give up their reasoning powers and offer themselves to die to serve the desired ends of Immortan Joe. As Han would explain, Immortan Joe's power over his followers is so significant that they do not think they are doing his bidding as much as they are having fun, exacting vengeance driven by their own sense of desire, and seeking immortality through war. Immortan Joe does not need to coerce them to do his bidding.

Lords and Immortans: Order and Power

Obedience may come from the threat of violence, but power is more stable when violence is not necessary, when the other internalizes the desires of the power holder. The *Mad Max* movies show that, even amid brutal violence, power is more effectively used when mediated by rituals, habits, myths, and titles that grant authority to the holder of power. This is a cautionary lesson that applies beyond the Thunderdome and in our world too.

Notes

1   Thomas Hobbes, *The English Works,* vol. III (Leviathan 1651), I, 13, 78, at http://files.libertyfund.org/files/585/Hobbes_0051-03_EBk_v6.0.pdf.

2   Ibid., I, 13, 185.

3   Niccolò Machiavelli, *The Prince: Cambridge Texts in the History of Political Thought,* ed. Quentin Skinner and Russel Price (New York: Oxford University Press, 1988).

4   Max Weber, *Economy and Society: An Outline of Interpretive Sociology*, ed. Guenther Roth and Claus Wittich, with multiple translators (Berkeley: University of California Press, 1978).

5   Byung-Chul Han, *What Is Power?* trans. Daniel Steuer (Medford, MA: Polity, 2019).

6   Thomas Hobbes, *De Cive* [1641], at http://public-library.uk/ebooks/27/57.pdf, accessed February 7, 2022. Curiously, the first appearance of the idea of a "werewolf," or a human taking on lupine characteristics, appears in Plato's *Republic*.

7   See A. P. Martinich, *Hobbes* (London: Routledge, 2005).

8   See Weber.

9   Of course, police officers do threaten the use of force in some situations. However, as a function of all police officer–civilian interactions, these situations are very rare.

10 See Weber.

11 Hannah Arendt, *The Promise of Politics* (New York: Schocken, 2007).

12 See Han, 2019.

13 Thucydides, *The History of the Peloponnesian War,* vol. 89, trans. Benjamin Jowett, at https://www.perseus.tufts.edu/hopper/text?doc=Perseus%3Atext%3A1999.04.0105%3Abook%3Dintroduction. Translation slightly modified.

14 Han, 2019, 3.

15 Ibid., 5.

16 Byung-Chul Han, *In the Swarm: Digital Prospects*, trans. Erik Butler (Cambridge: MIT Press, 2017).

17 Han, 2019, 5.

18 Ibid., 40.

19 Byung-Chul Han, *The Scent of Time*, trans. Daniel Steuer (Medford, MA: Polity, 2017). Also see Byung-Chul Han, *The Disappearance of Ritual*, trans. Daniel Steuer (Medford, MA: Polity, 2020).

20 Ibid., vi.

3

Thomas Hobbes and the State of Nature in the Wasteland

Greg Littmann

Their world crumbled. The cities exploded. A whirlwind of looting. A firestorm of fear. Men began to feed on men. On the roads it was a white-line nightmare. Only those mobile enough to scavenge, brutal enough to pillage, would survive. The gangs took over the highways ready to wage war for a tank of juice. And in this maelstrom of decay, ordinary men were battered and smashed.

—*Mad Max 2*

What will you do when civilization collapses all around you? Will you get in your car and drive away to make it on your own in the desert? Will you join up with a tribe of survivors working an old refinery, or with a gang of mobile marauders in cars and bikes, plundering the remains of the old world? Or will you just be a pulpy red stain on the tarmac?

Fortunately, the English philosopher Thomas Hobbes (1588–1679) left us guidelines on what to do if we find ourselves in a state of anarchy. Based on his extensive studies of history, he believed he knew how societies form out of chaos and how society ought to be structured. In his masterpiece *Leviathan* (1651), he lays out his blueprint for the state. Asking how Hobbes might advise the survivors of post-apocalyptic Australia isn't just an intellectual exercise. While we might not have to rebuild society from scratch like Max and the others do, Hobbes's instructions on the form that society should take apply just as much to us as to the mohawked cycle warriors of the near future.

Mad Max and Philosophy: Thinking Through the Wasteland, First Edition.
Edited by Matthew P. Meyer and David Koepsell.

"My Name Is Max. My World Is Fire and Blood" — Max, *Fury Road*

Hobbes thinks that the key to understanding human politics is understanding human motivations, and he believes that people only ever act out of self-interest. Hobbes wrote, "No man giveth but with intention of good to himself."[1] Because humans are purely selfish, we'll commit any act we can get away with if it benefits us. Without laws to keep humans in line, we live in violent anarchy, a "war of every man against every man."[2] Hobbes calls this the "State of Nature," since it was the state humans allegedly were in before they developed societies. He believes that where there are no laws, living completely selfishly is the reasonable way to live. He believed reason tells us to place our self-interest over every other consideration.

Hobbes claimed that conflict arises for three reasons. First, we fight for resources. If you have a tank full of gas while I'm running dry, I have every reason to crack you over the head with an old pipe and siphon your petrol. Hobbes would be unsurprised to see the tribes of the *Mad Max* saga fight over the desert's remaining treasures. In *Mad Max 2*, Lord Humungus's Marauders lay siege to the refinery town to take the precious guzzoline they control. In *Beyond Thunderdome*, Aunty Entity and Master Blaster go to war to control Bartertown's pig-shit electricity plant. In *Fury Road*, Immortan Joe holds power because he's taken control of the water supply; anyone who wants to drink or water their crops must do as he says.

Second, people fight to defend themselves from danger, even if it means striking preemptively against potential threats. If your insane auto-gang lives near to mine, I've got every reason to want to see you wiped out. In *Fury Road*, one of the surviving matriarchs of Furiosa's old tribe tells Max, "I've killed everyone I've ever met out here."

Finally, people fight just for the glory. Hobbes would be unsurprised to find that in Max's world, glory is one of the main motivations for violence. In *Mad Max*, Toecutter's gang beats up and rapes townies, forces other cars off the road, and drags people behind their bikes just to prove how bad-ass they are. When Nightrider kills a cop and takes his car for a joyride, he raves about himself over the police radio: "Are you listening, bronze? I am the Nightrider! I'm a fuel injected suicide machine! I am a rocker, I am a roller, I am an out-of-controller!" He even imagines that his gang is watching, crying, "Do you see me, Toecutter? Do you see me, man?" Max later dismisses him to Jesse as "just another glory rider." Toecutter hates police because they stop his gang from chasing glory through violence. He explains to Johnny the Boy, "The bronze: They keep you from being proud."

Even Max's cop mate Goose seems driven to fight Toecutter's gang because their actions stain his reputation. He's unfazed by their attacks on civilians, but when Johnny the Boy is released from custody, he goes berserk, having to be held back by Max and Chief Macaffee, as he shouts, "They're laughing at us! Can't you see they're laughing at us!"

Glory is so important to the bandit leader Humungus in *Mad Max 2* that he employs a lackey to tell everyone how great he is. As Humungus's gang gathers before the refinery town, the weasel-hatted crier shouts, "Greetings from Humungus! The Lord Humungus! The warrior of the Wasteland! The ayatollah of rock-and-rolla!" Humungus's top warrior, the red-mohawked Wez, is no less eager to use conflict as an opportunity to show off—popping wheelies, backflipping into battle, and pulling a crossbow bolt from his arm where Max can see him, just to show him how little he cares about pain and injury.

In *Mad Max 3*, when Max picks a fight with Master Blaster, Master agrees to a battle in Thunderdome between Blaster and Max, instead of using his brilliance to come up with a less dangerous plan. He presumably agrees because he loves it when the ringmaster yells, "You know him! You love him! He's Blaster!" to the cheering crowd who have climbed all over Thunderdome's structure to watch the bloodletting. In *Fury Road*, when the War Boys are about to pull off a stunt in combat, like leaping from one speeding vehicle to another while carrying an explosive spear in each hand, they shout, "Witness me!" to their comrades.

Not Even Max Can Make It Alone

Life in the State of Nature, according to Hobbes, is "solitary, poor, nasty, brutish and short."[3] Nobody is safe in such chaos, no matter how strong and capable they are. The *Mad Max* saga illustrates this well. Max is as tough and able as a person can be. He may well be the best driver and best fighter in the Wasteland. In *Mad Max*, the Main Force Patrol considers him their "top pursuit man." In *Mad Max 2*, the gyrocopter pilot tells him that he's the first person to be fast enough not to be killed by his snake-trap: "Never seen a man beat the snake before!" By *Mad Max 3*, Max is so deadly in a fight that he's the only one to ever pass Aunty Entity's "audition" (which consists of a surprise attack from several warriors at once). But even someone as capable as Max isn't safe. He's faced with imminent death on a regular basis.

In *Mad Max*, Bubba blasts Max's left knee with a shotgun, leaving him with an injury he's still suffering from three sequels later. Then Bubba and Toecutter almost run him over as he lies writhing on the highway. In *Mad Max 2*, the gyrocopter pilot gets the drop on Max with a crossbow and could have impaled him. Later, Max is badly hurt when he overturns his V8 Interceptor in a road-battle with Humungus's gang, after Wez smashes in his windscreen. In *Mad Max 3*, he loses his caravan in a hijack and is left in the desert to die, is almost killed in combat with Blaster in Thunderdome, is sent into the desert to die with his hands bound, and after the final chase, is captured by Aunty Entity, only surviving because she decides not to be ruthless for once and lets him go. Apparently, she identifies with him, affectionately asking, "Ain't we a pair, raggedy man?" before driving off. In *Fury Road*, he's captured by the War Boys and used as a human blood bank, escaping only by means of (what else?) an extremely dangerous car chase, complete with acrobatics on poles and flaming guitars.

"Bartertown's Learned. Now, When Men Get to Fighting, It Happens Here, and It Finishes Here!"—Thunderdome Announcer

People like Max who live in the State of Nature seem to be left in a hellish predicament. Fortunately, reason offers us a way out of the State of Nature. Living in such danger is in nobody's best interest. What would be in our self-interest is to come to some arrangement with others for our mutual good. For instance, we could all agree to give up the freedom to attack one another. Of course, being free to attack you is in my best interest, but the only way I can make it in your best interest to agree not to attack me is by offering you the same in return.

The people of Bartertown seem to have entered into just such a social contract for mutual benefit, by resolving their disputes in Thunderdome. The announcer explains to the bloodthirsty crowd:

> Listen on! Listen on! This is the truth of it. Fighting leads to killing, and killing gets to warring, and that was damn near the death of us all. Look at us now, busted up and everyone talking about hard rain!

But we've learned! By the dust of 'em all, Bartertown's learned. Now, when men get to fighting, it happens here, and it finishes here! Two men enter, one man leaves.

Another law that the people of Bartertown have apparently accepted for the common good states: "Bust a deal, face the wheel." This means that those who break their word must face a random punishment, including amputation, death, "gulag," forfeiture of goods, or imprisonment in the underworld. Max gets "gulag," being driven out into the desert bound on the back of a donkey.

Hobbes believes that the only rights humans have are those granted by a social contract. In *Fury Road*, an old woman points a rifle at Immortan Joe and scolds him for keeping slave concubines, telling him, "They aren't your property. You cannot own a human being!" Contrary to Hobbes, she seems to think that there is a right not to be owned that exists whether a society recognizes that right or not. Most Western philosophers of Hobbes' era thought that rights were bestowed by God. For instance, the American Declaration of Independence of 1776, published some 125 years after Hobbes's *Leviathan*, claims that humans are "endowed by their Creator with certain unalienable Rights." Hobbes believed in God, but he could see that God was not intervening to ensure that people received any supposed God-given rights. According to Hobbes, if we want rights that matter in practice, we're going to need to make contracts with other humans.

"We Do It My Way"—Lord Humungus, Ayatollah of Rock-and-Rolla

Even if we enter into a social contract, the problem remains that it will often be in our best interests to break that pact. As soon as my back is turned, you have the advantage and can just bash me over the head and drive off in my car. We need some way for the contract to be enforced, or it's useless. Hobbes warns, "Covenants, without the sword, are but words."[4]

In *Fury Road*, Immortan Joe's escaped wives leave the optimistic message "Our babies will not be warriors" scrawled on the wall. Hobbes would likely have pointed out that babies who don't grow up to be warriors need social contracts with warriors they can rely on to defend them. Social contracts only work if enforced by an authority backed up with force.

What we need to do, in Hobbes's view, is appoint a leader who we agree to obey. The leader is then responsible for enforcing the social contract that protects us from one another. For instance, in Bartertown, Aunty Entity enforces both the law requiring challenges to be met in Thunderdome and the law that states, "Bust a deal, face the wheel." The leader must punish the disobedient to ensure that it is in everyone's best interests to obey. Appropriately, in Bartertown, a man who killed a pig is sent to work for life in the pig-shit power plant, while Max is sentenced to "gulag" for busting a deal. Where the leader is too weak to punish, they have no authority, and laws are broken. Toecutter and his gang turn outlaw, defying the Australian police, because the cops have lost control of the highways and can no longer stop banditry.

The leader must be given absolute power. Even matters of religion must be entirely up to the leader to decide. Allowing power to be divided invites conflict as different factions oppose each other, competing to secure their own best interests. This easily leads to civil war, which is far worse even than bad government. Hobbes wrote, "[T]he greatest [misfortune], that in any forme of Government can possibly happen to the people in generall, is scarce sensible, in respect of the miseries, and horrible calamities, that accompany a Civill Warre."[5] Hobbes was speaking from experience. He'd lived through the English Civil War (1642–1651) between supporters of the king and the parliament, a conflict that had brought death and destruction on a breathtaking scale. About 200,000 Britons died from the war and war-related causes like disease and famine. That's about 1 in 25 of those living in Britain at the time, the equivalent of the modern United States losing 13.2 million lives.

Loss of personal freedom is a small price to pay for safety. In *Fury Road*, one of Immortan Joe's escaping wives has second thoughts about leaving him, reasoning, "We were protected. He gave us the high life. What's wrong with that?" Hobbes could not have agreed more.

Appropriately, most gangs and Wasteland communities we see in the saga have a single leader whose orders must be obeyed without question. Toecutter, Humungus, and Immortan Joe are all Hobbesian absolute dictators, commanding their warriors like generals in an army. In *Mad Max*, when a frightened railway worker assures Toecutter, "Anything you say!" Toecutter answers approvingly, "Anything I say. What a wonderful philosophy you have." In *Mad Max 2*, when Wez tries to attack the refinery before time, Humungus chokes him out, reminding him, "We do it my way."

The refinery town from *Mad Max 2* and the tribe of children from *Beyond Thunderdome* are more egalitarian, which Hobbes would disapprove of, but at least they are still ruled by single individuals, with the refinery town tribe being led first by Pappagallo, then by the gyrocopter pilot, and finally by the grown-up feral child, and with the tribe of children being led first by Slake and later by Savannah.

Hobbes would be horrified, though, by the situation in Bartertown in *Beyond Thunderdome*. Aunty Entity and Master Blaster vie for being the sole leader. Aunty Entity rules the surface, but Master Blaster rules the power plant and uses power embargoes to force Aunty Entity to announce over the PA system, "Master Blaster runs Bartertown." To Hobbes's mind, it's less important which of them wins, as long as one of them takes sole control. As things stand, Bartertown could easily divide into two violent factions who tear the town down in a roar of engines.

Hobbes would also caution Immortan Joe against relying too heavily on his allies the Bullet Farmer and the People Eater. Though they are subordinate to him, they have their own troops and run their own settlements, making them a lot like rulers in their own right. Hobbes warns that independent rulers can never trust one another since, not being bound by an external authority, they will take advantage of one another whenever they can benefit from doing so. If the Bullet Farmer ever decides that he can grow more powerful by raiding Joe's citadel, then that's just what he'll do. The perfect Hobbesian model of how nations treat each other is provided by Humungus's gang's attack on the refinery town in *Mad Max 2*. To Humungus and his tribe, the refinery people are nothing but an obstacle standing between them and a valuable resource. Their actions are dictated purely by the interests of their own group, which is to say, they intend to kill the refinery tribe and take their oil.

Since the leader should have absolute power, there's usually no question of appointing a different leader to replace them. The all-powerful ruler will appoint their own successor. Hobbes claimed that in civilized societies, our ancestors entered into such a social contract in prehistoric times, agreeing on our behalf that we would be subject to it. Those of us born into kingdoms or dictatorships should follow the national leader with complete obedience. Those of us born into democracies need to replace those democracies with dictatorships, and then we must offer our new leaders our complete obedience.

Our duty to obey our leader does not depend on whether the leader rose to power by legitimate means or not. Whether they fought their way to the top like Humungus and Immortan Joe, or rose through public support like Pappagallo, or built a town from scratch like Aunty Entity, we must do as they say. Nor does our duty to obey the leader depend on the leader ruling justly, since even an unjust ruler is preferable to lawlessness. Furiosa is wrong to rebel against Immortan Joe just because he enslaved women to be his breeding partners.

Still, because our duty to obey our leader derives from our self-interest, we only have a duty to obey for as long as it's in our best interests to do so. Hobbes wrote, "The obligation of subjects to the sovereign is understood to last as long as, and no longer than, the power lasteth by which he is able to protect them."[6] So while the ex-subjects of Immortan Joe were quite right to obey him while he lived, they were also quite right to respond to his death by embracing his old enemies Max and Furiosa and taking Joe's water supply for themselves. Likewise, it's perfectly rational for the likes of Toecutter and his gang to turn outlaw, ignoring Australian law in favor of living by their own rules. After all, the Australian authorities clearly aren't able to protect anyone, so there are no benefits to siding with them.

Beyond the White Line Nightmare

So much for how Hobbes would advise the survivors of post-apocalyptic Australia. The important question is, to what degree is he right about politics? I think Hobbes is right that without rules, backed up by an authority with the power of force, human community life would be impossible. Hobbes is also right to recognize how bad war is and that we must weigh our principles of freedom against the human cost.

But Hobbes is wrong that humans only ever act out of selfishness. Stories like the *Mad Max* saga, in which people do selfless or heroic things, only make sense because we understand how someone could be motivated to act that way.

Max often acts unselfishly, even after he's gone to live alone in the desert. For instance, in *Mad Max 2*, he saves a wounded driver from a crossbow-wielding bandit. Max insists, "I'm only here for the gasoline," but the first thing he does is tourniquet the man's leg. Later, Max gives an old music box to the feral kid, even though it's the sort of treasure that he might be able to trade for food or fuel. After defeating Blaster in Thunderdome, Max decides that he can't kill him when he finds out that Blaster has Down syndrome. "He has the mind of a child! It's not his fault!" begs Master. Max spares Blaster even though it breaks the deal he had with Aunty Entity, a dangerous person to upset. Later, he decides to rescue a tribe of kids he finds stranded in the desert and eventually sacrifices his own chance to escape Aunty Entity so that they can fly away to safety.

In *Fury Road*, Max explains, "Once, I was a cop—a road warrior searching for a righteous cause." Now he's "haunted by those [he] could not protect." Though he needs Furiosa's help to escape, he's soon willing to sacrifice himself. When she has to stop to cool the engines of her War Rig, and Max heads off to face the pursuing gangs, she asks him what she should do if he isn't back by the time the engines have cooled. "Well ... keep moving," he answers. He even transfuses his blood to Furiosa to save her life. We only understand characters like Max because they reflect how good human motivations can be. If humans were purely self-centered, as Hobbes insists, such behavior would be incomprehensible.

Perhaps it's Hobbes's misunderstanding of human motivations that led him to make some overly authoritarian political recommendations. As the *Mad Max* movies continue to demonstrate, Hobbes is wrong that we must concentrate power in the hands of a single leader. Hobbes thought that such a concentration of power would reduce the risk of civil war, but it's a far less effective system for avoiding civil war than democracy is. When power is concentrated in a leader's hands, violence is the only way to remove that leader from power. The English Civil War might not have occurred if the English had had the right to vote King Charles I off the throne. As it was, violent revolution was the only recourse for those who wanted political change. As individuals, it might have been in the revolutionaries' interests to stay silent and so avoid violence and death. But they were willing to fight instead, at terrible cost. Consider how difficult it would be to remove a leader like Toecutter, or Humungus, or Aunty Entity, or Immortan Joe, without the use of organized violence. Such a leader could only be deposed through blood and death and the burning wrecks of trucks.

Likewise, it may be Hobbes's misunderstanding of human motivation that leads him to his conclusion that only fear of punishment keeps people from committing crimes. Such a mistake can easily lead to the belief that the best way to treat criminals is to be as punitive as possible, resorting to the sort of brutality Max shows to Johnny the Boy in *Mad Max*, chaining him to a car that will explode and walking away. Hobbes failed to see how punishment can brutalize and embitter people, and have the opposite of the intended effect. If we voters aren't careful, in our efforts to maintain law and order, and to stop civilization from sinking into the sort of chaos of violence, pillaging, and stunt-filled car chases we see in the *Mad Max* saga, we could easily turn into more cruel and dreadful rulers than any narcissistic bandit-dictator in bondage gear and a hockey mask.

Notes

1 Thomas Hobbes, *Leviathan*, ed. J.C.A. Gaskin (Oxford: Oxford University Press, 2009), 100.
2 Ibid., 85.
3 Ibid., 84.
4 Ibid., 103.
5 Ibid., 122.
6 Ibid., 147.

The Political Economy of Bartertown: Embeddedness of Markets, Peak Oil, the Tragedy of the Commons, and Lifeboat Ethics

Paul Thomas

It may be tempting to dismiss the world of *Beyond Thunderdome* as mere dystopian fiction, but the familiar roots of capitalism are still visible. The idea of a selfish man who wants to maximize his utility is the core assumption of neoclassical economics, and it is operative in Bartertown. Capitalism functions using the same rationale, but how long can it survive? Is there an alternative to capitalism? Is collective resource sharing possible among humans? This essay will analyze the economic structure of Bartertown and compare it with present-day markets.

Bartertown and the Embeddedness of Markets

Traditional economists view economy and society as two distinct systems and study economy as a separate entity. This paradigm deserves some scrutiny. A human being acts in various spheres—social, economic, political, cultural—and hence is an amalgamation of various agencies. Economic agents are also social agents. In fact, an individual first becomes a social agent and only later becomes an economic agent when they have to engage in economic activities. Modern-day neoclassical economics, which is considered the conventional doctrine in

Mad Max and Philosophy: Thinking Through the Wasteland, First Edition.
Edited by Matthew P. Meyer and David Koepsell.
© 2024 John Wiley & Sons, Inc. Published 2024 by John Wiley & Sons, Inc.

economics, makes unrealistic assumptions to smoothly separate economic agency from a person's agency. In reality the economy and markets are *embedded* in society. The economy is immersed in social relations and it can never exist independently without the society as a whole.

In studying the economy of Bartertown, it is not possible to just look at the economic aspects of the town, which is mainly trade, and neglect the political and social relations of the town. The economy of Bartertown is embedded in the social, political, and cultural context of the town. Bartertown is a market where people exchange goods. No money is involved in this exchange, hence the name. If people don't have anything to trade, they don't have an existence in Bartertown. We cannot call Bartertown a truly free market because there are regulatory bodies that govern it for smooth functioning. Rather, Bartertown is an authoritarian capitalist or illiberal capitalist system in which a capitalist market economy exists along with an authoritarian government. The best examples of this sort of political economy from the contemporary world would be China, Russia, and Singapore.

Capitalist exploitation still prevails in Bartertown. From a Marxist perspective, the class divide between the proletariat (the laborers of Underworld) and the bourgeoisie (the ruling elite of Bartertown) is evident. The conflict between Aunty and Master Blaster can be seen as a conflict between capital and labor. From Hegel's dialectical framework, the unstable interaction between thesis and antithesis results in the synthesis of a new order which then becomes a thesis. And this is a continuous process. The clash between Aunty and Master Blaster was the culmination of the tension between capital (thesis) and labor (antithesis). In the new order (synthesis), Master Blaster was enslaved by Aunty resulting in a new Imperial system. This system lasted only until Max and the children knocked down Bartertown completely in the end.

Peak Oil

Human wants are unlimited, but Earth's resources are limited. How to allocate resources efficiently is the basic problem of scarcity in economics. Natural resources like air, water, oil, and minerals are limited but not all of them are terribly scarce. For example, air and water are not very scarce resources (for now), but oil and minerals are quite scarce because it is costly to extract them to make them available to meet human demands. Consider that when Max first enters Bartertown, he encounters a man selling contaminated water. A few hundred years ago the idea of water and air as marketable commodities was unimaginable, but today bottled fresh water is a profitable product with significant demand.

Peak oil is a situation where the world has already extracted the maximum amount of oil from the earth, and the rate of extraction begins to diminish permanently after that as the costs of extraction begin to exceed the value of the final product. The global petroleum reserve is limited. And the supply of oil is not just dependent on the existing oil reserve, but also on an economically viable means to extract it. A decline of oil extraction can be caused either by the depletion of resources or by the decrease in demand for fossil fuels to reduce carbon emissions as a response to a climate change crisis.

Bartertown is run on the greenhouse gas methane which is made from pig shit. The Underworld is the energy production house of Bartertown where pigs are raised and their shit is used to produce methane to run lights, motors, and vehicles. Why does Bartertown use methane as its energy source? Is it because of the depletion of oil reserves? Or is it a conscious decision to reduce the consumption of oil to bring down carbon emissions? The latter is unlikely because methane is equally or more polluting than petroleum, and honestly we don't expect any concern about climate change among the people of Bartertown. Hence, the obvious reason for the use of methane is the depletion of oil reserves.

In the context of the movie, Bartertown is a product of a post-peak oil crisis in the world. We know that water and oil wars have left surviving Australians battling for drops of gasoline in the Wasteland. In *The Road Warrior* we see the oil refinery governed by Pappagallo and his tribe extracting precious petroleum day and night. Whatever the cost of extraction may be, if there is any resource, then they will extract it.

In our world, where climate change and the depletion of resources are pressing issues, *Thunderdome*'s Underworld offers food for thought. There have been many predictions regarding the timing of peak oil over the past century, but with advancements in technology, there has been an increase in the extraction of oil past many of these predictions. As of 2021, the latest predictions on peak oil ranged from 2019 to 2040. The predictions are dependent on factors like future trends in the economy, technological developments, societal and governmental initiatives to fight climate change, and so on. Reuters reported that COVID-19 pushed the timing of peak oil to happen a few years earlier than the predicted time due to dented fuel consumption during the pandemic.[1]

Bartertown's pig-shit alternative is not very appealing for the demands of our present day. Even though it is renewable, methane is not a sustainable energy resource in moderating climate change. It is a well-known greenhouse gas. In Bartertown, the resources are completely depleted and whatever arrangements are made for their use boil down to survival. We have not completely depleted our oil reserves yet, and they must be judiciously used in aiding the transition to renewable clean energy sources.

Tragedy of the Commons

The tragedy of the commons describes a situation in which individuals have free and unlimited access to natural resources unrestricted by any formal or informal rule. Under these circumstances, people will ultimately deplete those resources. The idea was first proposed by the British economist William Foster Lloyd (1794–1852) in 1833 and later popularized as the "tragedy of commons" by Garret Hardin (1915–2003) in 1968.[2]

The example of a common grazing field is often used to illustrate the idea. Suppose there is a common grazing field on which cattle owned by different people graze. Since the field is not owned by any of the cattle owners, there is no reason why a particular person should not exploit the field by bringing in an additional animal. An economically rational person will always take actions that maximize their individual benefit. In this case, that would mean overgrazing the field. All cattle owners think along similar lines, and eventually this will result in the depletion of grass in the field.

Can We Escape the Tragedy?

What is the best economic system to solve the tragedy of the commons? Gandhi rejects capitalism on the ground that it inherently carries the idea of Darwinism—survival of the fittest. Gandhi argues from a moral philosophical framework that this should not be the state of a modern civilized society because competition ultimately leads to catastrophe. If we choose competition and self-interest, then there will be no collective left. But if we choose cooperation, then we can at least think about having a commons. As Gandhi sees it, we need cooperation not competition. Cooperation is possible and it is preferable to competition in a world of scarce resources in order to avoid the tragedy of the commons.

The history of the Soviet Union is an example of how socialism fails to avoid the tragedy of the commons. In a socialist system, to have collective ownership of property, the state needs to enforce strict surveillance and laws, which becomes quite difficult when the administrative territory becomes very large. Smaller scales allow individuals to cooperate more easily. They can thus produce something more meaningful and greater than what they would if they were working independently. Master Blaster is a good example of how two individuals using their comparative advantage and cooperation can become something that is superior to their individual selves. The Master uses his intelligence, which is his greatest asset, and Blaster uses his physical strength. Together they become the mighty-brainy Master Blaster ruling Bartertown. In contrast, the competition for power between Aunty Entity and Master Blaster ultimately leads to the end of Bartertown.

A real-life example of how efficiently people can collaboratively work and produce something very meaningful and useful is open-source software. Open-source software is free software where users can inspect, modify, and enhance the source code. Anyone is free to submit proposed updates and upgrades to existing code for review by the supporting community. Open source looks like a "commons" without a tragedy. Although open-source software is gaining popularity and is widely used, there is a tragedy hidden in many of these open-source software projects. Consider Python, which is one of the most prevalent programming languages currently used. Many big tech companies use Python for their products. They make huge profits but do not bother to improve the open software. The pain of improving open-source software is on the commons, but the benefit from the software goes to the big companies. In an open conference, Linus Torvalds (originator of Linux, another open-source software platform) openly criticized Nvidia, a graphics hardware manufacturing company, for using Linux in their production process but not providing technical support for the Linux software. They use the commons but don't improve it.

Unlike software, natural resources may become depleted if they are used without improvement. This raises a question about the potential for order emerging without authorities. Open-source projects seem to succeed without a single authority taking control. Can this work in society generally? People behave most prudently when they make present decisions that have a future effect on themselves. Prudence is a selfish virtue. If the future consequences are to fall on others more than themselves, then people will make decisions just based on the present. The present system provides individuals with opportunities to pursue actions that benefit them while spreading the ill effects (negative externalities[3]) across the larger population. Optimizing or utility maximization for the self in the short run is not optimal for the population in the long run. What is good for each of us is not good for all of us, but what is good for all of us is good for each of us.

We can consider the population problem as a tragedy of the commons.[4] If the world is taken as a commons that provides food and other resources for living, we are the cattle that feeds on that commons. Most essential resources, like air and water, are common resources that are not individually owned. The rise in population is a problem that affects all of humanity. Since the consequence of having children is to be borne by the entire population in the future, many people do not care about the individual burden of population increase. So they make their decisions based on their present desires. Adam Smith in his *Wealth of Nations* (1776) popularized the idea of the invisible hand, where if all individuals pursued actions in their self-interest, it would ultimately promote the public interest. The tragedy of the commons contradicts the wisdom of the invisible hand. Yet, ever since the publication of the *Wealth of Nations*, the invisible hand doctrine has become the dominant theory in economic reasoning, which became the foundation for the modern-day free market economy.

We have known about the tragedy of the commons for generations, and yet we continue in competition for natural resources. Natural selection has favored the forces of psychological denial. Taking Hardin's own words: "The individual benefits as an individual from his ability to deny the truth even though society as a whole, of which he is a part, suffers." To be truly free, sometimes we must restrict our freedom to prevent outcomes that would harm society as a whole. As Hegel said, "Freedom is the recognition of necessity." In *Mad Max*, Aunty Entity's system of primitive laws helps to prevent disorder and undue competition, balancing the invisible hand's faults in post-apocalyptic Australia. Today in our world, anarchy, direct democracy, and worker cooperatives are discussed as possible alternatives to capitalist and socialist systems.

Lifeboat Ethics

The idea of lifeboat ethics was a further development of the "tragedy of the commons" by Garret Hardin in which he describes a situation where there is a lifeboat with 50 people on board and a capacity of 60.[5] The lifeboat is floating in an ocean surrounded by 100 swimmers trying to get on board. Should one let any swimmers on board? Under what circumstances? Which swimmers?

Climate change, pandemics, and other calamities have raised serious questions about the survival of the human species on Earth. This is one reason some billionaires have expressed their intentions to settle in space. There has been a shift from viewing Earth as a wasteful cowboy economy to a frugal spaceship economy. In the cowboy economic system, the continuous expansion of consumption and production generate growth. This model is based on a false assumption of unlimited resources. In truth, overexploitation of resources leads eventually to crisis. This realization led to the development of a new outlook: an Earth-spaceship model. "The closed economy of the future might similarly be called the 'spaceman' economy, in which the Earth has become a single spaceship, without unlimited reservoirs of anything, either for extraction or for pollution, and in which, therefore, man must find his place in a cyclical ecological system which is capable of continuous reproduction of material form even though it cannot escape having inputs of energy."[6] The spaceship economy considers Earth as a spaceship and understands that the resources are limited.

Bartertown can be seen as a prototype of spaceship economy. Resources in Bartertown are very limited, and there is a wise and efficient allocation of resources according to Aunty Entity's system of laws. There are no more resources to extract. Instead, the energy inputs of Bartertown come from a new unconventional source—pig shit. It is a cyclical ecosystem that continuously produces energy.

Hardin critiques the spaceship model of Earth for not having a single leader to manage the planet. He believes that without a supreme leader, the planet will not be a commons and will end in a tragedy. In Bartertown there is single authority who controls the town. An authoritarian regime violates the spirit of human nature, but the question is whether a spaceship can afford the luxury of being liberal.

If the Earth as spaceship metaphor is correct, then there needs to be a supreme controller who can captain the ship. The ship cannot survive if controlled by a committee or group of people who claim rights without taking responsibilities. Who is the captain of Bartertown? Aunty Entity and Master Blaster both claim to run Bartertown. Their claims are opposed to each other. One rules it with law, the other with energy. The movie shows us the power struggle between Aunty Entity and Master Blaster. The rift between them has disrupted the functioning of Bartertown; their dispute is not sustainable and leads to conflict. Law, brains, and brawn vie for ruling this nascent polity, and the dispute leads to the town's ruin in warfare. This is a classic lifeboat ethics problem.

Two-thirds of Earth's population are poor while the other one-third is comparatively rich. Likewise in Bartertown, the poorest two-thirds are the laborers in the Underworld and the rich minority is the elite of Bartertown. The divide between the elite of Bartertown and the Underworld is much like that between rich and poor nations in our world. The Underworld is the powerhouse built on the labor of the imprisoned, while the elite of Bartertown enjoys the benefits. Developed countries consume more energy and emit more carbon than developing countries, whereas the burdens of climate change in the form of pollution, poor living conditions, and environmental degradation are experienced disproportionately by the developing countries. The Underworld takes all the negative externalities of pollution, whereas Bartertown enjoys the benefits.

Every person who is on the lifeboat is selfish. Otherwise they would jump off the lifeboat and make room for another person. But there is no guarantee that the person who replaces the selfless person who jumped out of the boat will also do the same. There is no guilt in the lifeboat. Everyone in that boat is a lucky selfish person. According to the cliché, "Nice guys finish last." Max in the movie is a good guy. But what is his situation in the end? He could not find a place in the plane and is left behind in the Wasteland. Of course, this is "reel" life, and he can afford to be left behind for the continuation of the story. But in real life nobody wants to finish last or be left behind. The future of humankind depends upon the ethics of a lifeboat, and the ethics of a lifeboat is that of a selfish person.

The Future

The peak oil crisis, the tragedy of the commons, and lifeboat ethics result from the failure of the free market economy. For the survival of the human race, we need to change from the capitalist system, which values selfishness as a virtue. We need alternatives that promote the values of equality, justice, and cooperation. Aunty Entity and an authoritarian regime is not our only alternative. We can explore the possibilities of anarchism, direct democracy, or other systems that don't compromise our rights and freedoms. The future does not need to be a post-apocalyptic dystopia.

Notes

1   Reuters, "Factbox: Pandemic Brings Forward Predictions for Peak Oil Demand," *Reuters*, July 24, 2022, at https://www.reuters.com/article/us-oil-demand-factbox-idINKBN2870NY.
2   Garret Hardin, "The Tragedy of the Commons," *Science* 162 (1968), 1243–1248.
3   Negative externalities occur when the production or consumption of a commodity causes harmful consequences to a third party.
4   William Foster Lloyd, "W. F. Lloyd on the Checks to Population," *Population and Development Review* 6 (1980), 473–496.
5   Garrett Hardin, "Living on a Lifeboat by Garrett Hardin," *The Garrett Hardin Society*, February 25, 2022, at https://www.garretthardinsociety.org/articles/art_living_on_a_lifeboat.html.
6   Kenneth E. Boulding, "The Economics of the Coming Spaceship Earth," in H. Jarrett ed., *Environmental Quality in a Growing Economy* (Baltimore: Johns Hopkins University Press, 1966), 3–14.

5

From Wee Jerusalem to Fury Road: Does *Mad Max* Depict a Post-apocalyptic Dystopia?

Clint Jones

The *Mad Max* film franchise is often described as depicting a post-apocalyptic dystopian world.[1] However, this may not be an apt description of the story or, at least, not of *all* the films. As we will see, an apocalypse would be much more global than we have evidence for in the films, and a dystopia is not the kind of place where Max, or nearly anyone else, would choose to live.

Pox-Eclipse Full of Pain: Apocalyptic Themes

One meaning of the word *apocalypse* is "catastrophe," and it is clear in the film franchise that something catastrophic has occurred. We get this sense not only in the depiction of the world Max inhabits, but through the language applied to the world. For instance, the place where the majority of the action and lives of the characters take place is labeled the *Wasteland*.

However, not all catastrophes are apocalyptic. Think of Hurricane Katrina in 2005. Katrina was a catastrophic experience for the coast of the Gulf of Mexico, but Katrina was not an apocalyptic event. For a catastrophe to be apocalyptic, it would have to be global in its reach. Whatever events reshaped the world of *Mad Max,* we can be sure they were not totalizing even if they were devastating.[2]

In contrast to the major catastrophe of Katrina, consider the apocalyptic catastrophe depicted in *The Walking Dead*, where a virus rapidly wipes out the vast majority of humankind.[3] It is a world with no

Mad Max and Philosophy: Thinking Through the Wasteland, First Edition.
Edited by Matthew P. Meyer and David Koepsell.
© 2024 John Wiley & Sons, Inc. Published 2024 by John Wiley & Sons, Inc.

civilization and constant hostility among the survivors—not to mention the ever-present onslaught of zombies.[4] In *Mad Max*, human society continues to function on more than a mere subsistence level. Though *Road Warrior* does not include references to cities the way *Mad Max* does, the survivors hunkered down at the oil refinery do have knowledge about a sanctuary, possibly civilized, hundreds of miles from where they are located. There is also enough scavengeable material about that all the groups involved in the siege of the oil refinery can build incredible vehicles, maintain them, and find fuel enough to operate them throughout their territory in the Wasteland—including at least one helicopter. Two things immediately stand out in the depiction of the world across the first two films: first, society, while degraded, has not fully collapsed; and, second, there is no good reason to believe that whatever crises are plaguing humanity result in a totalizing destruction of human civilization. This concern carries through all four films and leaves open the possibility that *Mad Max* is not subject to an apocalypse and, therefore, is not post-apocalyptic.

You Can Shovel Shit Can't You?: Dystopian Themes

The concept of dystopia was introduced by John Stuart Mill (1806–1873) during a speech he gave condemning England's treatment of the Irish. His use of this term was meant to elicit the opposite of utopia. Utopia as a concept was introduced into the Western imagination by Sir Thomas More (1478–1535) in 1516 with the publication of *Utopia*. More's use of the idea is a literal pun on two Greek words. On the one hand, it sounds like *eu*topia, which means good place, and, on the other hand, it sounds like *ou*topia, which means no place. By utilizing only the *u*- prefix to *-topia*, More was able to create a "good no place" or, likely more accurately, a "no good place."

The real difficulty with utopias is that every utopia is, for someone, a dystopia. It is a little harder to argue that every dystopia is someone else's utopia, but it is possible. If what makes a place a utopia or dystopia is merely perspective, then we must explain why one utopian or dystopian reality is preferential. The real difficulty here is that it seems like a clear benchmark for a dystopian world is that it is a place where *no one* would want to live. Yet, when we are dealing with dystopian narratives, there are always people who want to—or seem to want to—live in those realities.

To clarify the concept of dystopia, it will be beneficial to exclude the views of the powerful or elite in a society. Such views are not representative of the majority of people who are suffering in a dystopian reality. Dystopias tend to be created out of a reorganization of human society, often with totalitarian political elements. The resulting society is not designed to serve the majority of the people. Rather, the majority of the people are expected to serve the minority of leaders.

Post-apocalyptic societies grow out of the erasure of human civilization. An apocalyptic event would not merely reorganize society but would destroy it. From the ashes of the apocalypse, it would be possible to build both utopian and dystopian societies. This is a crucial point because *Mad Max* may be post-apocalyptic, but that alone does not make it dystopic. As we will see, there is good reason to believe that Max and others outside the structures of power want to live in the world as constituted by the events that shape the story as we receive it in the films.

Nomad Bikers, Bulk Trouble

In *Mad Max* some of the primary action takes place in and around the town of Wee Jerusalem. While Wee Jerusalem appears to be nothing more than a few streets and rundown buildings bordering on nowhere, it also boasts a small population, a railway station, and operational businesses. The town and the society it is part of is in a state of slow decline and decay, but that decline is not so severe that the society looks significantly different than a residential area that has lost its primary industry—think of Detroit or the rural areas around Pittsburgh. Neither Detroit nor rural Pennsylvania would live up to the label post-apocalyptic or dystopian.

Though Toecutter's gang is violent and savage, operating throughout Sector 26, the presence of a gang is not, in itself, sufficient to warrant a claim of post-apocalypse or dystopia. The MFP counters the gang, and society seems to be continuing with normal rhythms and routines. For instance, there are roadside diners and cabarets and Jessie is able to buy ice cream at an operational beach resort. Plus, following her harrowing run-in with Toecutter and his gang, she and Max flee to May's Farm, which is pastoral and idyllic. Dystopias don't produce such scenery—to say nothing of picnics with rope swings. Add to this the well-maintained roads, the ongoing application of justice as evidenced by the attempt to bring Johnny the Boy to trial, as well as what must be both a functional economy (Max eats a peanut butter and honey sandwich, two things unlikely to exist in a post-apocalyptic dystopia) and infrastructure, and it is hard to place *Mad Max* under a dystopian, and certainly not post-apocalyptic, label.

A Maggot Living off the Corpse of the Old World

Road Warrior continues the story of Max Rockatansky just a short time, potentially a few years, after the events of *Mad Max*. By *Road Warrior*, the Outback has been transformed into a space known as the Wasteland. However, the transformation of the Outback does not require that society has fallen nor that some apocalyptic event has occurred. It is entirely possible that the events of *Road Warrior* take place outside the reach of the MFP as Max wanders the countryside bereft and adrift after the loss of his family. Of course, the events that unfolded between *Mad Max* and *Road Warrior* are recounted by the narrator of the film, a feral child of Pappagallo's oil refinery compound:

> I remember a time of chaos, ruined dreams, this wasted land .... To understand who [Max] was you have to go back to another time when the world was powered by the black fuel and the deserts sprouted great cities of pipe and steel. Gone now. Swept away. For reasons long for-gotten, two mighty warrior tribes went to war and touched off a blaze, which engulfed them all. Without fuel they were nothing. They'd built a house of straw, the machines sputtered and stopped. Their leaders talked and talked and talked. But nothing could stem the avalanche. Their world crumbled. Their cities exploded. A whirlwind of looting. A firestorm of fear. Men began to feed on men. On the roads it was a white line nightmare. Only those mobile enough to scavenge, brutal enough to pillage, would survive. The gangs took over the highways ready to wage war for a tank of juice. And in this maelstrom of decay ordinary men were battered and smashed.
>
> ... Max wandered out into the Wasteland. And it was here, in this blighted place, that he learned to live again.

Here we have a description of what could have been the events lead-ing up to, and including, *Mad Max*, though the remembrance could also be of the time between *Mad Max* and *Road Warrior*. If we assume the narrator is recalling the time between the two films, we can safely say that while fuel reserves were dwindling up to and during *Mad Max,* global fuel production must have stopped in order to spark something like World War III—a conflict capable of creating a conflagration that could sweep away civilization as we know it. However, this does not actually jibe with the content of the films because enough fuel is being produced to run settlements, vehicles, and airplanes. In fact, the primary action of *Road Warrior* takes place at an active oil well and refinery replete with flamethrowers as part of the defenses.

The compound, run by Pappagallo, is not a ramshackle, makeshift hideout, but rather, a formidable, well entrenched, fortress. Even though the compound is located deep in the Wasteland, it is well provisioned, including livestock, and must have had access to enough water and food to care for both human and animal inhabitants. Given that the inhabitants are willing to abandon their compound to escape further harassment by Lord Humungus and his marauders and travel a great distance to do so, we are left wondering at their motives and the state of the world.

Pappagallo and his companions occupied a superior position, and Lord Humungus was not in possession of any weapons that posed a real threat. The inhabitants of the compound could have survived a very long siege and could have even made use of the fuel to trade for ongoing protection from Lord Humungus. That is, the outcome of the standoff didn't have to happen the way it did. Rather, Pappagallo and his companions were tempted by the possibility of a *better place* far from the hard life of the Wasteland. We get a glimpse of this possibility when Max is shown postcards, presumably of the location in question where there was "sunshine, fresh water, and nothing to do but breed." Regardless of its reality, the point is that people *believe* such places exist. The possible existence of such places negates the postapocalyptic narrative and simultaneously suggests people wanted to live in the Wasteland (as we know Max has chosen to do), thus negating a hardline dystopian reading of the world of the *Road Warrior*.

By My Deeds I Honor Him, V8!

There are three ways to understand the timeline of the film franchise.[5] First, and most obvious, is that the films represent the chronological order of events as experienced by Max. Second, *Fury Road* can be placed between *Road Warrior* and *Beyond Thunderdome*. Finally, we might accept the story of Max to be one of a future legend, each film representing a recounting by a future narrator of a particular isolated event that they experienced, so that there is no obvious chronology after *Mad Max*. Holding this interpretation would ultimately lead us back to accepting one of the first two interpretations.

One reason to place *Fury Road* ahead of *Beyond Thunderdome* is because Max is still driving an Interceptor in *Fury Road*. Though the vehicle was destroyed in *Road Warrior*, it seems Max rebuilt the car—this is no easy feat if we're really post-apocalypse. Max is able to recreate his vehicle without having to resort to cobbling it together or making oddball modifications. The ability to reproduce this vehicle suggests there are enough around that scavenging or trading for parts is possible *despite* whatever calamity has befallen society. When *Beyond Thunderdome* begins, we see Max driving a completely different, caravan-style vehicle with camels providing the "horse-power." Clearly something has happened such that the circumstances no longer allow Max to viably rebuild his Interceptor after the car was, once again, destroyed in the mayhem of *Fury Road*.

Another reason for placing *Fury Road* before *Beyond Thunderdome* is that the world of *Fury Road* is only just starting to recover from the thermonuclear war suggested to have happened at some point after *Road Warrior* by Savannah—the primary narrator of *Beyond Thunderdome*. In short, there are oil wars, and then water wars, and eventually things turn nuclear. However, at the beginning of *Fury Road*, when Max is narrating the story that led to his overlooking a Wasteland valley, the periodic radio static voiceover that interrupts Max's narration refers to a *thermonuclear skirmish* making it impossible for a nuclear apocalypse to be in the backstory. It is one thing if global nuclear powers start dropping nukes on major cities and quite another thing for those same powers to bring about a nuclear apocalypse. A nuclear apocalypse would wipe out nearly all life. If enough bombs were detonated, they would create a nuclear winter that would kill whatever the blasts did not. So we can safely assume that some places may be irradiated voids, but much of the world, and with it human civilization, would be navigating the fallout and learning to rebuild and thrive in their new circumstances.

At the beginning of *Fury Road*, as Max narrates the film, he says two things that place the film ahead of *Beyond Thunderdome*. First, he recounts his past life by saying, "Once I was a cop, a road warrior searching for a righteous cause," suggesting a continuation of his life from *Road Warrior* rather than as a man having adopted an identity appropriate for the Wasteland. That is, Max still thinks of himself to some extent as an extension of his self as presented in *Mad Max* and *Road Warrior*. Second, he says, "[A]s the world fell, each of us in our own way was broken. It was hard to know who was more crazy, me or everyone else." Here Max seems to be drawing a direct line from the "fall of civilization" to his present circumstances, or, put differently, the fall of civilization is still the defining factor of life in the Wasteland. Beyond that, however, after his capture by the War Boys, Max is tattooed with all the necessary information about him relevant to his use by the War Boys as a "Bloodbag."

Two things also stick out here. First, he is tattooed with a number representing the days since the fall of civilization, or at least since the nukes started dropping around the globe. The number is 12,045 days, which is 33 years. Since we don't know exactly when the bombs started falling, it is entirely possible that the first explosions were contemporaneous with the events of *Mad Max*. This reading is complicated by the fact that Furiosa claims to have been gone from the Vuvalini for 7,000 days give or take a few, but prior to her kidnapping she was able to remember "the Green place," which suggests she is remembering a time at or before the outbreak of nuclear warfare. Thirty-three years is enough time that the world would be starting to recover from the fallout, and it encompasses Furiosa's 19 odd years.

This brings us to the second point brought out by the tattoo. There are still people around who are knowledgeable enough about medicine, and with access to the right technology, they can blood-type Max. More than that, they are capable of using Max as a blood donor for War Boys suffering from radiation poisoning. There are clearly deformities among the people depicted in the film that would align with a first generation of survivors living amid the fallout as well as people who suffered directly because of the blasts. However, if *Fury Road* takes place after *Beyond Thunderdome*, it is hard to believe that this type of knowledge and the requisite technology would still exist.

This, along with Immortan Joe's collection of milking mothers and breeding wives, suggests that healthy babies are starting to be born again, as evidenced by the fetus removed from Angharad. Pair this with the fact that there is still capacity for producing gasoline, and it is obvious that civilization may have had to hunker down for a few decades after the initial nuclear war, but the war did not eradicate human society. In fact, it is possible that there are places undevastated by the war and even that places like Sun City and Wee Jerusalem still exist and are operational. Living in the Wasteland, even in *Fury Road*, appears to be a choice for some people. While there are good reasons to assume that life is not great for a good many people, and it is clear that the leaders of the Citadel, Gas Town, and the Bullet Farm are all despotic and unhinged, it is also clear that the world is still capable of supporting societies with large populations as well as smaller groups, marauders roaming the Wasteland, and lone individuals like Max prior to his capture. The presence of a dystopian community does not demonstrate that the entirety of the world is dystopian.

Two Men Enter, One Man Leaves

It is clear in *Fury Road*, in a way it is not in *Road Warrior*, that the world has suffered a great calamity, but perhaps not an apocalypse. *Beyond Thunderdome* comes closest to presenting the post-apocalyptic, but, I think, again fails to deliver a decisive dystopian punch. Even positing *Fury Road* as a story element ahead of *Beyond Thunderdome*, the timeline still works out—in some ways, it works out better.

Consider Bartertown. The sign to Bartertown says, "Helping Build a Better Tomorrow." Bartertown represents a clear societal break with the compounds and social arrangements of the previous films (including those of *Fury Road*). Aunty Entity tells Max that prior to the apocalyptic event she was a nobody but that afterward she was somebody because she was one of the survivors. She tells Max, as they look out over Bartertown from her penthouse tower, "Look around. All this I built. Up to my armpits in blood and shit. Where there was desert, now there's a town. Where there was robbery, there's trade. Where there was despair, now there's hope. Civilization." And, she tells Max, she would do anything to protect that civilization. Max does not react to Aunty Entity's declaration of hope, which suggests his attitude toward the future hasn't changed since his experiences during *Fury Road* where Max tells Furiosa, "You know, hope is a mistake."

Bartertown boasts a lot of opportunity and amenities for the people who live in or pass through the town. In the original script, Bartertown contains "a brothel, barber, doctor, dentist, butcher's, open auction market, repair shop, a bar, various trading stands and of course the center of all disputes—the Thunderdome."[6] All of this *and* enough industry to convert pig feces into methane to power the whole city, allowing Bartertown's residents to conserve fuel for their vehicles— hardscrabble, yes, but hardly dystopian.

Finally, we get a glimpse of the apocalypse from Savannah, who recounts the story of the Waiting Ones to Max once he escapes from his gulag-inspired punishment. The Waiting Ones are a primitive tribe of children living in a secluded, yet idyllic, gorge complete with presumably clean water. They have built an anarchic society led primarily by the older children, but even these older children cannot recall pre-apocalyptic society and what they do know or remember is encapsulated in the Tell of Captain Walker. It is here, again, better to quote Savannah at length:

> This ain't one body's story, it's the story of us all. We got it mouth to mouth so you got to listen it and'member.'Cause what you hears today you got to tell the birthed tomorrow. I'm looking behind us now. Across the count of time down the long haul into history back. I sees the end what were the start. It's the pox-eclipse full of pain! And out of it were birthed crackling dust and fearsome time. It were full on winter and Mr. Dead were chasing them all but one he couldn't catch: and that were Captain Walker. He gathers up a gang, takes to the air, and flies to the sky.

The most important clue she provides is the claim that it "were full on winter." If Savannah is recalling a nuclear winter, then a considerable amount of time would need to have passed for that to clear up. Nuclear winter would most certainly follow a nuclear apocalypse, but it is unlikely that much would survive the nuclear winter. However, we know that camels, dogs, monkeys, horses, plants, and people do survive. So, best case, it was a mild nuclear winter isolated to those areas where major detonations occurred. If Captain Walker was attempting to flee an impending nuclear attack on Sydney, that might explain the turbulence that downed his plane. Even reading the films this way, it is entirely possible that nuclear bombs were only dropped on the eastern cities of Australia, and, say, Perth was not bombed. It is entirely possible that on the western shores of Australia a weakened, crippled society is still chugging along without any of the problems that plague the Wasteland. In fact, it's hard to imagine a lot of smaller cities having to deal with either bombs or much of the fallout—and that would be the case the world over.

Dealing with the fallout is another feature of *Beyond Thunderdome* that raises suspicion about the nature of the apocalypse. When Max enters Bartertown, he uses a Geiger counter to scan the water being offered by a street vendor. If all the water is irradiated, as we would expect from a nuclear apocalypse, there would be no need to scan it. But, if there is clean water in the world—and we know there is, both at the Crack in the Earth and the Citadel and probably in other places as well—then it does make sense to check it out. If Bartertown were a trading encampment that developed during a nuclear winter, then grew to be the settlement it was by the time of Max's visit, it is possible that Bartertown was growing and developing concurrently to the events of *Fury Road*. The important thing to note about Bartertown is that people want to live there. The inhabitants seem relatively happy, and Aunty Entity, though a tyrant, is a soft-hearted one who both enforces and mostly obeys the laws—she even spares Max at the end of their epic chase despite having issued a command of no quarter. These are hardly the actions of a dystopian ruler—despotic, perhaps, but not dystopian.

But He's Just a Raggedyman

Given what we know about the world of Max Rockatansky, it is clear that at some point a major calamity befell human civilization. Yet whatever that catastrophe was, it was not global in its reach, or at least not as severe everywhere. It also doesn't follow that the world of *Mad Max* is dystopian. Clearly, there are people who have chosen to live in the Wasteland prior to the nuclear conflict. After that conflict, life continues on an upward trajectory, and many people seem to be living happy lives in spite of their circumstances. Ultimately, the world depicted in the film franchise is less than ideal, but it is not a post-apocalyptic dystopia.

Notes

1   In this essay I am ignoring the novelization of *Mad Max* because that undertaking was done (in part) by people who were not responsible for the construction of the canon. I am also explicitly ignoring the comic book version of *Mad Max* because the underlying causes of the apocalypse and resulting dystopia are updated to conform with more contemporary environmental concerns, and this completely shifts the ground of analysis for the films. That is, the comic books represent a completely different telling of the story of *Mad Max*.

2   I discuss the difference between types of apocalypses in greater detail in *Apocalyptic Ecology in the Graphic Novel: Life and the Environment After Societal Collapse* (Jefferson, NC: McFarland and Co., 2020), 1–8.

3 I am here referencing the graphic novel, though I believe similarly successful arguments could be made about the television show; Robert Kirkman, *The Walking Dead*, Compendium One (Berkeley, CA: Image-Skybound, 2009).

4 For a more thorough analysis of what the world of *The Walking Dead* would look like, see *Apocalyptic Ecology*, ch. 3.

5 The timeline for the story is difficult to make sense of even with (or perhaps especially because of) George Miller's lack of help in interviews, where he is intentionally vague and sketchy as to what *Fury Road* represents with *respect to the original trilogy*; he seems uncertain himself as to whether *Fury Road* represents a continuation or a reboot of the franchise.

6 Bartertown entry, at https://madmax.fandom.com/wiki/Bartertown. Emphasis in original.

Part II

THE MAN WITH NO NAME: HEROES AND FINDING ONESELF POST-APOCALYPSE STYLE

6

"Pray He's Still out There": Heroism in the *Mad Max* Films

Karen Joan Kohoutek

The character of Max Rockatansky tells a tale of two heroes. One is a "hero with a thousand faces," a concept defined by author Joseph Campbell (1904–1987) and acknowledged by *Mad Max* creator George Miller. The other is the existential hero: a figure who reacts to a world with no intrinsic meaning, as described by Albert Camus (1913–1960) in *The Myth of Sisyphus*.

In a cycle of four films, Max faces the forces of chaos, destruction, and tyranny. He prevails to varying degrees, but his successes never last. In the first film, *Mad Max*, all his victories are pyrrhic, and the character, initially described as a hero, succumbs to the madness of the highway, meting out a violent form of vigilante justice. The other films all begin with Max alone in a desert full of violent and unstable people, who are clustered into dangerous groups, and they end with him back in the same place.

In the second and third films, Max positions himself as a loner, resisting the call to help the community at the oil refinery in *The Road Warrior* and declining the role of savior offered to him in *Mad Max: Beyond Thunderdome*. Ultimately, though, he can't help himself from acting heroically. Both films end with the people he's helped creating pockets of a more livable society, looking back on him as a mythic figure who led them to a promised land which he is not a part of.

In *Fury Road*, Max begins as a loner, captured by a stronger group based out of the Citadel, a reconstructed society rooted in a violent patriarchy. Eventually, he helps an escaping group of women, and they return with the hope of reforming the oppressive society. Max

Mad Max and Philosophy: Thinking Through the Wasteland, First Edition.
Edited by Matthew P. Meyer and David Koepsell.
© 2024 John Wiley & Sons, Inc. Published 2024 by John Wiley & Sons, Inc.

himself goes back into the Wasteland, "out there with the garbage," as it's judged in *The Road Warrior*. Throughout the series, he never enjoys the benefits of his endeavors, always remaining outside any nascent revival of civilization. While he saves some people's lives, Max still exists within a profoundly broken world, where there are always going to be more people than one man can help. So he is always left in the same unforgiving desert where, as Camus puts it, "the whole being is exerted toward accomplishing nothing."[1]

As a concept, heroism is embedded in a system of social storytelling, requiring a degree of moral coherence. Max, in contrast, exists in an incoherent world where "it was hard to know who was more crazy," him "or everyone else." Max not only performs heroic acts, if sometimes begrudgingly, but he does so when there is no social order able to define right action or differentiate between good and evil. He faces an existential reality in which there is no given meaning. Thus, Max's acts taken "by themselves" will always succumb to meaninglessness. However, those acts and Max himself are rendered into myth by the people he has helped. Perhaps their act of mythologizing helps to recreate a sense of a social order, perpetuating the idea of heroism, that it's good to help others even when it provides no personal benefit.

"Down the Long Haul, into History Back"

All the *Mad Max* films deal with the collapse of social order as we know it. Once its resources—whether oil or water—are depleted, civilization falls apart, and in an environment of might making right, stronger groups and lone individuals fight for the basics of survival. Each film, taken chronologically, depicts a slightly more developed path toward rebuilding a semblance of human stability, creating what are almost case studies of how civilization developed in the first place, from small groups in local conflicts, to towns brought together by trade, to a larger patriarchal structure.

In the original *Mad Max*, an existing, recognizable social order is collapsing. In *The Road Warrior*, small groups have banded together for survival, in a fairly straightforward conflict over resources. One group has embraced violence and cruelty as a way of life, and the other self-consciously attempts to hold onto its humanity with a more cooperative form of self-government. In *Mad Max: Beyond Thunderdome*, we see the beginnings of a restored social order based on trade, cooperation, and the restoration of authority, which has some benefits despite its frequent brutality. The budding civilization is contrasted with the harshness of the Wasteland outside its borders; a sign at the entrance to town reads, "Bartertown: Helping Build a Better Tomorrow." In *Mad Max: Fury Road*, there's an established social order and authority in the form of a powerful and oppressive patriarchy, complete with a (brutal) form of religion, and a rebellion against its tyrannical nature. This society is the most complex so far, with a whole population eager to worship the tyrannical Immortan Joe, who gives them both (limited) water and a reason for living. The film also depicts a group of women from "the Green Place," who have stayed alive in the desert on their own terms, but don't have a sustainable culture, with no young people to continue it.

Throughout the series, there are complications in the continuity of Max's character, appropriate to a figure more from myth than history. The films share a main character and thematic concerns with violence, society, and the environment, but there's no strict narrative consistency or chronology. Only the first sequel, *The Road Warrior*, links directly to the previous, starting with flashbacks to the first movie as an origin story, but it is so different in tone that it could be a different world. It is as if each film features a version of the same character, in a slightly different world, each farther along a path of social evolution/devolution.

When an interviewer pointed out that there "was some confusion about how the overall continuity of the *Mad Max* films work," Miller responded at some length. "Well, they're not really connected in any very strict way. They're another episode in a saga of a character who is pretty archetypal: the wanderer in the Wasteland, basically searching for meaning.... You can't really put a chronology [of the *Mad Max* films] together. They were never conceived that way."[2] Miller's tendency to use the same actor to play different but thematically similar characters hints at this kind of fluid reality. Bruce Spence, for example, played the Gyro Captain in the second film and airplane pilot Jedediah in the third; Hugh Keays-Byrne similarly served as both the megalomaniacal Toecutter and Immortan Joe.

In a similar way, the films make no claim that Max needs to be a psychologically consistent character. After the first movie, in which he's a young man tempted by the idea of heroism, he is always a version of a lone wandering survivor, reluctant to reconnect with the damaged remnants of human society, while always drawn in to help them. Within those parameters, though, there is no specific timeline,

and after *The Road Warrior*, no direct connection to previous install-
ments in the series

We Don't Need Another Hero with a Thousand Faces

Miller has compared Max to the "hero with a thousand faces," saying
that "Max is a character who gets swept up into this story. He's sort
of wandering the Wasteland looking for some sense of meaning in a
very stark world, and he gets caught up in this story."[3] The phrase
"hero with a thousand faces" is drawn from the work of author
Joseph Campbell, who codified an archetypal "hero's journey" narrative based on common elements from the world's folklore. In
Campbell's terms, "Once having traversed the threshold, the hero
moves in a dream landscape of curiously fluid, ambiguous forms,
where he must survive a succession of trials."[4] After a series of adventures and surmounted obstacles, the hero finds redemption from his
mistakes, embraces his destiny, and "returns from the mystic realm
into the land of common day," described as a world where "men who
are fractions imagine themselves to be complete."[5]

Miller adds, "I really was aware that the *Mad Max* stories were a
kind of corruption of the hero myth, and, you know, we all know the
great work that Joseph Campbell did studying comparative religion
and folklore and so on and basically huge scholarship there which has
influenced movies and the classic hero myth." Max's stories contain
some element of the Campbell-style narrative, but instead of complet-
ing a coherent hero's journey, Max is mythologized by other characters who, viewing him from the outside, project their need for a hero
or a potential savior onto his basic competence. They want to see him
as a more conventional hero, because that's the story they need to tell
themselves. Ultimately, they tell stories that turn the flawed man into
a figure of legend. His heroism exists in the context of relationships
with social groups, which collectively mythologize his actions.

In the first film, Max's commanding officer complains that "people
don't believe in heroes anymore," but also insists "we're going to give
them back their heroes," particularly in the form of young Max as the
sort of man the masses can look up to. Even in those early days, however, Max understood that the supposedly heroic job was leeching
him of his humanity: "Any longer out on that road and I'm one of
them ... a terminal crazy."

The sequels all show Max as more of a reluctant hero. Miller has said that "Mel Gibson often describes the character as a sort of a closet human being who denied his humanity because he thought it wasn't conducive to survival." Max must be convinced to help people escape violence and rebuild civilization.[6] In *The Road Warrior*, he first offers his help in mercenary terms. Eventually, his actions become more selfless, so a member of the group later admits, "I was wrong about you." The idea of Max as a Messiah figure was highlighted in the film's ad campaign: "Pray he's still out there."

In *Max Max: Beyond Thunderdome*, Pigkiller, a prisoner in the Underground, almost immediately latches onto Max as someone special. He refuses to believe Max's insistence that he's "nobody," replying, "No, Mister, I can feel it! The dice are rollin'!" The youthful tribe Max later encounters view him more explicitly as a long-awaited savior, equating him with the "Captain Walker" they expect to come back for them. While that is the name of the pilot of their crashed airplane, Max is often seen as a "walker" in this film, literally traversing the Wasteland on foot, his strong identification with automotive culture notwithstanding.

Max's Messianic tendency is deconstructed by *Fury Road*, which puts him in the least heroic position so far, overwhelmed and held captive by the central tyrant. Early in the film, Max remains passive, even strapped to the front of the car exactly as the hapless victims of the marauders were in *The Road Warrior*. He retains his coolness of mind, able to take maximum advantage of the slightest opportunity, along with the fighting and driving skills he previously used to help others. Before long, he has fallen into an unspoken alliance against the forces of Immortan Joe, so that the escaping women uncritically put their lives in his hands, and it's his idea to return and remake their society, rather than flee it.

Campbell's myth stresses the importance of the "hoarder of the general benefit," who is "the tyrant-monster" that the archetypal hero must fight.[7] This idea recurs throughout the sequels, to greater and lesser degrees. In the second film, we see it in the battle between the survivors, at the oil refinery, and Lord Humungus's brutal raiders who'd use it for selfish personal benefit. In the third movie, Bartertown's Aunty Entity oversees trade and the efforts to kickstart a more civilized world, which requires her to keep tight control of the community's resources. The theme is most fully developed in the fourth film with Immortan Joe, who openly hoards oil, water, and fertile young women to maintain his power. The films show a continuum of conflicts that involve communities, their leaders, and the resources needed for survival. Ever since civilization began to break down in the original movie, individuals have vied for power, and the measure of their success was in the hoarding of the general benefit.

Miller explains screenwriter Terry Hayes's perspective:

> [Terry] started talking about mythology and how where people are short on knowledge, they tend to be very big on belief. In other words, they take a few fragments of knowledge and ... using those little bits of the jigsaw construct very elaborate mythological beliefs, which explain the whole universe. Terry was saying if you had a tribe of kids after the apocalypse who had only a few fragments of knowledge, [they would construct] a mythological belief as to what was before. And what would happen if Max or someone like that ...[8]

The interview is interrupted at this point, but it's fairly clear where Miller was going.

We Don't Need Another Absurd Hero

Despite Miller's awareness of Campbell's classic myth structure, Max is not ultimately this kind of archetype. Though other characters try to put him in the position of a more traditional hero, the kind who would end up in Campbell's book, he always ends up in the same place, the implacable Wasteland, making his heroism absurdly existentialist.

In his influential essay "The Myth of Sisyphus," French writer Albert Camus defines the mythological Sisyphus as "the absurd hero," who exists in a situation "in which the whole being is exerted toward accomplishing nothing."[9] For finding ways to cheat death, Sisyphus was condemned by the gods to push a boulder up a hill where it would always roll back down. Camus used this tale as a metaphor for humanity and the absurdity of its attempts to find meaning. It is also strongly analogous to Max's experiences in the films. Despite Max's position as an alienated loner, he remains "one of the living," as we are reminded in the Tina Turner song that opens *Mad Max: Beyond Thunderdome*. He has "the habit of living" intrinsic to Camus' absurd hero, since "in a man's attachment to life there is something stronger than all the ills in the world."[10]

Camus places a dividing line between a person's life before "encountering the absurd" and "after the absurd," which aptly describes the position of Max and the rest of the world's population, before and after the devastating crises that plunge them into barbarism. In the before, "the everyday man lives with aims, a concern with the future or for justification ... he weighs his chances, he counts on 'someday' ... he still thinks that something in his life can be directed. In truth, he acts as if he were free."[11] This is Max as we first saw him, living happily with his wife and child and taking a vacation in the middle of the film, unaware that the increasing chaos on the roadways was a sign of world-altering doom.

Afterward, "everything is upset ... thinking of the future, establishing aims for oneself, having preferences—all this presupposes a belief in freedom, even if one occasionally ascertains that one doesn't feel it. But at that moment I am well aware that that higher liberty, that freedom to be, which alone can serve as basis for a truth, does not exist. Death is there as the only reality. After death the chips are down."[12] In Max's post-apocalyptic world, the chips are down. There are no more illusions. The reality of death and the absurdity of life are both on full display.

Talking about his hero myth in light of both mythology and psychological theory, Campbell says that the hero reaches a "higher spiritual dimension," which involves "a retreat from the desperations of the waste land to the peace of the everlasting realm that is within."[13] By the time of *Fury Road*, Max is clear in his position that "hope is a mistake. If you can't fix what's broken, you'll go insane." It might sound like he has made some hard-won internal peace with the state of the world, but it's difficult to view this as true inner peace. In Campbell's paradigm of the heroic experience, "a decisive victory is won,"[14] but Max never wins a lasting, decisive victory—certainly never a personal one.

In *Fury Road*, he is haunted by his failures, all the people he could have potentially saved but didn't. These are not characters from the films we've seen, since he did mostly help those people. Unfortunately, no individual can single-handedly hold back "Mr. Dead" forever, even when they carry him in their pocket, as Max describes himself to the tribe of children in *Beyond Thunderdome*. The graphic novel tying into *Fury Road* states this explicitly: "[I]n this hostile world, one man alone could never prevail."[15] Any acceptance of what Max experiences seems far from a kind of peace. Camus suggests that we must ultimately imagine Sisyphus as happy, but that is hard to do with Max.

"Where Must We Go, We Who Wander This Wasteland, in Search of Our Better Selves?"

In both *The Road Warrior* and *Beyond Thunderdome*, Max helps groups of survivors escape to places of sanctuary, places from which to start again. Both include epilogues to let us know they succeeded and that Max is remembered in their legends, but there remains an air of ambiguity. Max is absolutely certain that they can't go back to Tomorrow-Morrow Land, but they do get to a place of safety and even turn the electricity back on, proving him wrong. If there are better places or better futures, though, Max is always shut out of them.

Fury Road offers the fullest picture of civilization rebuilding, but the process is full of human suffering, and it has no utopia as an endpoint. Instead, the fight against tyranny is going to take work, as the groups from the earlier films likely found out, off-screen. It also lacks the epilogue, but it seems likely that Max would be similarly remembered for his actions.

At the end of these films, as Max helps characters find hope for a restored order, they slot him into inspiring narratives, turning him into an archetype, but Max never embraces the role of hero. Instead, he returns to the Wasteland, in the same way that Sisyphus always ends up at the bottom of the hill, aligned with the absurdity of human existence in a world where order and history have been wiped away.

As part of the mythic structure, Campbell expects his hero with a thousand faces to experience an apotheosis, a satisfying conclusion in which he becomes godlike in enlightenment and is further defined by a return, "a coming back out of that yonder zone."[16] For Campbell, "*the return and reintegration with society,*" so important that he italicizes it, is considered "indispensable" to the hero's journey.[17] Max never experiences an apotheosis, and his trials are simply that: trials. They don't earn him anything, not even enlightenment or true inner peace. All that's left are small victories, so the good he does is on a small scale, meaningful for those he helps, but he doesn't save the world or escape his own wandering in the Wasteland.

Unlike the framework of Campbell's hero myth, Miller's films do not occupy the realm of fairytale. Instead, they take a hard look at the realities of upheaval and change, recognizing with Max that sometimes you can't fix what's broken. People continue to desire happy endings, myths of Messiahs and Chosen Ones who will save them, but a heroic apotheosis can only take place within a stable social order, something that can no longer be taken for granted.

For Max, it's impossible to return and reintegrate back into a society that literally no longer exists. A reconstructed Tomorrow-Morrow Land, striving to recreate or substitute for the world that's been lost, cannot replace the world he knew. There's no going back to who he was or to the position of authority he once held. Max knows the nature of his reality, and he doesn't travel through the Wasteland as a kind of initiatory experience. He's staying there for good. As Camus put it, "[A] man who has become conscious of the absurd is forever bound to it. A man devoid of hope and conscious of being so has ceased to belong to the future."[18]

Notes

1   Albert Camus, *The Myth of Sisyphus* (New York, Vintage Books, 1991), 120.
2   "George Miller Interview: *Mad Max* and the Making of *Fury Road*," at https://www.denofgeek.com/movies/george-miller-interview-mad-max-and-the-making-of-fury-road/.
3   "Mad Max Director George Miller: The Audience Tells You What Your Film Is," at https://www.npr.org/transcripts/465989808.
4   Joseph Campbell, *The Hero with a Thousand Faces* (Princeton: Princeton University Press, 1968), 97.
5   Ibid., 216.
6   "George Miller Talks About Mad Max, Heroes & Tina Turner: The 1985 Interview," at https://multiglom.com/2015/05/12/george-miller-the-1985-interview/.
7   Campbell, 15.
8   "George Miller Talks About Mad Max, Heroes & Tina Turner: The 1985 Interview."
9   Camus, 120.
10 Ibid., 8.
11 Ibid., 57.
12 Ibid.
13 Campbell, 17.
14 Ibid., 23.
15 George Miller, Nico Lathouris, Mark Sexton, Leandro Fernandez, Riccardo Burchielli, Andrea Mutti, Tristan Jones, Szymon Kudranski, Clem Robins, and Tommy L. Edwards, *Mad Max: Fury Road* (New York: DC Comics/Vertigo, 2015).
16 Campbell, 217.
17 Ibid., 36.
18 Camus, 31–32.

Bloodbags and Artificial Arms: Bodily Parthood in *Mad Max: Fury Road*

Joshua L. Tepley

In *Mad Max: Fury Road*, Max Rockatansky has his hair chopped off, his head encased in a muzzle, and his blood siphoned from his body. These are all cruel violations of his dignity as a human person. But what are these alterations doing to his *parts*? Is his body any larger or smaller after these changes?

Most people agree that hair and blood are parts of a person's body, so removing these takes away some of Max's parts. His body is a little bit smaller and lighter after these changes. Most people would also agree that Max's muzzle is *not* part of his body. Being muzzled doesn't add to a person's body any more than putting on a motorcycle jacket or picking up a sawed-off shotgun do.

Common sense tells us that some things—such as hair and blood, but also hands, feet, skin, bones, and internal organs—are parts of a person's body, whereas other things—such as muzzles, jackets, boots, and shotguns—are not. But what explains the difference between these? Why is Max's skin, but not his jacket, part of his body? And why are Nux's eyes, but not his goggles, parts of his? Common sense doesn't tell us.

Neither does common sense tell us what to think about every conceivable object that could be part of a person's body. Consider tattoos—like the one Max forcibly gets at the start of the movie. Are tattoos parts of a person's body? Ask different people and you'll get different answers. Another hard case is artificial arms—like Furiosa's. Some people think these are genuine parts of a person's body, on a par with their biological limbs, whereas other people don't. Who's right?

Mad Max and Philosophy: Thinking Through the Wasteland, First Edition.
Edited by Matthew P. Meyer and David Koepsell.
© 2024 John Wiley & Sons, Inc. Published 2024 by John Wiley & Sons, Inc.

In this essay, we'll search for a criterion of what makes something part of a human body and then apply this criterion to hard cases, such as tattoos and artificial arms. We'll consider five criteria in total: *adhesion, bonding, life, function,* and *integration.* Along the way, we'll use *Mad Max: Fury Road* to furnish examples and test cases. Our discussion will cover not just Furiosa's artificial arm and the alterations to Max mentioned above, but also Nux's Bloodbag, Immortan Joe's breathing mask, and the five wives' chastity belts. So grab your steering wheel and hook up your Bloodbag. We're about to take a drive through the cruel wasteland of *metaphysics*.

Adhesion: "You Want That Thing off Your Face?"

What makes Max's feet, but not his boots, parts of his body? Here's a simple idea: something is part of a person's body if, and only if, the former *adheres* to the latter. When something adheres to something else, it can't be easily removed from that thing. Max's feet are parts of his body because pulling them off would require a great deal of physical force. His boots are *not* parts of his body because they can be pulled off fairly easily.

The *adhesion criterion* looks pretty good at first, but it has some serious problems. To start, consider Max's muzzle. Max has an extremely hard time getting this off. So, according to the adhesion criterion, the muzzle is part of Max's body. And the same applies to the horrific chastity belts worn by Immortan Joe's five wives. These are also hard to remove, from which it follows—if the adhesion criterion is true—that they are parts of their bodies, too. These implications are just absurd, aren't they?

But hold on a second. Are these things *really* that hard to remove? Max can't get his muzzle off with his bare hands, but he is able to get it off with the help of a metal file from Furiosa. And the five wives are able to remove their chastity belts easily enough with the help of a bolt cutter. Moreover, the only reason these things are hard to get off in the first place is because nobody has the keys. With the keys, removing these things would be easy—no harder than taking off a jacket or pulling off a boot. So, perhaps Max's muzzle and the wives' chastity belts aren't good counterexamples to the adhesion criterion after all. With the proper tools, their removal would be easy.

There are two problems with using tools to save the adhesion criterion. First, although the muzzle and chastity belts in the movie do have locks, we can easily imagine versions of them that don't—such as muzzles and chastity belts welded into place. These would be hard to remove even with the proper tools. Second, if tools are allowed to make the removal of something easier, then it follows that our hands and feet aren't really parts of our bodies. For these, too, can be removed easily with the right tools—such as an axe or a meat cleaver. But surely our hands and our feet *are* parts of our bodies. So, with or without tools, it seems that the adhesion criterion just isn't going to cut it (no pun intended).

Bonding: "Don't Damage the Goods"

Perhaps the reason why Max's feet but not his boots are parts of his body is simply because removing the former, but not the latter, would harm him. Let's express this idea by saying that Max's feet are *bonded* to his body. When something is bonded to something else, the former can't be removed from the latter without damaging it.

The *bonding criterion* would explain why Max's feet, hands, bones, and internal organs are all parts of him: removing these things—by chopping them off or cutting them out—would damage his body. It would also explain why Max's boots, jacket, and muzzle are *not* parts of him: these things can be removed without harming his body.

While the bonding criterion seems promising, it faces some serious objections. To start, portions of our hair (above the root), skin (on the surface), and fingernails (at the ends) can be removed from our bodies without harming them. These things are "dead," so their removal doesn't cause us any pain or trigger our bodies' self-repair processes. If anything, the regular removal of this dead material is actually *good* for a person. But from all this it follows that the bulk of our hair, the surface of our skin, and the tips of our fingernails aren't really parts of our bodies. That seems wrong, doesn't it?

And on the flip side, there seem to be clear examples of things that are *not* parts of our bodies but which are harmful to remove. Take, for example, Immortan Joe's breathing mask. Besides whatever role it plays in bolstering his sinister persona, this mask clearly serves the practical function of supplying him with clean air to breathe. So, taking it away would cause him harm—at least in the long run. And the same is true of Nux's Bloodbag: given Nux's health problems, using Max as a Bloodbag is good for Nux's body. So, detaching the Bloodbag from Nux would harm him, too. But surely Joe's breathing mask and

Nux's Bloodbag aren't literally parts of their bodies. In light of these two problems, the bonding criterion seems to be another dead end.

Life: "They've Got My Blood"

Common sense tells us that hands, feet, bones, and internal organs are all parts of a person's body whereas boots, jackets, muzzles, and breathing masks are not. What feature do the former have in common with each other but not with any of the latter?

A moment's reflection yields an obvious answer: the former are all *alive*. The latter, by contrast, are mere artifacts. Perhaps *life* is what distinguishes genuine body parts (such as hands and feet) from bodily accessories (such as boots and jackets). More specifically, perhaps something is part of a person's body if, and only if, it is alive and attached to that body.

Life might have something to do with bodily parthood, but it can't be as simple as being alive and being attached to a body. Consider Nux's use of Max as a Bloodbag. Max is definitely alive, and he is physically chained to Nux while his blood is being siphoned. But surely Max isn't part of Nux.

Max doesn't become part of Nux while he's being used as a Bloodbag, but some of his blood does. What's the difference? The difference is that Max's blood, once it enters Nux's bloodstream, gets caught up in the life processes of Nux's body. Perhaps this is the key to bodily parthood: something is part of a person's body if, and only if, it participates in that body's life processes.[1]

The *life criterion* looks promising. It explains why hands, feet, bones, hearts, and lungs are all parts of a person's body; it also explains why boots, jackets, muzzles, breathing masks, and Bloodbags are not. So far, so good.

Unfortunately, the life criterion has problems, too. First, like the bonding criterion, the life criterion implies that portions of our hair, skin, and fingernails—namely, the parts that can be removed without harming our bodies—aren't really parts of us. These portions don't participate in our bodies' life processes and so aren't technically "alive." But common sense tells us that these things *are* parts of our bodies, doesn't it?

Second, this criterion implies that artificial things, no matter how seamlessly integrated into our bodies, are never really parts of us. Furiosa's artificial arm isn't the best example of this, since it can be detached fairly easily and has limited functionality. But there are plenty of good examples from real life, such as artificial knees, pacemakers, and cochlear implants. And these are just the tip of the iceberg when we consider what's possible in the future. Scientists are working on artificial hearts that can replace organic ones, prosthetic arms that can be "hard wired" into a body's nervous system, and brain implants that can mitigate blindness. I'm inclined to say that such artificial things—both the ones that exist now (such as artificial knees) and the ones that might exist someday (such as artificial hearts)—*can* be parts of a person's body.[2] But in that case, the life criterion can't be true.

Function: "If You Can't Stand Up, You Can't Do War"

Hands, feet, hearts, and lungs are all biological things. They are also *teleological* things. That is, they are all *for* something; they all have some *function*. Hands are for grasping and manipulating objects; feet are for standing and walking; hearts are for pumping blood; lungs are for breathing oxygen. The functions of these things vary, but they all have one thing in common: they contribute to the proper functioning of the human body. In order for a human body to function properly, its parts must perform their functions properly.[3]

Perhaps *function* is the key to understanding bodily parthood. Perhaps what makes something part of a human body is not what it's made of (such as living organic tissue) but what it does (such as pump blood). More specifically, perhaps something is part of a person's body if, and only if, it has a function that, when performed properly, contributes to the proper functioning of that body.

The *function criterion* neatly avoids the two problems with the life criterion. First, the function criterion can explain why "dead" matter—such as portions of our hair, skin, and nails—can be part of our bodies. These things all perform bodily functions: hair keeps us warm, skin protects us, and nails are useful for a variety of things, such as picking and scratching. So, according to the function criterion, these are all parts of the body—just as common sense says they are.

Second, the function criterion can explain why artificial parts—such as artificial knees, pacemakers, and cochlear implants—are parts of a human body. These perform functions that contribute to the body's overall proper functioning. In some cases (such as artificial knees), they simply replace biological parts; in other cases (such as pacemakers), they enable a damaged biological part to work properly. Either way, these things contribute to the proper functioning of a human body and so count as parts of that body according to this criterion.

I wish I could stop there and tell you that we've finally found a criterion of bodily parthood that is free of problems. Unfortunately, I can't.

To start, the function criterion runs into problems with biological parts that have no function. Consider tumors, such as Nux's two "mates"—Larry and Barry. Tumors have no function, let alone a function that contributes to the proper functioning of a human body. And the same holds for vestigial organs, such as the appendix, which supposedly serve no function at this stage in human evolution. So, if the function criterion is true, then tumors and vestigial organs are *not* parts of human bodies. Doesn't that seem wrong? Doesn't it seem like tumors and vestigial organs *are* parts of our bodies?

Be that as it may, there is a bigger problem with using function as a criterion of bodily parthood. Consider the fact that human artifacts—such as boots, jackets, and breathing masks—have functions, too. And in many cases, these functions contribute to the proper functioning of a human body. Boots protect our feet and make walking easier, jackets keep us warm and block the sun's harmful radiation, and breathing masks purify the air we breathe and keep our lungs free of toxins. If the function criterion is true, then these things are all parts of human bodies. Another dead end.

Integration: "Got Everything You Need"

Let's consider one final criterion. Immortan Joe's breathing mask performs a function: it filters the air he breathes. So, its removal would cause him harm—at least in the long run. But removing his mask wouldn't necessarily cause him any harm *over and above* the harm caused by the loss of its function. Of course, its removal in the movie does cause him additional harm—his face gets ripped off! But this is an accident of how it gets removed. Under normal circumstances, removing Joe's mask doesn't cause him any harm in addition to the harm caused by the loss of its function.

Compare Joe's breathing mask with his lungs. His lungs, too, perform a function: they allow him to breathe. So, removing his lungs would certainly cause him harm by depriving him of this vital function.

But notice that removing his lungs would harm him in other ways, too. Cutting them out would damage his tissue and cause him to bleed. So, unlike his breathing mask, Joe's lungs can be removed only by causing him harm over and above the harm caused by the loss of their function.

Let's introduce a piece of terminology. Let's say that something is *integrated* into a human body when it performs a function for that body and its removal would harm that body over and above the harm caused to it by the loss of that thing's function. So, arms and legs are integrated into a human body, whereas jackets and breathing masks are not. Removing any of these would (or at least could) harm a person's body, but only the removal of the former (arms and legs) would harm a person's body in addition to the harm caused by the loss of their function. Turning this idea into a criterion of bodily parthood: perhaps something is part of a human body if, and only if, it is integrated into that body.[4]

According to the *integration criterion*, arms, legs, hearts, lungs, pacemakers, artificial knees, and blood are all parts of a person's body. Each of these performs some function in the body, and its removal would harm the body in addition to the harm caused by the loss of its function. Things that are *not* parts of a person's body, according to this criterion, include muzzles, breathing masks, Bloodbags, boots, jackets, shotguns, and shrapnel. Some of these things (muzzles and shrapnel) aren't parts of a body because they don't have functions that contribute to the proper functioning of the body as a whole; the others (breathing masks, Bloodbags, boots, jackets, and shotguns) do have such functions, but they can all be removed without damaging the body over and above the damage caused by the loss of their functions.

These results conform to our commonsense intuitions about what things are and are not parts of human bodies. Unfortunately, the integration criterion has a couple of counterintuitive consequences as well. First, like the function criterion, the integration criterion implies that tumors and vestigial organs are not parts of our bodies. For although their removal would cause our bodies some damage, they serve no function. Second, like the bonding and life criteria, the integration criterion implies that the "dead" portions of our hair, skin, and fingernails aren't really parts of us. For although these things do perform functions, their removal causes no harm over and above the harm caused by the loss of their functions. So, while the integration criterion has a lot going for it, it's not problem-free.

Life or Integration: "We're the Only Ones Left"

None of the criteria of bodily parthood examined in this essay aligns perfectly with common sense. Each of them implies that things we would expect to be parts of human bodies aren't or that things we wouldn't expect to be parts of human bodies are. This leaves us with two options: either we keep searching for a criterion that doesn't violate common sense in these ways, or we bite the bullet and admit that common sense is wrong. In what follows, I take the latter option. Readers unwilling to follow me in this rejection of common sense are welcome to pursue the first option on their own. I wish them luck!

Of the five criteria discussed in this essay, two stand out as being the most plausible: the life criterion and the integration criterion. Both criteria imply that hands, feet, hearts, lungs, eyes, and blood are parts of a person's body; and both imply that boots, jackets, breathing masks, shotguns, muzzles, Bloodbags, and shrapnel are not. These are commonsensical results. Where these two criteria diverge from common sense is in what they imply about the "dead" portions of our hair, skin, and fingernails—namely, that these things aren't really parts of our bodies. That's hard to swallow. But if these are the best criteria of bodily parthood on offer, and they both agree on this point, then perhaps we have no other choice.

Even so, how do we decide which of these two criteria is true? We can start with the ways in which they disagree. According to the life criterion, artificial objects—such as artificial knees, pacemakers, and cochlear implants—aren't really parts of our bodies, whereas according to the integration criterion they are. And whereas the integration criterion implies that living things that serve no function—such as tumors and vestigial organs—aren't really parts of our bodies, the life criterion says that they are. Which of these consequences is less counterintuitive? What's less strange: that artificial knees and pacemakers aren't really parts of our bodies, or that tumors and vestigial organs aren't?

Arguing for Integration: "That's My Head!"

My intuitions aren't strong enough to answer this question. My gut tells me that artificial knees and tumors *both* belong to a person's body, and I can't tell about which of these things I feel more strongly.

At times like these, when our intuitions peter out, philosophers rely on rational arguments to help them decide what to believe. Here is one such argument in favor of the integration criterion.

Consider a future in which our technology has advanced to the point where parts of human brains can be replaced with artificial parts (like silicon chips) that duplicate the functions of the parts they replace so perfectly that the people who have them can't tell the difference. They think and act just like they did before they got the implants. Taken to the extreme, it seems possible that a person's entire brain could be replaced, bit by bit, with artificial parts and yet the person feels no different afterward. In such a world, people with artificial brains think and act just like people with organic ones.[5]

I'm inclined to say that such a future is possible. I'm also inclined to say that in such a world the artificial brains would be parts of the persons who have them. The integration criterion can accommodate this intuition, for artificial brains would be integrated (in the technical sense of "integrated," defined above) into human bodies. The life criterion, by contrast, can't explain this. According to the life criterion, something is part of a body only if it is caught up in the biological processes of that body. Since an artificial brain isn't alive, it can't be part of a person's body any more than a piece of shrapnel can be. Therefore, assuming the scenario described above is possible, and artificial brains would be parts of human bodies, we have a reason to prefer the integration criterion over the life criterion. Personally, I find this argument pretty compelling.

Tattoos and Artificial Arms: "Now We Bring Home the Booty"

One reason to identify a criterion of bodily parthood is to help us decide what to think about hard cases. I mentioned two such cases at the opening of this essay: Max's tattoo and Furiosa's artificial arm. Let's take a look at what the integration criterion says about these. We can compare this to what the life criterion says about them as well.

Both of these criteria—life and integration—imply that Max's tattoo is *not* part of his body. According to the life criterion, this is because the ink of the tattoo isn't caught up in the life processes of his body. His body tolerates the tattoo, to be sure, but being *tolerated* by a body's life processes isn't the same thing as being *involved* in those processes. According to the integration criterion, Max's tattoo isn't part of his body because it doesn't contribute to his body's proper functioning. His body isn't any better off because he has the tattoo.

What about Furiosa's artificial arm? Both criteria give a negative answer here, too. Furiosa's artificial arm isn't part of her body according to the life criterion because it isn't alive, and only living things (or very small things, like proteins and molecules) can participate in a body's life processes. It's not part of her body according to the integration criterion because it isn't integrated into her body. Its removal doesn't harm her over and above the harm caused by the loss of its function, as evidenced by the times she removes it during the movie and seems no worse for wear.

That being said, we can easily imagine an artificial arm that would be part of a person's body according to the integration criterion— namely, one that is tied into a person's nervous system such that its removal would require surgery. Since its removal would harm the body over and above the harm caused by the loss of its function, such an artificial arm would be a part of that body—at least according to the integration criterion.

Conclusion: "He Doesn't Know What He's Talking About!"

To be perfectly clear, I don't think that George Miller—the writer and director of *Mad Max: Fury Road*—intended for his movie to raise questions about bodily parthood. But that doesn't mean that the movie doesn't raise these questions anyway. The greatest works of human culture, including pop culture, are rich with opportunities for philosophical reflection. *Mad Max: Fury Road* is a perfect example of this. Intentionally or not, it raises all sorts of interesting philosophical questions, including the ones discussed in this essay. This richness is partly what makes *Mad Max: Fury Road* such a great movie.

Notes

1 The life criterion is commonly credited to the English philosopher John Locke (1632–1704). See his *Essay Concerning Human Understanding*, Book II, chap. XXVII, secs. 4–7. Two contemporary defenders of this criterion are Peter van Inwagen and Eric T. Olson. For van Inwagen's view, see his *Material Beings* (Ithaca: Cornell University Press, 1990);

for Olson's view, see his *The Human Animal: Personal Identity Without Psychology* (New York: Oxford University Press, 1997). See also Eric T. Olson, *What Are We? A Study in Personal Ontology* (New York: Oxford University Press, 2007), esp. 23–29, 71–75.

2 For a defense of the view that human bodies can have artificial parts, see Andy Clark, *Natural-Born Cyborgs: Minds, Technologies, and the Future of Human Intelligence* (New York: Oxford University Press, 2003). See also Lynne Rudder Baker, "Technology and the Future of Persons," *The Monist* 96 (2013), 37–53.

3 The idea that parts of bodies are defined by their function (teleology) is owed to the ancient Greek philosopher Aristotle (384–322 B.C.E.). See, for example, his *On the Parts of Animals.* For a contemporary discussion of function as it relates to the parts of organisms, see Joshua Hoffman and Gary S. Rosenkrantz, *Substance: Its Nature and Existence* (London: Routledge, 1997), ch. 4.

4 I'm unfamiliar with any philosophers who endorse the integration criterion exactly as I've stated it here. But one account that comes close is that of Hilary J. Yancey. See her *Is That My Heart? A Hylomorphic Account of Bodily Parthood* (Ph.D. dissertation, Baylor University, 2020). On Yancey's view, "[B]odily parthood is defined by the performance of functions that aid in the sustainment of a human being's biological life and is restricted additionally by the need for body parts to be integrated and interdependent on one another," 16.

5 This thought experiment of replacing a person's organic brain with artificial parts is not original to this essay. See, for example, Peter Unger, *Identity, Consciousness, and Value* (New York: Oxford University Press, 1990), 121–122.

8

The Meaning of Life According to *Mad Max: Fury Road*

Kiki Berk

> Where must we go ... we who wander this Wasteland, in search of our better selves?
>
> —The First History Man

Mad Max: Fury Road might not strike us as a film about the meaning of life, and George Miller may not have intended it as such. Nevertheless, it provides excellent illustrations of contemporary philosophical theories about meaning in life. What's more, the film clearly weighs in on which of these theories is best, and it even advocates for a specific kind of meaningful life. This essay sketches the different theories of meaning illustrated in the movie—in particular, by examining the lives of Nux, Max, and Furiosa. By the end of this essay, we'll have an answer to the question: What is the meaning of life according to *Mad Max: Fury Road*?

Nux's Faith, Crisis, and Purpose

When we first meet him, Nux is one of Immortan Joe's "War Boys." These half-clad, bald, skinny, pale, hollow-eyed men, who only live a "half-life" because of the effects of radiation following "the Fall," make up Immortan Joe's personal army. They consider Immortan Joe their father and, more important, their god. There is a myth that Joe is immortal (hence "Immortan" Joe) and will reward the War Boys for their service to him with admission to Valhalla, the afterlife. As a

Mad Max and Philosophy: Thinking Through the Wasteland, First Edition.
Edited by Matthew P. Meyer and David Koepsell.
© 2024 John Wiley & Sons, Inc. Published 2024 by John Wiley & Sons, Inc.

result, the War Boys worship Immortan Joe and are obsessed with entering Valhalla, often exclaiming, "Witness!" when they think their time has come. Nux is no exception. Raised as a War Boy since he was a "pup," Nux venerates Immortan Joe. When he gets Immortan Joe's attention during the wild car chase through the Wasteland that makes up most of the film, Nux is overjoyed: "Immortan Joe! He looked at me! He looked right at me! ... I am awaited in Valhalla!" It's not an exaggeration to say that Nux's life is meaningful because of Immortan Joe. Being a War Boy gives his life purpose, Valhalla is his promised land, and Immortan Joe is the god who makes it all possible.

Nux can be classified as a Supernaturalist. One of the main beliefs of Supernaturalism is that life can be meaningful only if God exists. In addition, Supernaturalists believe that God exists, and so life is meaningful. This theory is commonly (but not always) held by religious people who think that God bestows purpose on the universe and on their lives. As William Lane Craig, a contemporary Supernaturalist, says, "[I]f there is no God, then man's life becomes absurd."[1] Immortan Joe isn't actually a god. But the War Boys think he is, and he plays the same role in their lives that God does for conventional Supernaturalists (like Craig).

The promise of an afterlife, which often accompanies belief in God, serves an important function here, too: it guarantees eternal existence to those lucky enough to make it. A common corollary of Supernaturalism is the idea that things that don't last forever are insignificant. Death, therefore, would deprive life of meaning. But if we can survive death, for example by entering an afterlife, then our lives can retain their significance. Nux's faith in Immortan Joe as the source of his life's purpose and his belief in life after death make Nux a Supernaturalist—until Nux's crisis of faith, at least.

In the hot pursuit that follows the discovery that Furiosa is making a run for it with Immortan Joe's wives, Nux has an opportunity to "shine." His and Immortan Joe's pursuit vehicles pull up aside the War Rig at the same time, and Nux volunteers to kill Furiosa and "rescue" Immortan Joe's five wives. After asking the War Boy's name, Immortan Joe hands Nux his gun and makes him a deal: "Stop the Rig, return my treasures to me ... and I, myself, will carry you ... to the Gates ... of Valhalla." Nux double-checks: "Am I awaited?" Joe reassures him: "You will ride eternal ... shiny and chrome." When Nux jumps on the rig, however, the chain attached to his arm gets caught, causing him to stumble and drop Immortan Joe's gun. This less-than-smooth performance elicits a "Mediocre!" from Immortan Joe.

This is the moment when things start to go south for Nux. He loses face in full view of Immortan Joe and realizes that he will never be restored to Immortan Joe's good graces. What is worse, he has missed his opportunity to enter Valhalla. As a result, Nux spirals into a depression and crisis of meaning. When one of Immortan Joe's wives, Capable, finds him in the back of the rig, he opens up to her: "He saw it all. My own Bloodbag [Max] driving the rig that killed her.... Three times the gates were open to me.... I was awaited in Valhalla. They were calling my name. I should be walking with the Immorta. McFeasting with the heroes of all time.... I thought I was being spared for something great." Instead, he finds himself alone (or, rather, among those whom he considered until moments ago to be his enemies), ashamed, and without hope of gaining immortality or Immortan Joe's approval. His life has lost all meaning.

At this point, Nux's view can best be described as a kind of Nihilism. Nihilists agree with Supernaturalists that life can be meaningful only if God exists, but Nihilists believe that there is no God and, therefore, that life is meaningless. Some people regard this as a depressing view, whereas others, such as the contemporary philosopher Thomas Nagel, are less fazed and think that it doesn't really matter that nothing matters: "If ... there is no reason to believe that anything matters, then that does not matter either, and we can approach our absurd lives with irony instead of heroism or despair."[2] Even though Immortan Joe still exists, Nux doesn't believe anymore that he can bring him salvation. Nux no longer has a role to play in Immortan Joe's plans, and he won't be rewarded with eternal life. Because Nux feels cut off from him, Immortan Joe loses his god-like status, and Nux loses his purpose, hopes, and dreams. His worldview is shattered, and nothing is meaningful to him anymore.

Fortunately, this phase of Nux's development doesn't last long. Soon after he is discovered on the War Rig and has a heart-to-heart with Capable, he switches sides. His new companions quickly come to accept him as one of their own, and Nux finds new meaning in supporting their mission. After Furiosa's party discovers that the Green Place no longer exists and endeavors to double back past Immortan Joe's army in order to capture the now undefended Citadel, Nux fully embraces his new purpose. He ends up playing a crucial role in the success of Furiosa's mission by using the War Rig to collapse a thruway, thereby blocking Immortan Joe's army from its pursuit of the other members of her group who are riding ahead on motorbikes. Nux thus sacrifices his own life to save his new friends. After losing his faith in Immortan Joe and his resulting crisis, he has now given his life (and death) meaning and significance by choosing his own purpose.

In this final stage of his life, Nux has become a Naturalist. Naturalism can mean many different things in philosophy, but in this context it means that people can make their own lives meaningful, regardless of whether or not there is a God or an afterlife. Some Naturalists believe in God and others don't, but they all agree that the question of God's existence is independent from the question of life's meaning. Instead of relying on a higher power to provide a purpose, Naturalists think that we imbue our own lives with meaning and that we *can* do so, even if there is no purpose in the grand scheme of things. After his supernaturalist upbringing and nihilist crisis, Nux manages to make his short life meaningful by helping Furiosa and playing an important role in the liberation of the wives.

Max: From Survival to a Meaningful Life

At the start of the film, the only thing Max cares about is his own survival. Having lost his family in the Fall, he has worked and fought his way through the Wasteland. He has made several alliances and been betrayed every time, losing everything and ending up alone again and again. He has tried helping other people and is still haunted by those he was unable to save. When he is captured by Immortan Joe's army, brought into the Citadel, and turned into a "Bloodbag," his only aim is to escape and save his own life. In Max's own words: "I am the one ... who runs from both the living and the dead. Hunted by scavengers. Haunted by those I could not protect. So I exist in this Wasteland. A man reduced to a single instinct: survive."

This changes when Max ends up on the War Rig with Furiosa after the wild car chase for which Max is brought along to serve as Nux's Bloodbag. After some initial mutual distrust between them, Max reluctantly agrees to help Furiosa get to the Green Place to try to save the wives. Following the sad discovery that the Green Place no longer exists, Furiosa's group sets out to ride across the salt flats for 160 days on motorbikes, and Max takes off to make his own way. But not for long. He soon changes his mind, chases down the others, and convinces Furiosa that their best strategy is to turn around and try to take the Citadel: "It'll be a hard day. But I guarantee you that a 160 days' ride that way ... there's nothing but salt. At least that way, you know, we might be able to ... together ... come across some kind of redemption." This time, there is nothing reluctant about Max's help. He has made Furiosa's mission his own, cares about getting her group to safety, and is willing to risk his own life for the cause. He even literally gives Furiosa his own blood after she gets injured on the War Rig, saving her life and coming full circle as a "Bloodbag"—this time voluntarily.

With which theory about meaning in life do Max's beliefs fit most closely? Naturalism. We can infer this from a simple process of elimination. Max doesn't believe that the purpose of his life depends on a higher power, and there's no reason to think he believes that his life is meaningful only if there is an afterlife. He is, therefore, not a Supernaturalist. Furthermore, Max doesn't seem to think that life is necessarily devoid of meaning, as Nihilists do. His past actions, rather, suggest that he thinks that life can be meaningful if one succeeds in making it so oneself. After all, he keeps starting anew and trying, again and again, to find new allies and to help other people.

These are all reasons to think that Max should be classified as a Naturalist. But there is more to say. As we have just seen, Max—just like Nux—goes through a process of personal development over the course of *Fury Road*. Max remains a Naturalist throughout, but he moves through different "flavors" of Naturalism, so to speak. Let's get a taste of each one.

As we discussed in the previous section, Naturalists believe that we can make our own lives meaningful. But how exactly do we do this? Naturalists of different kinds disagree with one another. To start, there are Subjective Naturalists who believe that your life is meaningful if, and only if, it is worthwhile to *you*. It doesn't matter what you choose to do with your life. As long as you find your life worth living, it is. According to Subjective Naturalism, meaning is entirely dependent upon the person who grants it—just like beauty is often said to be ("Beauty is in the eyes of the beholder," as the saying goes). A meaningful life can be spent writing books, raising a family, or even counting blades of grass—as long as the person finds the endeavor worthwhile. Richard Taylor, a well-known Subjective Naturalist, writes that "the meaning of life is from within us, it is not bestowed from without."[3] When we first meet Max in *Fury Road*, his life might be meaningful according to this version of Naturalism. He is fully engaged in the project of escape and survival, which is meaningful to him, even though it is arguably meaningless in itself. Subjective Naturalists would say that Max's life during this stage has meaning in virtue of the fact that he cares about what he is trying to accomplish: staying alive.

Other Naturalists agree that we can make our own lives meaningful but disagree with Subjective Naturalists about how exactly this can be done. According to these Naturalists, who are called Objective Naturalists, our lives are meaningful when they exhibit value that is independent of our personal judgment. Their idea is that some projects are inherently valuable (for example, writing a book or raising a family), whereas others are not (for example, counting blades of grass or staring at a blank wall). Objective Naturalists think that no particular person or group of people decides which projects are valuable; rather, they believe that value is something that exists in the world independently of people and their opinions. Some things simply *are* more worthwhile than others, and therefore some lives (namely, those filled with these more worthwhile things) simply *are* more meaningful than others.

Saving someone's life is a project that many Objective Naturalists think has intrinsic value. They think that this is a worthwhile project for anyone to undertake, even if someone isn't really invested in it. Consider Max when he first joins up with Furiosa on the War Rig. He's going through the motions of helping her, but he's really in it to save himself. Even though what he's doing is a good and valuable thing for him to do (objectively), we can't say this is his main motivation (subjectively). So, Max's life would be meaningful according to Objective Naturalism but not according to Subjective Naturalism. His life has meaning, according to Objective Naturalism, because he is doing something worthwhile, even though he doesn't find it particularly worthwhile himself.

A third kind of Naturalism combines Subjective and Objective Naturalism into what is called "Hybrid Naturalism." Hybrid Naturalists think that a person's life is meaningful only if two conditions are met: (1) that person finds their own life to be meaningful and (2) that person's life exhibits objective value. As Susan Wolf, the most famous proponent of Hybrid Naturalism, puts it: "Meaning arises when subjective attraction meets objective attractiveness."[4] One reason why Hybrid Naturalists think that Subjective Naturalism falls short is that, on this view, a life spent doing seemingly meaningless things (such as counting blades of grass or staring at a blank wall) can be meaningful—so long as the person doing them believes they are meaningful. In fact, such a life could be just as meaningful as a life spent as a doctor, an artist, or a parent. This is a conclusion that Hybrid Naturalists think we should resist.

A reason why Hybrid Naturalists think that Objective Naturalism falls short, on the other hand, is that on this view we are forced to say that someone's life is meaningful even if that person doesn't find their life to be worthwhile. This seems wrong. Think again of Max when he is first helping Furiosa: he's doing something valuable but his heart just isn't in it. Hybrid Naturalists will say that Max is doing a meaningful thing, but his life isn't meaningful because he doesn't find it meaningful.

At the end of the film and in the final stage of his development, Max's life is meaningful by the standards of Hybrid Naturalism. Not only is trying to bring Furiosa's group to safety an objectively valuable thing to do, but Max is now invested in this project himself. Such a subjectively engaging and objectively valuable project is a good example of one that Hybrid Naturalists think is meaningful.

Furiosa as a Role Model for a Better Self

We have seen how Nux's and Max's developments illustrate different theories about meaning in life. But what *is* the meaning of life according to *Mad Max: Fury Road*? Does the film contain a message about how to live a meaningful life? It does.

The theory of meaning that comes out most favorably in *Mad Max: Fury Road* is Hybrid Naturalism. Two pieces of evidence support this claim. First, Nux's and Max's developments both culminate in this position. If we consider their developments as paths of personal growth resulting in "better selves," then the fact that they both end up being subjectively engaged in objectively valuable projects is an indication that this is considered a good way of living one's life according to the film. The fact that this is where Nux and Max end up is, therefore, a vote for Hybrid Naturalism.

Second, Furiosa is a very good example of someone living a life that Hybrid Naturalists would consider meaningful, and she is, arguably, the main hero of the film. She doesn't go through a developmental process, as Nux and Max do, because she already has it all figured out. She used to be one of Immortan Joe's warriors, guarding his wives. But she slowly changes sides until, one day, she decides that the right thing to do is to liberate the wives, despite the costs and risks to herself. As she explains to Max on the rig, she is looking for "redemption." She realizes that supporting Immortan Joe was wrong, and she tries to make amends by doing what is right. What is more, she is fully engaged in this project. Thus, Furiosa's life exhibits both objective value and subjective engagement—the key ingredients of a meaningful life according to Hybrid Naturalism. This is another reason to think that the film supports this particular theory of meaning.

Objective Values

According to Hybrid Naturalism, if we want to live meaningful lives, then all we have to do is take up objectively valuable projects and be subjectively engaged with them. It's not hard to grasp what it means to be subjectively engaged with a project because we all know the difference between caring about a project, on the one hand, and feeling alienated, bored, or checked out, on the other. When an activity (or your life as a whole) feels worthwhile to you, this subjective condition is met. But the other requirement is not quite as straightforward. What exactly are objectively valuable projects?

This is a hard question to answer because which activities, projects, and lives are more valuable than others are, on this view, objective facts—like the facts of science and mathematics. Just as some scientific facts are hard to establish (for example, exactly how many stars there are in the Milky Way), so are facts about value. This doesn't mean that these facts don't exist; it just means that it's hard to find them. Some philosophers have proposed short lists of objectively valuable things, called "Objective List Theories." The items on these lists are supposed to be good for anyone—at any time and any place— even if a person doesn't subjectively value them. After all, that's just what it means for these values to be *objective*: they are independent of people's preferences and opinions. (Remember that the subjective side is taken care of by the first condition!)

It may help to have some concrete examples of Objective List Theories. Thomas Hurka, for example, writes: "There isn't just one intrinsic good but many, not just pleasure or virtue but also knowledge, achievement, and maybe more."[5] Jean Kazez, by comparison, offers the following, slightly different list: happiness, autonomy, self-expression, morality (virtue), and progress. Kazez calls these "fundamental goods that are necessities" for a good life.[6] And finally, as a third example, Christopher Belshaw suggests that relationships, pursuing a plan or project, and moral goodness (virtue) are "the sorts of things that sit, often, towards the centre of the meaningful life."[7]

Are there any specific values exhibited by the lives of Furiosa, Nux, and Max in *Mad Max: Fury Road*? I think there are three: virtue, autonomy, and relationships. Let's start with virtue. It's clear that helping other people is one of the biggest themes in the film. After all, the whole plot turns on Furiosa's attempt to liberate the five wives. Max is haunted by the people he was unable to save. He is so dejected that he cares only about himself, but then he comes around to help his new friends. Nux was caught up in his worship of Immortan Joe and his obsession with the afterlife, but he ends up sacrificing his own life to help his new friends. It should be noted that all three of these characters help others at a cost to themselves, and all three of them help others because they think it's the right thing to do.

But the film isn't just about doing the right thing; it's also about becoming a better person. That is to say, the end product is important, but so is the (fury!) road that leads you to a better self. Nux and Max both experience important developments in their moral character: they become better people over the course of the film. Furiosa serves as their role model, having already gone through this process herself. When Furiosa reaches the Citadel and is hailed as a hero (and the new leader?) of the people who were left behind, Max goes his own way—but as a changed person. There's a hint that more adventures and personal growth are in store for him in the quote with which the film ends: "Where must we go ... we who wander this Wasteland, in search of our better selves?" This quotation also confirms that becoming a better person is an important value in the film. Virtue, especially developing virtue, is therefore a central value promoted in *Mad Max: Fury Road*.

Another value that plays a crucial role in the film is autonomy. Many of the characters lack autonomy to start, most notably Immortan Joe's wives, who are held as "breeders." Max is physically in chains and used as a Bloodbag against his will, while Nux is psychologically bound to Immortan Joe as a War Boy. Furiosa used to serve and obey Immortan Joe as one of his warriors until she decided to break with him and go her own way. The operation to liberate the wives, the core of the story, puts the value of autonomy front and center. Max breaks free from his captivity, and Nux learns to think for himself and make his own choices. The fact that so many important characters in the film gain their freedom and independence is a clear indication that, according to the film, autonomy is not just worth fighting for but also an indispensable value for living a meaningful life.

Finally, relationships play an important role in the film. Even though they have little else going for them, Immortan Joe's War Boys enjoy a close comradery. The wives are close friends who look out for each other and grieve deeply when one of them (Splendid) dies. The heart-to-heart Nux has with Capable on the War Rig is a transformative moment for him, and Furiosa and Max bond as they slowly form a team. The women from the Green Place live together in a tight-knit community, and in the end the whole group works together to reach a common goal. For all of these characters, their interpersonal relationships form a valuable part of their lives, but they seem the most life-changing for Max, who was all alone to start. Even though he chooses to go off on his own again at the end of the film, it's clear that the connections he's made have had a significant impact on him and his life.

These three values—virtue, autonomy, and relationships—make up the Objective List Theory of *Mad Max: Fury Road*.[8] This is not to say that these are the only things that have objective value, but they are clearly the most important values in the film. Specifically, then, the type of meaningful life for which *Mad Max: Fury Road* advocates is one containing (at least) these three values.

A Meaningful Life on the Fury Road?

We are finally ready to answer our original question: What is the meaning of life according to *Mad Max: Fury Road*? According to the film, a life is meaningful when the person living it is autonomous and subjectively engaged in objectively valuable projects, especially doing the right thing (virtue) and maintaining relationships. This explains why, at the end of the film, Max's life is meaningful: he has formed valuable connections with others, whom he has been able to help and save, and he is free again to pursue his own path. The same applies to Furiosa. A life exhibiting these particular values might not be the only kind of meaningful life there is, but it is the one endorsed by *Mad Max: Fury Road*.

Notes

1   William Lane Craig, "The Absurdity of Life Without God," 2001, at https://www.youtube.com/watch?v=_fOIWRiC3vQ.

2   Thomas Nagel, *Mortal Questions* (Cambridge: Cambridge University Press, 1979), 23.
3   Richard Taylor, *Good and Evil* (Amherst, NY: Prometheus Books, 2000), 334.
4   Susan Wolf, "Happiness and Meaning: Two Aspects of the Good Life," *Social Philosophy & Policy* 24 (1997), 224.
5   Thomas Hurka, *The Best Things in Life: A Guide to What Really Matters* (Oxford: Oxford University Press, 2011), 163.
6   Jean Kazez, *The Weight of Things: Philosophy and the Good Life* (Malden, MA: Blackwell Publishing, 2007), 6.
7   Christopher Belshaw, *Ten Good Questions About Life and Death* (Malden, MA: Blackwell Publishing, 2005), 116.
8   The Objective List Theory proposed by *Mad Max: Fury Road* thus shares some commonalities with Hurka's, Kazez's, and Belshaw's lists.

Part III

BUILDING A BETTER TOMORROW! ETHICS IN *MAD MAX*

What Saves the World? Care and Ecofeminism

Leigh Kellmann Kolb

"Who killed the world?" The Splendid Angharad yells at Nux, verbalizing the graffiti in the vault that she and her fellow wives escaped. That question, implied throughout the *Mad Max* films, is past-tense. However, in *Mad Max* (1979), the question would be present-tense: "Who is killing the world?"

In *Ecofeminism as Politics: Nature, Marx and the Postmodern*, the Australian sociologist Ariel Salleh says that "Global crisis is the outcome of a capitalist patriarchal system that treats both women and nature as 'resources.'"[1] George Miller's *Mad Max* films reveal the horrors that patriarchal capitalism can lead to.

Mad Max sets the landscape of brewing social, environmental, and political downfalls. Subsequently, each film has used Max to trace the catastrophes and glimmers of hope at what appears to be the end of civilization. The common thread throughout the films is the destructive nature of capitalist patriarchy run amok, contrasted with the persistent and healing forces of what philosophers call an ethic of care and ecofeminism. Dystopian, post-apocalyptic fiction often warns us about the horrors percolating in our own times, and the *Mad Max* franchise is no exception, offering both warnings and salves.

Who Killed the World?

The original *Mad Max* was the prelude to the full-blown apocalypse that would set the stage for the following films—*The Road Warrior*,

Mad Max and Philosophy: Thinking Through the Wasteland, First Edition.
Edited by Matthew P. Meyer and David Koepsell.
© 2024 John Wiley & Sons, Inc. Published 2024 by John Wiley & Sons, Inc.

Beyond Thunderdome, and *Fury Road*. Even in the original film, it's apparent that Max embodies what Carol Gilligan calls an ethic of care, a way of being that can and should be valued by men as well as women. Gilligan's book *In a Different Voice* (1982) was a ground-breaking work that established the theory of the ethics of care: an ethics that focuses on relationships, emotions, and the situated nature of nuanced ethical decision-making. Such an ethics was the result of what Gilligan found lacking in the models of moral development created by previous moral psychologists, which had focused on individual responsibility and abstract principles of justice. Even though the elements of the ethics of care in American society are often seen as "feminine," Gilligan argues they can and should be "human."[2]

Mad Max opens with examples of careless, violent, misogynistic men. A police officer aims his gun at a couple having sex in the distance; a father berates a mother as their child wanders away. However, when we meet Max, he's caring for a baby—he makes coffee and breakfast and seems comfortable in a domestic space and at ease with an equal relationship with his wife, Jessie. He is also a police officer—but wants to quit, lest he turn into something he doesn't want to be (like the crazed, violent officers from the opening scene, who are his colleagues). Max talks about his emotions with Jessie and displays comfort with their egalitarian relationship. Our hero demonstrates the ethics of care: he is concerned with relationships and human connection more than power and justice. (In contrast, remember the Bullet Farmer in *Fury Road*, screaming, "I am the scales of justice.")

The villains in the original film are a chaotic, violent biker gang led by Toecutter—embodying toxic masculinity, the patriarchal antithesis to care. Terrorizing and mauling others, they are styled in excessive ways that are a prelude of the villains to come in Max's future. The gang sets their sights on Jessie—especially after she initially fights back and knees Toecutter in the crotch, a symbolic act that displays her power and further enrages Toecutter. They hunt her, kill her dog, and take baby Sprog. When they see her, they say, "There's our little mother." Aunt May arms herself and initially saves Jessie and Sprog, but she can't save them once they get on the road where Max goes mad.

Our introduction to "Mad" Max suggests that the apocalyptical disease, as seen in *The Road Warrior*, is the toxic masculinity that terrorizes communities with chaos and violence, and which leads to the war, "maelstrom of decay," and the "Wasteland." The logical outcomes of this terror are the ecological and social disasters that follow.

Mad Max's first appearance in 1979 came at the end of a decade that began with the fights and hopes of the feminist movement and the burgeoning ecofeminist movement. As British sociologist Mary Mellor says, ecofeminism "sees a connection between the exploitation and degradation of the natural world and the subordination and oppression of women."[3] By the 1970s and into the 1980s, feminist and ecofeminist concerns had become more mainstream, but the changing sociopolitical landscape was filled with setbacks. The original *Mad Max* trilogy (1979–1985) has this as its global backdrop: the erosion of much of the hope of social and ecological movements as the world buckled under deregulation and social and financial inequities. *Mad Max* sets the stage for consistent themes throughout the films: capitalistic patriarchal systems are destructive. However, an ethic of care and ecofeminism are remedies or alternatives that both men and women can embody for the hope of future civilizations. Max goes "mad" at the end of the original film, and at first glance he may look like a typically male lone wolf and reluctant savior who cares mainly about survival and chooses the "just" course of action. But a closer look reveals that "care" also motivates his actions, and we see that the post-apocalyptic landscapes he encounters are most destructive when they resemble patriarchal capitalism.

From the beginning, Max embodied an ethic of care. He was about to quit his job instead of going down a path of unhinged violence and a twisted sense of justice, as he saw happening with his colleagues. The cultural markers of toxic masculinity—aggression, violence, misogyny, control, objectifying/suppressing women (and anything coded feminine), sexual assault, belief in male supremacy—all reveal themselves in the *Mad Max* films as indicators of destructive villainy. Many male characters display these traits, but in a patriarchal capitalist incubator of toxic masculinity, women can also embody these destructive characteristics.

I Thought You Girls Were Above All That

The Road Warrior begins with a black-and-white montage of modern institutions we rely upon, and which also seem to be dangerously on the edge of destruction. A male narrator refers to a war, their world—of black fuel, cities, steel—crumbling. This "blighted" place is where "ordinary men" like Max learn to live again. The second film once more shows the villain as a biker gang of excessive, violent men who hoard fuel and resources and murder women. Lord Humungus and his marauders, villains who are reminiscent of Toecutter's gang and foreshadow *Fury Road*'s War Boys, again display a hypermasculinity that is both terrorizing and ludicrous. In contrast, residents of the Oil Refinery compound solve internal disagreements by debating; men's and women's voices are heard and respected. Women are decision-makers and fighters. The better civilization is shown as more egalitarian between men and women, and while they will fight for gas and resources, they also conserve and live relatively modestly.

Though Max attempts to position himself as a selfish outsider, he often ends up embodying the ethic of care. When Max arrives at Bartertown (*Beyond Thunderdome*) as a stranger, he can detect radiation in the water that a peddler tries to sell him. From an ecofeminist perspective, he can detect literal and figurative poison.

Aunty Entity is the architect of Bartertown. As she bargains with Max, she tells him that society was crumbling but is now organized. She built the place to provide an arena for goods and services, and she's clearly proud. An indoor swine farm generates energy from methane gas, and the Thunderdome provides a colosseum-like outlet for public violence. Aunty Entity is a woman in charge, but she's built a patriarchal capitalistic system that is literally and figuratively toxic and runs on greed, pollution, and violence. She says, "You think I don't know the law? Wasn't it me who wrote it? And I say that this man has broken the law. Right or wrong, we had a deal. And the law says: bust a deal and face the wheel!" Her society, centered on cruel justice ("Two men enter; one man leaves!"), is built on oppression and degradation of people and animals, all for the sake of order and the free market. Clearly, capitalist patriarchy can persist even with women as its acolytes.

When banished to the desert, Max is saved by a woman, Savannah, who brings him back to her oasis—a village mostly of children who have not been pulled into the destructive and violent capitalism of Bartertown. They believe that the pilot of the crashed plane will come and rescue them, and they immediately identify Max as their savior. Max resists the call to help, as usual, but ends up helping them to flee to safety. Savannah and the other survivors develop a new community and remember Max as the one who helped them get there.

Savannah ends the story, holding a baby and telling the new, saved community that their future rests in the importance of storytelling, history, and connection: "[T]his ain't one body's Tell. It's the Tell of us all." The focus on community and generational memory is in stark contrast to how we've seen the post-apocalyptic communities respond and certainly embodies a more feminist ethic of care and connectivity. Indeed, the original trilogy upholds a feminist ethic of care and ecofeminism as the most functional and healthiest ways of being in a world that has been ravaged by destructive patriarchal forces.

We Are Not Things

Fury Road takes the feminist messaging of the first three films and boosts its engine with siphoned gasoline. It's crystal clear that ecofeminism is the salve to the patriarchal monstrosity of Immortan Joe and his Citadel. In addition to the continued commodification of "guzzolene," *Fury Road* pushes the commodification of nature to the extreme. Water ("Aqua Cola") is rationed, gas and bullets are traded in towns named for their products, breastmilk is a commodity, and the green hope of nutritious food is seen high at the top of the Citadel—far away from the throngs of desperate people (the Wretched) below. Nature is owned.

Fury Road opens—like *Road Warrior*—with a montage of news headlines bringing us up to date; there have been oil, thermonuclear, and water wars (these wars have extended into nature in new ways). Then we hear women's voices: "Our bones are poisoned," "We have become half-life," "The earth is sour." These women's voices echo the calls in ecofeminism. Truly, women are often the ones who first know something is wrong with nature because of their proximity to it in patriarchal capitalism. There is, though, discomfort among some feminists in too closely aligning women and nature, because that coupling has historically led to the subjugation of both. Beyond that, the association can be read as gender essentialism, the theory that men and women are inherently different due to their biology and that women are "naturally" aligned with nature.

The Citadel is the culmination of the horrors of the original trilogy—Toecutter's biker gang has built a city.[4] It is no surprise, then, that the next step in this post-apocalyptic patriarchal community-building is making the women's bodies part of the trade. Salleh observes, "Women are human, but still treated socially as simple reproductive sites or commodities, made use of and exchanged like any other natural resource."[5] Breeders are stored in a vault; Milking Mothers are strapped to milking machines; breastmilk is traded for fuel and ammunition. *Fury Road* was ostensibly released in a relatively new world—2015 versus 1985—but the themes that grew out of the original trilogy were neither shocking nor surprising. Enslaving women, starving the impoverished class, using boys and men to fight wars—these are all extensions of patriarchal capitalism.

The natural world has withered, and human behavior (nods to nuclear warfare) has resulted in "half-life" War Boys and an increase in birth defects. Max is abducted and pulled into the Citadel, and when they discover his universal blood type of O negative, he is used as a "Bloodbag" for Nux, a War Boy evidently at the end of his half-life. Nux desperately wants to go to war and die heroically in the eyes of Immortan Joe. "I live, I die, I live again" is his refrain. Here Nux exemplifies what men will do with the promise of patriarchal favor and salvation.

The central conflict is introduced early on, as Immortan Joe finds his "prized breeders" have disappeared. Miss Giddy is in the vault holding a gun on him: "OUR BABIES WILL NOT BE WARLORDS," "WHO KILLED THE WORLD?" and "WE ARE NOT THINGS" have been painted in the room. Miss Giddy yells, "They are not your property. You cannot own a human being! Sooner or later, someone pushes back!" Imperator Furiosa—trusted and respected by Immortan Joe and his men due to her masculine-coded abilities—has taken the war rig on a routine mission, but has smuggled away the wives to take them and herself to "The Green Place of Many Mothers."

The villains in *Fury Road* mirror the villains in *The Road Warrior*: the over-the-top motorcycles and cars and the excessive displays of hypermasculinity. Humungus and his crew can be seen as representing queer culture in a way that allows *Road Warrior* to be read as homophobic, since they are the villains.[6] Some of this imagery persists in *Fury Road*, particularly in the Bullet Farmer. However, the characterizations of these men throughout the films can also be seen as satirical of performative masculinity—an obsession with cars, bikes, chrome, and bullets. By *Fury Road*, the War Boys—descendants of Toecutter— are dying of patriarchal capitalism and environmental degradation, stealing blood from unwilling donors and policing wives and mothers. They are foot soldiers for toxic masculinity.

Breeding Stock and Battle Fodder

During the chase, the wives are referred to as "the goods" and "the assets." Immortan Joe yells at Splendid when she uses her pregnant body as a shield, "That's my child, my property!" It's unclear if he means the child is his property or she is. Probably both. He sees himself as owning and controlling it all, as the patriarch of the Citadel. He is the means of all production, and reproduction.

Immortan Joe's wives/breeders are chosen because of their youth, beauty, and fertility. The Milking Mothers are strapped to milking machines and hold baby dolls, which ostensibly help to inspire milk production, but also remind us what an inhumane and horrifying system this is. Their milk is drunk by Immortan Joe and traded for bullets and guzzolene. In *Fury Road*, forced reproduction is part of the system; women have no choices. The commodification of women's bodies without their consent is presented as a horror to fight against.

After Splendid and her baby die ("Was it a male?" Immortan Joe asks, and we know his grief will depend on the answer; indeed, it was a "perfect" boy), the inhabitants of the War Rig divide labor and develop a moving communal resistance against the army behind them. When the rig gets stuck in mud, Nux suggests they tie a rope to "that thing"—he didn't know what a tree was (the women did). Nux and the War Boys had been far removed from nature, laboring underground on vehicles and being shielded from the elements outside.

Soon after, Max returns from an off-screen battle. He brings Nux's steering wheel and boot and is covered in blood (not his own). As he starts to splash his face with liquid coming out of the rig's tanker, he asks, "What is this?" The Dag replies, "It's mother's milk." The baptismal act of washing himself with breastmilk acts as a transformative, natural moment. Max and Nux had already proven themselves as allies to Furiosa and the wives, but this scene marks a turning point— especially for Max's outward displays of care. He asks Furiosa about the Green Place and what she's looking for. He still hasn't shared his name, but he's connecting to Furiosa in an emotionally vulnerable way that shows him embodying care in a way that again shows that he isn't the selfish survivor that he says he is. Of course, this scene occurs shortly after he and Furiosa would have killed one another if the gun had been loaded. They are both lone road warriors, but as Max allies with Furiosa—who is also dedicated to saving subjected women—his egalitarian ethic of care shows itself.

Out Here, Everything Hurts

The Green Place, Furiosa's fertile matriarchal birthplace, is no more. It's been destroyed, and the Vuvalini of Many Mothers had to move further into the desert: "The soil, we had to get out. We had no water. The water was filth. It was poison, it was sour. And then the crows came. We couldn't grow anything." The plan of rebirth in the Green Place is over.

Ecofeminism's awareness of nature being gendered as feminine allows for approaches that both embrace and reject that mythology. Nature-as-female has long been used as a patriarchal excuse for nature-as-object-to-be-dominated (even in nature, the feminine is virgin or whore). Because of patriarchal systems, women have typically been the ones at the forefront of recognizing and exposing environmental degradation. Mellor and Salleh both provide abundant examples of women's campaigns that began with women seeing and experiencing the toxification of nature (water, air, food, and related health outcomes) because that is often what they are tasked with managing in and out of the household.[7]

Another common trope depicts nature as Eden, "a pristine garden of natural delight." Michelle Yates examines the Edenic recovery narrative that features a "desire to protect and/or recover Edenic nature" that is "often a central narrative within Western environmentalism."[8] She points out that *The Road Warrior* is an example of an Edenic recovery narrative; postcards in the Oil Refinery show "Paradise" (beautiful natural settings and objectified women). In *Fury Road*, we briefly experience a similar "environmental nostalgia"[9] about the Green Place, but when it's not there, the recovery narrative is disrupted.

Max presents the plan for going back to the Citadel. Showing the women a map, he suggests the logic of returning to the Citadel, where there are crops and water. He says, "At least that way, we might be able to together, come across some kind of redemption." This isn't a heroic man providing a solution—it will be a difficult journey, but one with possibility. Hearing our "Mad" Max point out the power of togetherness is poignant and shows his continued ethic of care. They will return (in an anti-Eden recovery narrative) to the monstrous place they fled in hopes that they can retake but respect, communally, the nature that's been commodified—because the rest of nature has been stripped and destroyed.

We're Not Going Back

On the way back, the gang of women (and Max and Nux) work together to get "home," suffering casualties along the way. Amid the bullets and machines, the ethic of care and the spirit of ecofeminism fill the War Rig. Nux experiences human love. Max gives his

O negative blood to save Furiosa's life and shares his name with her. The Keeper of the Seeds gives her bag of seeds to the Dag before dying (she had told her earlier, "Trees, flowers, fruit. Back then everyone had their fill. Back then there was no need to snap anybody").

The promises of a matriarchal paradise are unfulfilled. From Aunt May to the Keeper of the Seeds, elder women are shown having to rely on "anti-seeds" to fight back—the world that both Toecutter and Immortan Joe inhabited was too far gone. Instead, the best chance for not only surviving but thriving is to retake the Capitol—the patriarchal capitalist nightmare—and ensure that resources are preserved and equally distributed. No more worries about addition to Aqua Cola. At the end, we see the Milk Mothers releasing water to the throngs of people below, who are celebrating Immortan Joe's death. Not only are the women shown to be in powerful positions (the Milk Mothers as well as Furiosa, Capable, Toast the Knowing, the Dag, and Cheedo the Fragile, who are being raised up), but the young boys, the "War Pups," are seeing and participating in this celebratory moment. They too are transformed. Change is possible. Life-giving resources have been mined and hoarded, but they don't have to remain that way. Ecofeminism suggests emancipation is possible for not only nature, but for women and men as well.

A pre-credits screen offers the quote: "Where must we go ... we who wander this Wasteland, in search of our better selves?" credited to the First History Man. The "we" suggests a kind of togetherness, and the question mark leaves the audience with something to think about. The *Mad Max* films show the devastating effects of toxic masculinity and patriarchal capitalism, yet they also show the redemptive possibilities of fighting back with an ethic of care and ecofeminism. There's no Eden; there's no paradise. But can we reshape the Wasteland that we've created?

Maybe, just maybe, the world isn't dead yet.

Notes

1 Ariel Salleh, *Ecofeminism as Politics: Nature, Marx and the Postmodern*, 2nd ed. (London: Zed Books, 1997, 2017), 209.
2 Carol Gilligan, Interview, "Network," *Ethics of Care*, June 21, 2011, at https://ethicsofcare.org/carol-gilligan/.
3 Mary Mellor, *Feminism & Ecology* (New York: New York University Press, 1997), 1.

4 The late British-Australian actor Hugh Keays-Byrne played both Toecutter and Immortan Joe.
5 Salleh, 253.
6 Michelle Yates, "Re-casting Nature as Feminist Space in *Mad Max: Fury Road*," *Science Fiction Film and Television* 10 (2017), 357.
7 Mellor examines grassroots movements such as the Himalayan Chipko movement, the Kenyan Green Belt movement, the Love Canal activism, and more, all of which were active in the late 1970s–1980s, 17–22.
8 Yates, 356.
9 Ibid., 359.

Seeking the Good Life in the Wasteland

Andrew Kuzma

Is it possible to be a good person in the Wasteland? At the beginning of *Mad Max: Fury Road*, Max's answer is an emphatic "No." "I exist in this Wasteland," he says, "a man reduced to a single instinct: survive." With the road wars and the fallout, it's hard to argue with Max. Doing what it takes to survive isn't always pretty. Morality is a luxury of the world before. Again and again throughout the *Mad Max* film series, however, Max denies this instinct. He chooses to help others, even when it puts his own survival in jeopardy. What does Max find out there in the Wasteland that convinces him that he can do more than just survive—that he can also be good?

Life in the Wasteland

The idea that you need civilized society to be a "good" person seems like common sense. Imagine a world without governments or laws. There would be no industry or economy, no building or infrastructure, no art or culture. There would be nothing to do except survive and nothing to keep you safe. Once society collapses, morality goes out the window. You join the roving biker gang or you die. Everyone would live in perpetual fear of violence and death. Life would be solitary, poor, nasty, brutish, and short.

This scenario sounds a lot like the Wasteland in which Max exists, but it is also how Thomas Hobbes (1588–1679) describes what it would be like to live in the "state of nature."[1] Hobbes was

Mad Max and Philosophy: Thinking Through the Wasteland, First Edition.
Edited by Matthew P. Meyer and David Koepsell.
© 2024 John Wiley & Sons, Inc. Published 2024 by John Wiley & Sons, Inc.

a philosopher during the English Civil War. Even if you have never heard of him, you are probably familiar with some of his ideas, which influenced modern political philosophy so much that we tend to take them for granted.[2] He is probably the reason you might think that to "survive" is the only thing possible to strive for in the Wasteland.

The "state of nature" or "the naturall condition of mankind," as Hobbes describes it in his 1651 work, *Leviathan,* is the way that human beings would live without a political authority reigning over them. "Natural" here does not mean "original," as if referring to the way that human beings lived before society came along. Hobbes is making a more fundamental claim about human nature. He says that we each have a natural right to preserve our own lives at all costs.[3] I might not want to steal my neighbor's guzzolene, but how do I know that my neighbor won't kill me for my guzzolene and my Pursuit Special? The safest thing for me to do would be to kill my neighbor before he can kill me. After all, there is no "right" or "wrong" in this world. Hobbes is very clear on this point. There is no justice or injustice because there is no political power to impose or enforce said "justice" prior to the establishment of that political power. Everyone has the natural right to do whatever they need to do to protect themselves. In a world without the security provided by a political authority, the "natural condition" of human beings would end up being a war of "every man against every man" and life would be "solitary, poore, nasty, brutish, and short."[4] Because most of us do not find this sort of existence very appealing, Hobbes explains, we agree to give up some of our natural freedom by submitting to a political authority—thus, the "social contract" theory of government.

Max acts very much like he's read *Leviathan* (who knows, maybe a copy survived). At the beginning of *Fury Road*, we see Max bearded and unkempt casually gulp down a two-headed lizard that scurries past his feet. This image reflects his moral state of being: nothing but the drive for self-preservation. In *The Road Warrior* and *Beyond Thunderdome*, he outfits his V8 Interceptor with various kill-switches and booby-traps because he does not trust anyone. Or, to put it another way, he trusts that everyone will do anything to survive. In *Fury Road*, for instance, he attempts to steal Furiosa's War Rig and abandon her and the wives to Immortan Joe. The only reason he lets them back on the rig (at gunpoint, mind you) is because Furiosa installed a kill-switch of her own.

Life in the Wasteland is a war of all against all. If we look at it this way, seeking the good life *is* impossible. There is no good; there can't be when your choice is to kill for Aqua Cola or die of thirst.

Who Killed the World?

Then again, maybe the Wasteland is more complex than it first appears. In terms of moral systems, it is pretty diverse. Max has options. Bartertown in *Beyond Thunderdome* has strict rules to enforce trade ("Bust a deal, face the wheel!") and uses the Thunderdome to resolve disputes ("Two men enter, one man leaves"). The Citadel in *Fury Road* has its own religion centered around Immortan Joe. Or Max could continue following a Hobbesian view of the world, which the roving biker gangs also seem to hold. None of these, unfortunately, can help Max seek the good life.

Here one might object: why can't Bartertown or Immortan Joe's promise of "Valhalla" represent the good life for Max? *We* might not want to follow either, but somebody might. Bartertown's rules might be harsh, but aren't harsh rules better than anarchy? Of all the communities in the *Mad Max* films, Bartertown most resembles "civilization." By the same token, Immortan Joe's cult-like religion might look ridiculous to us, but the War Boys certainly have faith that they will ride eternal, shiny and chrome. Who are we to take that away from them? Maybe we should let Nux keep on yearning for Valhalla. While this "live and let live" attitude sounds reasonable, I would guess that most of us would still say "no" to Aunty Entity and Immortan Joe.

Contemporary philosopher Alasdair MacIntyre can help us explain why Max should reject these moral systems. In his most famous work, *After Virtue*, MacIntyre argues that modern moral systems are failures. Just look, he says, at the way that moral arguments today tend to drag on and on. People might think that they debate with open minds the "rights" and "wrongs" of abortion or immigration or taxes, but in the end, everyone leaves believing what they believed already. The problem, MacIntyre explains, is that when people today talk about "morality," no one is talking about the same thing.

Consider two of the most popular moral theories today: utilitarianism and deontology. Utilitarians say that the right action is the one that leads to the best result. Deontologists say that we have a duty to perform certain actions regardless of the results. If you think that a good result is the most important consideration, then you might justify torture if it keeps a city safe. If you think that you have a duty to never intentionally harm a human being, then you might condemn torture in all cases. There is no rational or objective reason to choose one over the other. There is no way to resolve this disagreement. The problem is that both claim to be *rational* and *objective* accounts of morality—both think that any reasonable person should agree with their conclusions. In the end, they just turn out to be arbitrary personal preferences. It all comes down to whether one happens to prefer "results" or "duty." Both use the words *right* and *wrong*, but both use them to mean something different.

Modern morality is a wasteland just like the world of *Mad Max*. This is not an exaggeration. MacIntyre compares modern morality to a post-apocalyptic world. Once, he says, we could resolve our moral disagreements because we all spoke the same moral language. Then the world of moral philosophy suffered a catastrophe.[5] Something important was lost—the very thing that gave this shared morality its meaning. What we have now are moralities cobbled together from its pieces. We have the words, but not the meanings. Without this shared context, morality became arbitrary—*right* and *wrong* can mean whatever you want them to mean—which is why utilitarians and deontologists don't agree. The Wasteland in *Mad Max* is similarly fragmentary. It is built out of the debris of the old world. Vehicles, like Furiosa's War Rig and Max's Interceptor, are a hodge-podge of random parts. Clothes and structures are stitched and bolted together from scraps and fragments. Nothing is new. Indeed, one of the fun things about the films is deciphering the visual chaos of Max's world to discover how mundane things have acquired drastically new purposes.

Consider Immortan Joe's "religion." The first thing that we notice is that the War Boys are devoted to the V8 engine. When they are not using their steering wheels, they place them carefully around an altar. They make a "V8" sign (interlocking four fingers on each hand in the shape of a "v") in prayer. Anything good or powerful they refer to as "shiny" and "chrome." Many, like Nux, have scarified engine diagrams into their bodies. These devotions are all directed to a single, greater purpose: serving Immortan Joe. He alone has the power to open the gates of Valhalla, and death in his service will grant them the reward to "ride eternal, shiny and chrome." Nux follows the dictates of this religion with a childish innocence. We feel his agony when he trips and Immortan Joe utters, "Mediocre." But we also know that Nux is better off without Joe as his savior.

Unlike Nux, we can see all the ways that the world has been broken. We know that V8 is just an engine, not a divinity. We know that "Valhalla" has been appropriated from its original cultural religious meaning to give Immortan Joe and his cult the veneer of legitimacy. We know where these fragments come from so we can see how they have been misused. When we then see the way that "Immortan" Joe is wasting away, we know that this "religion" is just a ruse to trick the War Boys. "Valhalla" is a lie. Immortan Joe uses fragments of an older morality to give a sense of legitimacy and objectivity to what is ultimately his personal preference.

Moral Force Patrol

According to MacIntyre, the catastrophe that led to modern morality was the rejection of the *telos*. The concept of a *telos*, which means "goal" in Greek, is the foundation of virtue ethics. Unlike modern theories, which tend to fixate on rules and principles, virtue ethics focused on building character. Once upon a time, societies each followed a *telos*, a shared vision of the "good life." The good life was not a physical destination so much as a way of being. "Virtues," accordingly, were those traits or habits that someone living the good life would possess. Virtue ethics also had room for rules and principles, but these were meant to help us to improve; to get us from who we are to who we should be. This is the original morality that MacIntyre says was lost.

Why was it such a catastrophe? The whole idea of a *telos* is that it is *shared*. Virtue ethics presume human beings are fundamentally social; we all strive together to live the good life and we all agree on what that life looks like. Modern moralities see human beings as fundamentally individual. By rejecting the *telos*, they embraced the idea that we are just a bunch of isolated individuals with no common cause holding us together. As a result, all the virtues, laws, and principles that were aiming at this *telos* suddenly lost their meaning. That's why MacIntyre says that modern morality is fragmentary; all these bits of the virtue tradition carried on, but without any agreed upon purpose (kind of like how the Main Force Patrol tried to maintain "justice," but wasn't much better than the roving gangs terrorizing the highways). Thus, without a shared goal, morality boils down to individual preference. It's also why Hobbes thought that the state of nature would be a war of all against all. There is no "good" in this world because "good" can mean whatever each of us wants it to mean.

Bartertown is the perfect representation of individualistic modern moralities. There is a "shared morality" in the sense that everyone agrees to the rules, but there is no *telos*. These rules do not make anyone better. They do not promote any vision of the good life. Their only purpose is to prevent individuals from killing each other (right away). Bartertown's rules presume that human beings are fundamentally just individuals in conflict. The Thunderdome as a means of resolving *any* conflict offers the clearest distillation of this concept: "Two men enter, one man leaves!" Bartertown's "morality" lets individuals make their own arbitrary choices about what is "right" and "wrong." It's probably better than nothing, but it doesn't give Max any "good life" to strive toward.

The War Boys of the Citadel, on the other hand, possess something that looks like a shared *telos*. Each War Boy knows his function—to serve Immortan Joe—and knows where fulfilling this function will lead him—Valhalla. What makes it different from the sort of Aristotelian account that MacIntyre promotes is the fact that this *telos* is a lie. The War Boys *telos* is not truly shared by the community. It was invented and imposed by an individual, Immortan Joe, to manipulate the community. Unfortunately, we don't always realize when we're members of a cult following the insane promises of a false god. The realization can come as a shock, as we see with Nux. MacIntyre calls this experience an "epistemological crisis." In this case, the crisis comes from the realization that everything you believed was wrong.[6] When that happens, we need to find a newer, better, and hopefully truer way of looking at the world.

Nietzsche or Aristotle? Immortan Joe or Furiosa?

Ultimately, the choice that Max faces in *Fury Road* is between rejecting all these moralities to "make his own way" or joining Furiosa's community. In the post-apocalyptic wasteland of modern morality, MacIntyre says that this is a choice between Nietzsche and Aristotle.

Friedrich Nietzsche (1844–1900) got one thing right according to MacIntyre: he recognized that modern moralities are not based on "reason." Deciding that the "best result" or that "duty" should be the ground of morality is not a rational choice; it's a preference. For Nietzsche, all morality is just an expression of someone's will. We ought then, he says, reject all moralities and follow our own individual will. The person who does this fully is what Nietzsche calls the *Übermensch*.

Immortan Joe could be an example of Nietzsche's *Übermensch*. Consider the evidence. He claims the Citadel's aquifer for himself, he manipulates the War Boys with the V8 religion to serve his will, he imprisons and rapes his "wives" out of his desire to create a healthy male heir, and he willingly sacrifices numerous lives in his pursuit of Furiosa. Immortan Joe follows no will but his own and he masks his will to power to manipulate others.[7]

Max could choose Nietzsche without becoming a dictator. As a loner and drifter, he repeatedly decides to "make [his] own way." In *The Road Warrior*, he initially opts to take his guzzolene and go, rather than drive the tanker for the community. In *Beyond Thunderdome*, he makes a deal with Aunty Entity but busts it as soon as it goes against his own will. Finally, in *Fury Road*, he makes every effort to leave Furiosa and the wives. He is, as he says at the beginning, "the one who runs from both the living and the dead." Choosing Nietzsche, we must admit, is more honest than putting his faith in the rules of Bartertown (which, it turns out, just mask the will of Aunty Entity) or in the promise of Valhalla (which just masks the will of Immortan Joe). Max, at least, recognizes the façade.

The other choice, and the one that MacIntyre prefers, is Aristotle (384–322 B.C.E.). Aristotelian virtue ethics, unlike modern morality, assumes that human beings are fundamentally social. Community, in this view, is the only place in which we can seek the good life. For example, the times that Max joins others are really the only times that we could call him "good." In *Mad Max*, it is the loss of community that turns him "mad." Toecutter kills Max's family, and Max abandons the Main Force Patrol to seek vengeance alone. In *The Road Warrior*, he helps a community escape from the Humungus. In *Beyond Thunderdome*, he helps a tribe of children fly to the ruins of Sydney. He becomes "good" when he finds a common cause with others. In *Fury Road*, Max finds it with Furiosa and the wives.

What the First History Man Knew

Let's revisit the opening of *Fury Road*. Max tells us that he's been reduced to a single instinct, but he also tells us his story:

> Once I was a cop. A road warrior searching for a righteous cause. As the world fell, each of us in our own way was broken.... Here they come again, worming their way into the black matter of my brain. I tell

myself they cannot touch me. They are long dead. I am the one who
runs from both the living and the dead. Hunted by scavengers, haunted
by those I could not protect.

Max is aimless because he has lost his family, his community, and his
mission—all the social things that give one purpose. He might *act*
like he's living in Hobbes's state of nature and his tendency to "make
his own way" might resemble Nietzsche's will to power, but the fact
that Max feels "haunted" tells us that he is in despair over what he
lost. He had a role—protector, road warrior—and he failed. He still
feels the pull of that identity, but he lacks a community in which to
practice it. Maybe MacIntyre felt like Max when he was writing
After Virtue; a virtue ethicist alone in the wasteland of modern
morality.

The *telos* of virtue ethics is not just an end goal; it is a way of life.
MacIntyre explains that a *telos* presumes a certain function. A "good
watch," for instance, is accurate, precise, and easy to carry around.[8]
We must know what a watch is supposed to do before we can know
what makes it "good." Really, though, we must *agree* on what a
watch's function is supposed to be. This tells us two things: (1) we
must know our *telos* before we can know how to be a "good" human
being, and (2) we can only know our *telos* in community. Without a
community, Max has no function or purpose. He remains haunted
because he had a role that he can longer fulfill.

It is important for us to remember Max's story because narrative is
a necessary part of virtue ethics. Modern moralities view human
beings as essentially abstract, rational individuals. Their systems, consequently, start by asking what an individual would agree to if stripped
of all historical circumstances and personal commitments that might
bias a "rational" decision. The fatal flaw with this approach, says
MacIntyre, is that human beings don't actually think this way. We
don't ever make decisions in a vacuum. We need to know the context
and the intention to understand anyone's actions, especially moral
ones. We understand why Max drifts aimlessly and avoids getting
close to others because we know his story: "Once I was a cop...."
A human being, MacIntyre observes, is not an abstract individual but
"essentially a story-telling animal."[9]

We learn morality from stories. The stories that people share make
them a community, both the stories that a community tells and the
story of the community itself. MacIntyre even calls attention to how
important fairy tales can be in the moral education of children.[10]

We all start somewhere, whether it be ancient Athens or the future Wasteland. Our identities and our actions are formed by these communities. We learn our *telos* through stories about the "good life." We learn it from stories about honorable road warriors and patriarchal warlords, about who killed the world, and about places where things still grow green.

We can see the importance that stories play in shaping identity and community through Furiosa. When she finally meets the Many Mothers, she tells her story: "I am one of the Vuvalini, of the Many Mothers! My initiate mother was K.T. Concannon! I am the daughter of Mary Jabassa! My clan was Swaddle Dog!" We never learn what any of these details mean, but they convey something important: Furiosa and the Vuvalini are guided by their stories. There are "initiate mothers" and "clans." There is a structure and roles and purpose. The wives presumably know these stories. We know that Furiosa has told them about "The Green Place."

Bartertown and the Citadel have stories too. Everyone has a story. One of MacIntyre's criticisms of modern moralities is that they try to act as if they are not shaped by their own stories. Utilitarianism and deontology are products of particular narratives; they just won't admit it. Sometimes we must choose among stories (the "epistemological crisis" that Nux goes through). In those situations, the main question that we need to ask is: which story offers me the best explanation of the world? Aunty Entity's narrative of a restored civilization and Immortan Joe's narrative of Valhalla are both, for different reasons, unconvincing. Both claim to benefit the people, but really just further the aims of a despot.

"We Might Be Able to ... Together ... Come Across Some Kind of Redemption"

The Green Place is the *telos* of Furiosa's community and the *telos* that allows Max to seek the good life. At first, the Green Place is a literal place. It was where Furiosa was born and the home to which she was trying to escape. Even though it is gone—things stopped growing once the water was poisoned—the Green Place remains the metaphorical, moral goal for this community. When one of the Vuvalini tells the Dag that she's killed everyone she's met in the Wasteland, the Dag sighs: "Thought somehow you girls were above all that." The Vuvalini responds by pulling out a bag of seeds, noting that she plants one every chance she gets. The Vuvalini resort to violence out of necessity, but growing things is their way of life, their *telos*. In the end, the Citadel, free from Immortan Joe's tyranny, becomes the new "Green Place," confirming that their goal was never a place. Their goal was *living a certain kind of life.*

Max is only able to seek the good life when he embraces this *telos*. He initially rejects Furiosa's offer to join her and the Vuvalini in riding across the salt desert. "No, I'll make my own way," he replies. He has helped them and saved their lives many times already. Up until this point in the film, everything that he has done could just be seen as serving his own will. Perhaps cooperating with Furiosa happened to be the best way to ensure his own survival. Only when he turns Furiosa back toward the Citadel does Max put his survival at risk unnecessarily. This is the moment that he embraces their *telos*. By committing to their goal of finding the Green Place, Max is finally able to seek the good life because he has a community and a role within it: "Look, it'll be a hard day.... At least that way we might be able to ... together ... come across some kind of redemption."

"Where Must We Go, We Who Wander This Wasteland in Search of Our Better Selves?"

The Wasteland is still a wasteland. There's no returning to the old world, but Max can find a new way to seek the good life. For Furiosa, the wives, and the Vuvalini, the good life is the life spent seeking the Green Place. The last we see of them, they are being lifted into the Citadel, carrying up the wretched masses with them, finally letting the waters flow freely, and ready to plant the seeds of a new world. Max does not join them. We should not take this departure to mean that he has rejected their *telos*, but as confirmation that he has embraced it. Had Max stayed, we could have interpreted his actions as just another way to guarantee his long-term survival. Leaving demonstrates that he truly was trying to help his community achieve their *telos*. The Green Place, after all, is not a place, but a way of life. We can seek it anywhere. Having found redemption in this community, Max can now continue to seek the good life, even in the Wasteland.

Notes

1 Thomas Hobbes, *Leviathan* (New York: Penguin, 2017), 100.
2 David Graeber and David Wengrow, *The Dawn of Everything: A New History of Humanity* (New York: Farrar, Straus and Giroux, 2021), 2–3.
3 Hobbes, 106.
4 Ibid., 102–103.
5 Alasdair MacIntyre, *After Virtue: A Study in Moral Theory*, 3rd ed. (Notre Dame, IN: University of Notre Dame Press, 2007), 1–2.
6 Alasdair MacIntyre, "Epistemological Crises, Dramatic Narrative, and the Philosophy of Science," *The Monist* 60 (1977), 453–472.
7 MacIntyre, *After Virtue*, 258.
8 Ibid., 57–58.
9 Ibid., 216.
10 Ibid.

11

"We're Not to Blame!" Responsibility in the Wasteland

Justin Kitchen

Assigning responsibility is usually pretty straightforward. You broke a promise? You can be blamed for doing something bad. You kept a promise? You can be praised and thanked for doing something good. You intentionally hurt somebody? You're blameworthy. You helped somebody? You're praiseworthy. You broke the law or a contract? You're held accountable and punished. You're a law-abiding citizen? You might not be praised, but at least you deserve to be left alone.

But what happens when there is no more government, no more law? What happens when it's expected that you'll do *anything* to survive—scavenge, pillage, steal, kill. What happens when everyone acknowledges that you *must* intentionally hurt other people or break promises sometimes in order to stay alive? To steal in order to stay moving? To wage war for a tank of juice? Let's try to make sense of moral responsibility in the Wasteland. In doing so, we can also make sense of why the Road Warrior, Max Rockatansky, sometimes feels blameworthy and guilty for what he did while fighting to survive.

Henchmen and Marauders: A Problem of Many Hands

There are different ways to look at someone's actions in order to determine whether they should be held morally responsible—whether they should be praised or blamed. The most common way is to use

Mad Max and Philosophy: Thinking Through the Wasteland, First Edition.
Edited by Matthew P. Meyer and David Koepsell.
© 2024 John Wiley & Sons, Inc. Published 2024 by John Wiley & Sons, Inc.

cause-and-effect reasoning: you caused it; you're responsible. This is aptly called *causal responsibility*.

When the character Blaster is killed in *Beyond Thunderdome*, we can ask who was responsible. If we narrow our focus, it seems obvious that Aunty Entity's henchman, Ironbar, was responsible. He pointed his crossbow at Blaster and pulled the trigger. Point, shoot, dead. Ironbar was causally responsible because he caused the short chain of events that ended with Blaster's death. But fans of the movie know it's not that simple. When we broaden our focus, the question of who's responsible becomes a bit more complicated—Ironbar could not have pulled it off on his own.

Earlier in the story, Max made an agreement with Aunty Entity: he would take out her rival, Master Blaster, in exchange for supplies and safe passage. She wanted to eliminate Blaster (Master's muscle) but in a way that would not rouse suspicion of treachery. The plan was this: Max draws Master Blaster into a dispute; Aunty and her henchmen interrupt and remind Master of the law (disputes must be settled in Thunderdome); Master agrees and volunteers Blaster for a fight to the death in Thunderdome with Max; Max then kills Blaster fair and square and Master is left defenseless. Notice all the people who are needed to help carry out this plan: Aunty and her henchmen must work behind the scenes (including Ironbar); Max must deceptively engage Master Blaster in a dispute; the citizens of Bartertown must rally around the idea of Thunderdome as the arena for settling disputes; and Master Blaster himself must demand Thunderdome to seek justice. Ultimately, Max refused to carry out the deed, but he still helped coordinate things so that Ironbar could kill Blaster as a legitimate way to enforce the law—"Two men enter, one man leaves" and it seemed like Max won the fight.

So now that we have a fuller picture, who was really responsible for Blaster's death? Nobody seemed *sufficient* to bring it about on their own, but each person seemed *necessary*. Maybe that's what we mean when we say that someone is responsible: someone is responsible for an outcome if it wouldn't have happened without them. We could excuse Max to *some* degree since he changed his mind at the very end, but he cannot be excused completely if we're taking this approach. Blaster would not have died if Max wasn't in Bartertown getting involved. He played a necessary role and should be partially blamed.

Let's complicate this just a little bit more. What if nobody involved was either sufficient *or necessary*. Imagine if Ironbar caught the sniffles and couldn't attend the Thunderdome event that night. It's likely that another one of Aunty's henchmen would have used his own weapon to kill Blaster once Max defeated him in combat. Because an understudy henchman is always waiting in the wings, Ironbar is neither *sufficient* to kill Blaster on his own (because of everyone else involved) nor was he *necessary*. How about this: we can also imagine Max was not robbed on the road and did not need to make a deal with Aunty in the first place. It's unlikely, but someone else might have discovered Blaster's weakness (a high-pitched whistle) and leveraged it to beat him in Thunderdome. So Max might not have been necessary either. In these situations, it could be difficult to assign responsibility to anyone aside from Aunty Entity herself since the event was likely going to happen with or without them. This can be called *the problem of causal overdetermination* or simply *the problem of many hands*. It describes the common difficulty of assigning responsibility to any single person among a large group.

In the Wasteland, feuding political groups are less common than *war parties*. But war parties of marauding psychopaths still have to cope with the problem of many hands. Like all wars, a road war in the Wasteland seems to require many unspecialized soldiers to wage it. Yet, if one warrior goes AWOL, there are other warriors waiting in the wings to take up his role. Almost every warrior— considered in isolation—is unnecessary in this way. The war would still be fought and the same results would likely play out. So, it's difficult to point the finger at anyone for the results of the battle or campaign. This is how soldiers have tried to excuse themselves from war atrocities. If they actually assess any events of the war they participated in as atrocities, they may try to wash their hands clean of guilt with the common refrain "I was just one person ... it would have happened with or without me ... if not me, then it would have been someone else." And we can imagine some warriors in a large road gang or road army giving similar excuses: "Hey, I was just one marauder ... those folks would have been brutally slaughtered with or without me." It seems like the problem of many hands makes it difficult to blame any single individual among the marauding horde—they can all be let off the hook.

Recall in *Fury Road* when the wives accuse people like Nux and their husband, Immortan Joe, of "killing the world." In exasperation, Nux yells, "*We're not to blame!*" That could easily have been the response of the henchmen in Aunty Entity's circles. But it sounds strange that nobody in the Wasteland is blameworthy for all the violence and mayhem.

"Witness!" War Boys and Responsibility

Most of the baddies in the Wasteland would find this strange too—especially the War Boys in *Fury Road*. They certainly don't think they're blameworthy, but they don't want to be let off the hook either—they want to be held responsible for their actions so that they can be *praised* and welcomed at the doors of Valhalla. To *guarantee* that they are held responsible when they see an opportunity to go full-tilt kamakrazee, they single themselves out from the group and demand to be "witnessed." In doing this, they're plucked out from the marauding horde and become the single cause of whatever happens next. If Ironbar yelled, "Witness!" while shooting his arrows into Blaster's chest, we would feel compelled to hold him more responsible—it would make him seem like a rogue agent who demands that our attention be focused on him instead of an instrument of justice who is just doing what any law-respecting henchman would do.

Max Rockatansky does something like this when he makes it a point to act alone. The Road Warrior is an army of *one*. Though he doesn't draw as much attention to himself, he does mark himself as distinct from any group. And like the singled-out War Boys and the rogue henchman, he can't really use any of the excuses that members of large groups, armies, and gangs might use. If something bad happens, there's no place where Max can pass the buck. Likewise, if he steps away from a task or mission, it's unlikely that anyone is waiting in the wings to pick up the slack. All blame (and praise) lies with him. This fact helps explain why Max is riddled with guilt at times—there are very few excuses that he can use to avoid causal responsibility.

So these singled-out War Boys and the lone Max avoid the problem of many hands and make themselves responsible for their behavior. But there's still one other problem with causal responsibility. Causal responsibility doesn't completely track our intuitions about moral responsibility in general because intentions matter to us. At times, we may even care *more* about intentions than who caused what.

"Some Got the Luck ... and Some Don't"

Max feels guilty for the results of his past interactions with people—those he couldn't protect who haunt his memories, including his wife and little Sprog. But maybe he's too hard on himself. Maybe there are other kinds of responsibility besides casual responsibility that we can point to and say, "You're not to blame, Max. Don't worry about it." Perhaps his actions caused some bad results, but perhaps there were good intentions behind those actions that might relieve him of blame and guilt.

If we see something wrong with relying too much on causal responsibility, it's likely because we recognize that *luck* often influences the results of our actions despite our best intentions. Not holding ourselves accountable for the good and bad luck that is ultimately out of our control seems intuitive. The philosopher Thomas Nagel uses the term *moral luck* to capture this intuition and its relationship to moral responsibility.[1] More specifically, the luck that influences the results of our actions is called *resultant luck*, and the luck that influences the circumstances in which we find ourselves is *circumstantial luck*. Max is affected by both: the results of his actions are influenced by things outside his control and these actions were necessary responses to circumstances that he couldn't avoid. Max didn't choose for a perverse and violent biker gang to stalk him and his family during the events of *Mad Max*; he didn't choose to be ambushed and have his dromedaries stolen in *Beyond Thunderdome*—he was in the wrong place at the wrong time. Unlucky circumstances like these force Max to make tough decisions that may then have unlucky results. But bad luck should not determine whether someone should be held morally responsible.

The problem here is that the biker gangs and War Boys also cope with moral luck, but we don't necessarily want to let them off the hook because of that. They didn't *choose* to live in a post-apocalyptic Australian wasteland, so we should cut them some slack for acting a bit uncivilized considering the circumstances. But the gang did choose to stalk Max and his family; they did choose to chase and kill innocent bystanders. The War Boys in *Fury Road* didn't *choose* to be born and raised in the Citadel, but they did choose to go into battle and kill others for gasoline, ammunition, and slaves. The malicious intentions—regardless of circumstances and results—are what distinguishes the bad guys from the good guys.

But let's complicate things yet again: aren't the intentions that we form a matter of luck too? All the War Boys were once innocent War Pups. Gradually, over time they were indoctrinated by the older members of the Citadel into becoming the fanatical marauders that would ultimately confront Max in the Wasteland. They were raised in unlucky circumstances that they couldn't avoid or control and it's these circumstances that—over time—form a distorted sense of right and wrong which leads to reprehensible actions. It does indeed seem to be a matter of luck; if they were raised in slightly different circumstances, then their sense of right and wrong would be more sound. Think of the Feral Child in *The Road Warrior*, who was apparently raised by Pappagallo and his group. If he was raised in the Citadel, he would surely have become a gloriously bloodthirsty War Boy.

If this is the case, then shouldn't we say that the War Boys are actually free from blame considering that so much of their upbringing was out of their power to influence? Max faced resultant luck and circumstantial luck. The War Boys faced what Nagel calls *constitutive luck*—the constitutions of their psychology, which tend to produce malicious intentions and horrible behavior were influenced by things beyond their control. If we can't blame Max for the actions that are forced by his poor circumstances, how can we blame the War Boys for the actions that ultimately came from their poor upbringing? Yet again, it seems like *nobody* can be held responsible in the Wasteland.

Murderer or Just Kamakrazee?

The philosopher Harry Frankfurt identifies two types of freedom that someone must have in order to be held morally responsible regardless of luck.[2] First, someone must have *freedom of action*—freedom to act in whatever way they think is best. This means that my actions align with my intention or desire to act in that way and I'm not being coerced or compelled to do so. Next, someone must have *freedom of the will*—freedom to desire in whatever way they think is best. This means that not only do my actions align with my desire, my intentions align with some deeper sense of identity—I sincerely endorse or approve of that intention. Freedom of the will requires that a person reflect and make sure their intentions all align with their deep-seated values or self-image that they take to be their "real" self. Susan Wolf calls this a *Deep Self View* or *Real Self View* of moral responsibility.[3] Let's test it out.

Both Max and the indoctrinated War Boys have freedom of action, but Immortan Joe's imprisoned wives (and anyone else enslaved in the Wasteland) do not. They are not morally responsible for whatever they do under duress. Max has freedom of action when he's not chained to the front of a speeding war machine or coerced into a particular course of action. When he has some time to think, he seems to have freedom of the will too—he often revises his desires to better align with his real self ... and we suspect that his real self is a *good guy*. For example, he often debates with himself about who to cooperate with in the Wasteland, and he evaluates and revises these desires as events progress: often he desires to leave someone behind, but later we find him desiring to help or cooperate with them. If he endorses the desires that he ultimately acts upon, then Max has freedom of the will and is morally responsible for those actions. So far, so good: Max can be held morally responsible for his well-intended actions despite unlucky results and he's let off the hook if he's coerced or faces unlucky circumstances.

The question now is whether the War Boys can be held morally responsible. Has their upbringing and the social constraints within the Citadel made it impossible or practically impossible for the War Boys to even reflect on their desires and revise them like Max does? Imagine three War Boys who all have the desire to murder some poor wretch. All three have the freedom of action to pursue their desires and so they decide to join a war party and chase Mr. Wretch down. All three hope they can murder him by the end of the day—fingers crossed. Now imagine that we've stopped these War Boys in their tracks, taken them aside, and asked them what they think of their desire for murder. They all desire to murder Mr. Wretch, but upon reflection do they *want* to have this desire? Does this desire reflect their real selves?

The first War Boy—we'll call him Maniac—doesn't even hesitate and accuses us of being an enemy of the V8 cult. How dare we distract him from finding glory on the Fury Road and McFeasting with the heroes of all time! OK ... onto the next one. ... The second War Boy—named Fanatic— actually considers our question: "Do you *want* to have the desire to murder Mr. Wretch?" Quickly he says yes—he's committed himself entirely to the V8 and really enjoys murdering people—it aligns with his deep-seated values and self-image. So he thinks he'll really enjoy murdering Mr. Wretch and have fond memories of it in the future. OK ... onto the next one.... The third War Boy—named Addict— also considers our question and hesitates. He certainly wants to murder (don't get him wrong) especially when he gets caught up in the excitement of it all, with his adrenaline surging, and the Doof Warrior rocking *hard*. But when he gets back to the Citadel after a long day of murdering, he's not really happy with himself. He doesn't seem as fulfilled as his fellow V8 cult members. Upon reflection, he wishes he didn't have these desires. He wishes he could change, but it often feels like he's *addicted* to murder and ingratiating himself to others.

Maniac doesn't seem to have freedom of the will *at all*—he has been so indoctrinated that he is practically and perhaps pathologically incapable of self-reflection. This means that Maniac is not morally responsible for his actions and we can't blame him (though we should stay away from him). This is why we may want to excuse unruly cult members for their behavior (though we should arrest them if they break any laws and deprogram them if possible). Fanatic definitely has freedom of the will—he is capable of reflecting upon his desires and revising them, but he chooses not to revise his bloodlust because he claims it aligns with his real self. This means that Fanatic is morally responsible for his actions and we can freely blame him despite his rough upbringing. Addict is capable of reflecting upon his desires, but it is questionable that he is capable of revising his desires. If he absolutely cannot revise his desires so that they align with his real self, then he doesn't seem to have freedom of the will. This question depends on whether he is truly addicted or otherwise psychologically constrained from changing. If he has no control over his bloodlust, then he is pathological like Maniac and it would be difficult to blame him for the same reasons—he appears to be a victim of his unlucky upbringing, which has left him with a poorly constituted psychology. This is why we may want to excuse drug addicts for their behavior (though we should help them with their addiction).

The character Nux seems to be like Addict. He is addicted to a sense of brotherhood, a sense of purpose that Immortan Joe and the V8 gives him, and he's addicted to proving himself to Joe, despite the agitation it causes him. This lack of freedom of the will is immediately recognized by Splendid when the wives prevent Furiosa from killing Nux:

SPLENDID: "No unnecessary killing!"
FURIOSA: "This War Boy wants me dead!"
SPLENDID: "He's Kamakrazee! ... He's just a kid at the end of his half-life."
NUX: "No! I live, I die, I live again!"

Splendid is treating Nux as if he is not morally responsible for trying to murder—and *wanting* to murder— Furiosa because he does not have freedom of the will.

One of the wives, Capable, talks with Nux and asks him questions (as *we* did with Maniac, Fanatic, and Addict), and it seems like he eventually achieves or actualizes freedom of the will. He comes to realize, as Max often does, that deep-down he cares about fostering real relations with other people and protecting them. He probably starts the chase for Furiosa like Maniac—acting without thinking—until he is actually prompted to question his desires with the help of Capable. At that point, he realizes that he is not acting in accordance with his real self and so resists his harmful tendencies by teaming up with Furiosa, Max, and the wives. Once he has freedom of the will, we are free to praise or blame him for what he does.

"Where Must We Go ...?" Who's Responsible?

So with the help of philosophers like Nagel, Frankfurt, and Wolf, we have a better handle on who's responsible in the Wasteland.

By default, if Max causes an event to happen, then he is a candidate for moral responsibility; in normal circumstances, he would be blamed (or praised) for whatever he did. We would excuse Max if something he couldn't control or account for intervened to cause poor results despite his good intentions—that would be bad resultant luck as Nagel would say. We may give Max some slack overall considering that he's trying to survive in a post-apocalyptic Wasteland among armies of marauding psychopaths—that's bad circumstantial luck. What we care about most are the intentions behind his actions. If he has freedom of action—freedom to act in whatever way he thinks is best—then it seems like he's responsible. But if he was actually brought up in horribly oppressive conditions like those in the Citadel, this upbringing may influence his psychological constitution so much that he has distorted views of right and wrong—this would be bad constitutive luck. Frankfurt insists that someone must also have freedom of the will—freedom to desire in whatever way they think is best upon evaluation—to be morally responsible regardless of their constitutive luck.

All of the War Boys face circumstantial and constitutive bad luck, being raised in the Citadel just to be battle fodder for Immortan Joe. Many of them should not be blamed since they can't reflect on their desires and intentions and revise them if they don't align with their real selves. If anyone at the Citadel reflected upon their desires and said, "Yes, this is representative of my real self," then they would be to blame for any actions that came from those desires. Moral responsibility of course includes causal responsibility, but what seems to matter most is whether we have freedom of action and will.

Surely Immortan Joe, Aunty Entity, and the other leaders have freedom of action and freedom of the will. They are in control of their own lives and have plenty of opportunities to reflect on what they're doing. It's likely that fanatical War Boys like Nux's partner, Slit, also have freedom of the will—they all seem to *really* love what they're doing. That means that they all are morally responsible. The wives and many of the slaves and indigents in the Wasteland do not even have freedom of action. So they can't be morally responsible at all until they are freed. Furiosa and the wives who run away are reclaiming their freedom of action and only kill in self-defense (otherwise, it would not align with their real selves). They are all morally responsible. The story of Nux is a story of someone who reclaims his freedom of the will and is morally responsible—praiseworthy—up to the last moment of his life.

Mad Max is morally responsible most of the time. When he's all alone for a long time, he gets a little crazy. But like Nux, he reclaims his capacity to reflect on himself and his intentions when called upon to help others. Recall the old proverb of the First History Man (at the very end of *Fury Road*):

> Where must we go ...
> We who wander this Wasteland
> In search of our better selves?

But it must be stressed that you can't just wander *aimlessly* in the Wasteland. Like Max, you have to encounter other people who can help *you* search and discover your real self—to help you reflect on what you're doing and align your desires with your real self. Max should certainly not feel guilty for his encounters with others. In a poetic way, they are what help him reclaim his freedom of the will and his moral responsibility.

Notes

1   Thomas Nagel, *Mortal Questions* (Cambridge: Cambridge University Press, 1979), 24–38.
2   Harry Frankfurt, "Freedom of the Will and the Concept of a Person," *Journal of Philosophy* 68 (1971), 5–20.
3   Susan Wolf, "Sanity and the Metaphysics of Responsibility," in Ferdinand Schoeman ed., *Responsibility, Character, and the Emotions: New Essays in Moral Psychology* (Cambridge: Cambridge University Press, 1987), 46–62.

12

"Look, Any Longer out on That Road and I'm One of Them, You Know?": Madness in *Mad Max*

Matthew P. Meyer

Madness runs throughout the *Mad Max* films. In fact, almost all of the villains and even some of the heroes could be seen as mad. But context matters: when so many people have accepted a lifestyle so different from the civilization we are used to, how do we distinguish madness from its opposite? The philosopher Michel Foucault (1926–1984) and his masterpiece *Madness and Civilization* can help us address this question. In addition to a close look at Mad Max himself, we'll focus on four main relationships: Toecutter and Johnny the Boy (*Mad Max*), Lord Humungus and Wez (*The Road Warrior*), Master and Blaster (*Beyond the Thunderdome*), and Immortan Joe and Nux (*Fury Road*). Through these relationships we'll consider important themes of madness: contagion, morality, animality and confinement, and manipulation. We'll also examine the way that responsibility and blame are associated with insanity.

Terminal Crazies: Madness and Contagion

In the original *Mad Max*, there are some pretty mad characters: Nightrider speeding down the road and talking "crazy" in the beginning, Toecutter and his gang, and even Goose who seems a little mad. But this begs the question: what is madness? In *Madness and Civilization*, Michel Foucault creates a genealogy of madness. Why a

Mad Max and Philosophy: Thinking Through the Wasteland, First Edition.
Edited by Matthew P. Meyer and David Koepsell.

genealogy and not simply a definition? Because madness, like so many social constructions, is an affliction that gets treated differently at different times by different cultures.

Foucault points out that there was a time when what we now call *madness* was seen as divine insight, as an inspiration from another world. But in the period from roughly 1600 to 1800, madness became an enemy in the war against "unreason." The enemy was anything that could be seen as interfering with reason: the body and its flaws, illness, passion and desire, and errors in thinking. Foucault notes that even before it was considered curable, madness was associated with another important feature of physical illness: contagion. Many of the earliest centers of confinement for the insane were former lazar houses for the confinement of lepers. "People were in dread of a mysterious disease that spread, it was said, from the houses of confinement and would soon threaten the cities."[1] Though today madness is clinically seen as neither contagious nor incurable, these earlier social constructions continue to taint our notion of madness.

From the middle of *Mad Max* until almost the end of *Fury Road*, Max is preoccupied with going crazy. One major element of this fear is contagion. At the beginning of *Mad Max*, we see the Nightrider wreaking havoc on the Australian countryside—he appears to be crazy and is a self-described "fuel-injected suicide machine." This is clearly the type of crazy that Max wants to avoid becoming himself. About midway through the film, Max wants to quit his job with Main Force Patrol (MFP). In reasoning about this to his boss, Max says:

> I'm scared, Fif. It's that rat circus out there, I'm beginning to enjoy it. Look, any longer out on that road and I'm one of them, you know? A terminal crazy. Only, I've got a bronze badge to say I'm one of the good guys. You know what I'm trying to say?

There are a few things worth noting about Max's expression of concern. First, this is before his wife and child are killed in front of him and before Goose gets burned up by Toecutter. In other words, at this point in the film there was no catalyst for a breaking point. Which means that, second, Max's main concern here is expressed as fear of a kind of contagion by exposure. The road itself and being on it with other crazies can make one crazy. And not just any crazy—a terminal crazy. What is a terminal crazy? It is someone whose mind has become so diseased that one or both of the following happen: either they become delusional and therefore have a break from reality, or they become unmoored in terms of morality, and therefore can no longer tell right from wrong. The genius of Max's acknowledgment about his bronze badge is this: it could be the case that if he becomes terminal that he is basically behaving the same way as the people he is trying to stop (foreshadow alert!), and the *only* difference is that he has a bronze badge *to say* that he is one of the good guys. The logic is reversed from the way it should be: usually, a person would have a bronze badge because they are good. Max is worried that he will be considered good only because he has the bronze badge. Which brings us to the third key point of Max's beautiful confession: terminal craziness precludes morality. To be crazy *is* to be bad.

The relationship between the terminal crazy and righteousness is explored at the very beginning of *Fury Road* as well where Max reminds us: "Once, I was a cop. A road warrior searching for a righteous cause—to the terminal freak-out point." As we know, at the end of *Mad Max*, Max does indeed snap. When he finds Johnny the Boy after Toecutter and the rest of the gang were killed during the chase with him, he sets up an elaborate way to kill Johnny the Boy—one that ends with Johnny the Boy dying in the same way that Goose had died at the hand of Toecutter. Max handcuffs Johnny the Boy to a wrecked car that is leaking gasoline as Johnny the Boy pleads with him:

JOHNNY THE BOY:	Listen, man, will you? Listen to me! They were a hell of a lot of crazy people back there, man. Some kind of bad people. I'm not responsible for anything.... Hey, listen. I'm not a bad man. I'm sick, see? Sick. What do you call it? Psychopathic, you know. Personality disorder. The court, man, he said so. You're not gonna hurt me, are you? ...
MAD MAX:	The chain in those handcuffs is high-tensile steel. It'd take you ten minutes to hack through it with this. Now, if you're lucky ... you could hack through your ankle in five minutes. Go.
JOHNNY THE BOY:	You're mad, man! ... Please sweet Jesus, I was sick!

"I Was Sick!": Responsibility and Madness

In the above exchange, Johnny the Boy is trying to make the case that he is not "responsible" for anything—namely, what happened to Goose. In fact, in the documentary *The Madness of Max*, Tim Burns, who plays Johnny the Boy says as much: "I was trying to show that there were reasons for behaving the way I [Johnny the Boy] had and an intelligent, moral, compassionate man would recognize this, which he [Max] fails to do."

Philosophers distinguish between two kinds of responsibility: *causal* responsibility and *moral* responsibility. An insane person may be *causally* responsible for what they do—they have done it, after all—but they are not *morally* responsible. Why? Because if a person doesn't know what they are doing, or cannot control themselves, then they cannot be held responsible for what happens. In legal terms a crime has two components: *mens rea* or guilty mind (that is, one intended to do harm), and *actus reus* or guilty act, the external (non-mental) component. From a philosophy of law standpoint, the legal analysis of insanity *ought to* have two prongs. One prong is called the cognitive prong: this asks did the person *know* that what they were doing is wrong? The second prong is called the *control* prong: did a mental defect get in the way of the person being able to control their behavior? But I said *ought to* have two prongs, because while there are a handful of philosophers who argue for a "control" test of insanity, the legal standard does not.

The legal standard operating in most states today is based on the M'Naghten rule. In an 1843 case before the House of Lords, M'Naghten tried to kill a lord thinking that the lord was constantly pestering him (he was not). According to this rule, acquittal is required if "the party accused was labouring under such a defect of reason, from disease of the mind, as not to know that nature and quality of the act he was doing, or as to not know that what he was doing was wrong."[2] Importantly, if a person knows the action they are doing is wrong, then it doesn't matter how "in control" of that action they are.

In Johnny the Boy's instance, though he does appear to have awful judgment in marauding with Toecutter, one could fairly claim he is not responsible for Goose's ultimate demise in both ways. He is not causally responsible for Goose's demise in that he does not throw the cigarette that burns him up; Toecutter does. And he may not be morally responsible if what he says above is to be believed. In fact, there is reason to believe others see Johnny the Boy as incompetent in the relevant sense. His nickname is the "the Boy," and clearly people associate his personality disorder with immaturity and a lack of self-control. Not every mental disorder qualifies for the "not guilty by reason of insanity" defense of "personality disorder," but what Johnny the Boy says he is diagnosed with, most likely would. Still, the question is: does Johnny know that what he did (in this case, throw the brake rotor at Goose's truck) was wrong? Unfortunately for him, he seems to recognize this in his confession to Max. At that point, whether he could control himself—from a legal standpoint—is immaterial.

The problem of responsibility and madness can also be seen in Max's fight with Blaster in *Beyond the Thunderdome*. Recall that Blaster is half of Master Blaster. Master is a person of small stature who is the "brains" of the duo (and rides on Blaster's back), and Blaster is the "brawn," a gigantic man covered in armor who seems impossible to defeat. But what we do not immediately realize about Blaster is just how little intelligence he has. Max is given the choice to fight Blaster in the Thunderdome ("Two men enter, one man leaves") to earn his freedom and get his Interceptor back. While it seems like the odds are against him, Max cleverly uses a whistle to disorient Blaster and then a gigantic hammer to knock his helmet off. Once his helmet is off, we see that Blaster has a rather small head and is clearly developmentally disabled. Master pleads with Max: "No, no! Look at his face! He's got the mind of a child. It's not his fault. Blaster, I'm sorry." Max clearly agrees with Master and says to Aunty Entity (the leader of Bartertown): "This wasn't part of the deal." In fact, for going back on his deal to follow the Thunderdome rules ("Two men enter, one man leaves"), Max has to face a punishment from "the wheel of fortune." As a result, he is exiled from Bartertown.

To be clear, Blaster is not "mad" in the conventional sense. But Blaster's cognitive limitations certainly fall under what would be called *incompetence*. We do not hold incompetent people morally responsible for their actions, even if they are *causally* responsible for harm, because they fail to the meet the criteria for moral/legal responsibility: they act neither voluntarily nor with ill intent. It is clear that Blaster is merely following the orders of Master (hence the name).

As Foucault documents, both madness and cognitive disability would be classified as "unreason," that is, as one of many things that are opposed to "reason." In this schema, anything against reason—madness, ignorance, error, passion—is to be avoided. All forms of unreason can be classified into roughly two forms: error and sin. Error is what comes about when we have misapprehended reality. Perhaps we have a hallucination due to extreme sleep deprivation. Or maybe we thought the person who grabbed the nice lady's purse was wearing glasses, when CCTV footage shows they were not. In either case, error in sensation—or our understanding of what we saw—has led us astray. The second way unreason can go awry is in the failure to follow what Immanuel Kant (1724–1804) famously calls "practical reason," that is, in behaving the correct way. Reason is supposed to give us accurate information, truth, and guide us toward good behavior, righteousness. Madness threatens both: "Being both error and sin, madness is simultaneously impurity and solitude; it is withdrawn from the world, and from truth; but it is by that very fact imprisoned in evil."[3] There is a paradox in this thinking: in the very feature that makes the mad not guilty (namely, in being cut off from reason), there is also an evil to be avoided. Max himself ponders this evil throughout the series. We've already seen his concern in *Mad Max*, where Max tells his boss he's afraid of being "like them." In *Fury Road*, Max admits: "It was hard to know who was more crazy: Me ... or everyone else."

That said, even if Max is not insane, he is no saint. We may relish the poetic revenge he takes on Johnny the Boy, but under any just system, an agent of law cannot be judge, jury, and executioner. One wonders if Max here had reached his "terminal freak-out point." Tim Burns, the actor playing Johnny the Boy, again sheds some light on this: "He is a person who, when given a moral choice, he becomes a crazed killer. The cop kills more people in that film than anybody."

Similarly, Max in *Fury Road* is a morally ambiguous character. He seems willing to help Furiosa and the five wives only after it becomes clear to him that he needs them (not the reverse). The near abandonment of the women happens on the back of a past littered with his failure to save people. Ultimately, Max does the right thing, even though he has a chance to escape on his own motorbike. Instead, he drives after Furiosa and convinces her not to travel 160 days across the salt flats. Then he helps her retake the Citadel.

Hanging by a Thread: The Furrow of Reason

In *Mad Max*, we see Max's fear of going insane. He opines that perhaps a bronze badge is all that sets him apart from the crazies on the road. In *Fury Road,* in the midst of a series of delusions, he mutters, "If you don't fix what's broken, you'll uh ... You'll go insane." This appears to be a warning to himself.

Foucault notes that this idea of a thin "sane" line was all too common during the eighteenth century. For instance, one dictionary of the time writes of the word *delirium*: "This word is derived from *lira,* a furrow; so that *deliro* actually means to move out of the furrow, away from the proper path of reason."[4] In other words, madness is just a step out of the path of reason.

The idea that insanity is only one small step away is present in Aunty Entity's view that "all of our lives hang by a thread," thus motivating her devotion to the laws of Bartertown. As Heraclitus (ca. 500 B.C.E.) reminds us: "One must fight for the law as for the city walls." If there weren't laws—not law enforcement in the form of agents of the law, but laws themselves—all of Bartertown would fall apart. That's why the crowd is beholden to the law that ultimately winds up saving Max's life. Recall that Max refused to kill Blaster, so Aunty Entity had her henchmen kill the giant. Then she wanted to kill Max for breaking the rule in refusing to kill Blaster; but the crowd chants, "Two men enter, one man leaves" as reminder of the law, and Max is spared. This leads Aunty to profess her second law: "Break a deal, face the wheel."

The point here is not whether these laws themselves are *rational* or typical. The point is that law is supposed to be an expression of reason—a universalization of moral principle. Aunty seems to believe—and perhaps rightly so—that any law is better than no law, and that laws prevent the disintegration of society. And if we're not rational citizens, we may become ... animals.

"Unleash My Dogs of War": Confinement and Animality

Confinement and animality, two themes associated with madness, appear often, sometimes simultaneously, in the *Mad Max* films. First, a very brief history lesson from Foucault. In the 1700s, the houses of confinement in France were used to house anyone who was considered a vagrant or deviant, be they indigent, criminal, or mad. In March 1790, in the spirit of the Declaration of the Rights of Man, the French Assembly emptied houses of confinement of all vagrants *except* those convicted, those facing charges, and "madmen." It became clear, however, that there was a great friction between the categories of the criminal and the mad. While certain people argued it was unfair to the mad to remain incarcerated, some criminals argued it was unfair *to them* to be housed with the mad (again, hinting at contagion). Regardless of the reason, many mad people were eventually set free prior to any other arrangements for their care, resulting in a second decree "remedying the disagreeable events that may be occasioned by madmen set at liberty, and by the wandering of vicious and dangerous animals."[5] Thus, the mad were thought of in the same way as rabid dogs. Finally, after still not having any infrastructure in place, but attempting to be humane, authorities released mad people to the care of their families (none of whom were equipped to provide such care) in 1791.

Foucault explains the problem well: "By this detour around their liberation, madmen regained, but this time within the law itself, that animal status in which confinement had seemed to isolate them; they again became wild beasts at the very period when doctors began to attribute to them a gentle animality."[6] The problem of animality is then twofold: first, how do we protect human beings from danger? And second, how do we recognize the relative innocence of the mad-as-wild animal? But let's not think that this second question always has humane answers: when a bear attacks a human and escapes, authorities will often track it and kill it regardless of its moral innocence.

Confinement and animality go hand-in-hand. A dog is kept on a leash in public. The most dangerous animals are caged when brought into proximity with humans who do not know how to handle them. Recall that in *The Road Warrior* Lord Humungus says to the people of the refinery, "Again you have made me unleash my dogs of war!" In making this pronouncement, he also physically unchains Wez, his best warrior. He continues to the rest of his "Smegma Crazies" and "Gayboy Berserkers": "Attack, my vermin, attack!" Thus, Lord Humungus dehumanizes and exploits his followers—and in doing so he reduces them to animals. Or think also of the time when, in *Fury Road*, Max is also on leash: he too acts more feral under those conditions.

The problem of animality pertains to responsibility and self-control. In *Rex v. Arnold* (1724), "the 'wild beast test' emerged: the judge ruled that a defendant is insane and criminally irresponsible if he did not know what he was doing and was doing no more than a 'wild beast' would do."[7] Such a view, while perhaps antiquated, does seem to square with the viewer's intuition that Blaster, Johnny the Boy, Wez, and perhaps Nux are not to blame for their actions—they are just doing what a wild beast would do. But if that is the case—that the right-hand men of the villains in each film are made innocent by their animal status—then who is to blame?

124

MATTHEW P. MEYER

"I Am Your Lord!": Cults, Shared Psychosis, and Responsibility

In the cases of Immortan Joe (*Fury Road*) and Lord Humungus (*The Road Warrior*) and perhaps Toecutter, there is a collective delusion that may qualify as mass shared psychosis. Put another way, the followers of Humungus and Immortan Joe have undergone mind control and have become members of a cult. How else to explain Humungus's claim—"I am your lord!"— or the worship of Immortan Joe and his claim that he can take his followers to Valhalla? In both cases, the villains have taken extraordinarily desperate populations and exploited their insecurities by providing minimal survival needs (water, food, guzzolene) and a promise of something better. "Common characteristics" of cults "are members' adherence to a consensual belief system, the maintenance of a high degree of social cohesiveness, strong behavioral mores that influence member behavior, and the recognition of members or group leaders as charismatic or divine."[8] According to that definition, the followers of Immortan Joe and Lord Humungus would qualify as cults.

Yet, despite the commonsense idea that many cults use mind control to manipulate their followers, there has not been one successful NGRI (Not Guilty by Reason of Insanity) defense in appellate cases in the history of the United States.[9] What this means is that jurors weren't convinced that the defendants in such cases met the M'Naghten test. This is significant because while we may be inclined to blame Toecutter, Humungus, Aunty Entity, and Immortan Joe for the damage their followers inflict, it turns out that Johnny the Boy's plea would not usually work in court. Again, the issue comes down to the fact that Johnny the Boy, the War Boys, the Berserkers—or most of them—could discern right from wrong. Except for Wez, the others all come to a moment of self-effacement wherein they recognize the wrongness of their prior actions, even if they were in service to a villain and not acting fully volitionally. They'd been manipulated into madness by the mind control of their leaders.

"... One of Them, You Know?"

The *Mad Max* franchise provides myriad opportunities to view philosophical issues concerning madness. We've seen the tentative status of Max's own sanity and considered the criminal and moral responsibility of Johnny the Boy, Wez, Blaster, and Nux. We've seen the way that the cult leaders—Toecutter, Aunty Entity, Lord Humungus, and Immortan Joe—likely have ultimate moral responsibility for their followers' actions (even if a court may not agree). We've looked at the way that "terminal crazies" are treated like animals and often confined. As of this writing, I do not know what happens in *Furiosa*, but I'm pretty sure the "madness" will continue.

Notes

1   Michel Foucault, *Madness and Civilization,* trans. Richard Howard (New York: Vintage Books, 1980), 203.
2   Paul Litton, "The Mistaken Quest for a Control Test," in Mark White ed., *The Insanity Defense* (New York: Praeger, 2017), 186.
3   Foucault, 175.
4   Ibid., 99.
5   Ibid., 236.
6   Ibid., 238.
7   Meron Wondemaghen, "Insanity Constructs," in Mark White ed., *The Insanity Defense* (New York: Praeger, 2017), 133.
8   Brian Holoyda and William Newman, "Between Belief and Delusion: Cult Members and the Insanity Plea," *Journal of American Academic Psychiatry and Law* 44 (2016), 53.
9   Ibid., 60–61.

13

Justice, Reason, and the Road Warrior: A Mechanic Reads Plato

David H. Gordon

Growing up, the kids on my block were fascinated by anything attached to a motor. We trafficked in go-carts, minibikes, dirt bikes, mopeds, and, later, cars. During my undergraduate and graduate days, I pulled several tours of duty working at the local garage. Learning how to work on cars involved learning the language game associated with this form of life: ohm meter, choke butterfly valve, cold cranking amps, high lift cam, harmonic balancer, OBD-II, intake manifold, and so on. *Mad Max* (with American voiceover) and *The Road Warrior* were like *Sesame Street* for learning the lingo of garage speak. Who are the people in your neighborhood? Bubba Zanetti, Johnny the Boy, Mudguts, Cundalini, the Goose, Sprog, Fifi, Aunt May, and the Feral Kid. The cult of the V8 was a real thing. If you drove a four banger, you weren't fully human.

Because I would go back and forth from the classroom and the garage, I would often see parallels between them. Socrates was a street philosopher. Max too lives on the street, but inside a car. So what is a car? A car is more than just a mechanical object one owns and leaves sitting in the parking lot. A car is a machine, a technological device, an instantiation of a rational system. A car in need of repair has somehow diverged from that rational system. To fix it, you must learn the system that governs it. Diagnosing what is wrong with a car that won't run involves following a logical procedure, deducing from its condition what has caused it not to work (Does it have spark? Does it have fuel?). When one climbs into a car, one is not just getting inside

Mad Max and Philosophy: Thinking Through the Wasteland, First Edition.
Edited by Matthew P. Meyer and David Koepsell.
© 2024 John Wiley & Sons, Inc. Published 2024 by John Wiley & Sons, Inc.

a material object, one is getting inside the thoughts and ideas of the engineers who built the car. If the car runs as it was intended on a consistent basis, then those thoughts were good thoughts. But who put those thoughts into the engineer's head? Those thoughts really represent years of training in the applied sciences, in which the engineer assimilated the collective wisdom of the scientific community, which reflects centuries of humans grappling with the world trying to understand what makes it tick.

In the sense just outlined, working on cars is a rational enterprise, and the automotive technician possesses a certain kind of rational esoteric knowledge, a valuable skill the public lacks. Technological skill or know-how is a form of instrumental reason, which is itself a mode of human rationality. In *Mad Max* and *The Road Warrior*, the gangs Max confronts appear to operate under only instrumental reason. They might know how to construct and maintain engines of war, but their use of instrumental reason is geared only toward their own self-interest, with no regard for the objective ends or good of society. Instrumental reason focuses on finding the most efficient means to achieve your ends, but it doesn't tell you which ends are worth pursuing. Consider that a gun can be used as a deterrent to protect the lives of the innocent, but it can also be used to rob a bank. One is a proper end; the other is not. Only by melding these two forms of reason together, instrumental with objective reason—that is, a concern for proper ends such as justice—can technology be utilized in appropriate ways. Max doesn't drive just any car, but a Main Force Patrol Interceptor. As such, Max participates in the state's concern for the public good and is charged with enforcing the principles of justice that ideally stand behind the rule of law. In *The Road Warrior*, Max says to Pappagallo, "Two days ago I passed a vehicle that will haul that tanker. You wanna get out of here, talk to me." On the surface, Max is speaking about his ability to fix a mechanical problem, but as it turns out, Max has more to offer. He possesses not only the means to resolve their problem, but knowledge of the right purpose of the rig.

Reason Belongs in the Driver's Seat

The *Mad Max* films are about who rules, who rules the towns, who rules the streets, who rules Bartertown, who rules the Citadel, and who has access to and control over the scarce resources of water and fuel. Max's primary opponents for the most part lack any concern for justice. Instead, they are lawless, raping, pillaging, and killing for a tank of juice to fuel their frenzied existence. In *Mad Max*, there is a fragile political order, a society on the verge of collapse, but one that still has a nominal legal system. In *The Road Warrior*, this political order has collapsed because of a nuclear war, and society has devolved into an anarchic state of nature. In *Thunderdome*, Aunty Entity rules Bartertown, but Master Blaster challenges her because he keeps the electricity on. In *Fury Road*, Immortan Joe rules the Citadel not by principles of justice, but through control of an underground aquifer of uncontaminated water. Wherever Max goes, he challenges those who rule unjustly. Max often would prefer just to be left alone, but when forced to choose between serving the just or unjust, Max is willing to risk his own interests in the fight against injustice, which means he has some grasp of what justice is.

In the *Republic*, Plato argues that only people who know what justice is are qualified to govern.[1] To illustrate this, Plato makes use of several allegories, one of which is the analogy of ship of state. Suppose there is a ship where everyone onboard thinks they are a little smarter than the captain. Eventually they mutiny, seize the ship, and toss the captain overboard, then promptly consume the ship's liquor and food. Who should now be in charge of the ship? If they are out in the middle of the sea, the only way for them to return home safely is to appoint someone who is knowledgeable in the art of navigation, one who knows how to read the stars and winds. In other words, the navigator has a certain kind of knowledge the rest of the crew lacks. As the captain/navigator is to the ship, so the ruler is to the state. It is their knowledge of justice that legitimizes their reign.

Max not only has an intuitive understanding of justice, but he also possesses the virtues of courage and fortitude in pursuing it, as well as the virtue of prudence in determining who is just and who is not. Max may have a hard time articulating the love he feels for his wife, but what is more important is that the love is there. The same is true for his sense of justice, which is akin to the North Star. One doesn't have to know ontologically what the North Star is. One only needs to know that it can serve as an objective guide by which to gain one's bearings. Similarly, Max's internal moral compass seems to be pointing toward justice.

In the opening scene of *Mad Max*, Roop and Charlie argue over who should be driving their patrol vehicle. Similarly, in the *Republic* and the *Phaedrus*, Plato tells the Myth of the Charioteer.[2] Reason should be in command of the chariot, the charioteer holding the reins of the two horses pulling it. The white horse is Spirit, which is responsive to the reins, but not always. The black horse is Bodily Appetite, which wants to go its own way and can be subdued only when Reason and Spirit join forces. Similarly, Justice is the proper balance between the soul's parts—Reason, Spirit, and Bodily Appetite. The role of the affective and appetitive parts of the soul is not to rule, but to remain subordinate to reason.

On a macrolevel, this same theory can be applied to the state: reason should be in control. Using this metaphor, Max is attempting to rein in and control the willfulness of those he encounters, who often are resistant to the reins of reason. The Nightrider with his feverish passion is an example of what happens when the spirited aspect of the soul, rather than reason, winds up behind the steering wheel. Only Max has the ability to restrain him.

Why should reason rule? Why does reason belong in the driver's seat? In Book IV of the *Republic*, Plato argues for a functionalist interpretation of justice that says each person should perform only that function in society for which they are best suited. Shoemakers should not try to be physicians, and soldiers should not try to govern.[3] Only the wisest and most rational among us should hold the reins of power. At the end of Book 1, Plato argues for a functionalist interpretation of the human soul as well.[4] What makes humans essentially different from all other species is our ability to reason. If reason is our essence, then a good person is one who reasons well. Max throughout the films is calm, cool-headed, and deliberative. Reason also allows humans to deliberate over their actions, to deliberate over the nature of the good, and to try and act justly. Animals cannot do this.

Toecutter's biker crew act and behave more like animals than humans; they hoot and howl the way animals do and they prey upon people. Like pack animals, they follow the lead dog and don't seem capable of thinking for themselves or behaving according to principles of law. They live in the moment and react only to the material, to visual stimuli, chasing after whatever grabs their attention. Max is more than just an animal; he is a rational animal who possesses both intellectual and moral virtue. He can think for himself, and his behavior is principled. Some of the characters that Max faces have amiable qualities. But they all lack the kind of conscience, the kind of moral compass, Max has. After Goose goes down, Max says to his wife, "Here I am trying to put sense to it, when I know there isn't any." Often we hear talk of "senseless gun violence." How do you make sense of senseless violence? You can't. There is no rhyme or reason to it. Evil acts suffer from a deficiency, a failure to abide by the principles of rational conduct.

Administrator of Street Justice

A central theme in the *Mad Max* series is that the scales of justice have been upset. Justice demands that the scales be balanced by punishing those who have brought harm and by making restitution to those who have been harmed. Questions arise: Was Max's administration of justice proper, or was it excessive? Did he go too far? Should Max have apprehended his suspects and delivered them over to the justice system to be given due process? Did Max exceed his authority as a police officer in chasing down and killing Toecutter and his crew? Plato argued against retaliation; a good person should never injure anyone, even the unjust. On top of that, retaliation is ineffective. Plato argues that much as horses and dogs don't benefit from harm, humans are not improved by being injured.[5] So, what we should desire to befall unjust people is not harm, but for them to change from their unjust ways and behave justly. In other words, Plato prefers rehabilitation of the wrongdoer to retaliatory punishment. One could argue that Max tried to follow this course by arresting Johnny the Boy and turning him over to the courts, but the courts failed to prosecute Johnny or send him to prison. Instead of securing justice, they freed him so that he could then go on to commit more terrible crimes. Fifi, in whatever authority he had, gave Max permission to take matters into his own hands—"As long as the paperwork is clean, you boys are free to do what you like out there."

One of the first attempts to define justice in the *Republic* is when Polemarchus cites the poet Simonides and claims that justice is "to render to each his due."[6] This definition has an element of just deserts theory in it—we should get what we deserve. We ought only expect and receive what we are due, and if we take more than that, we have unjustly procured more than our fair share. Toecutter's biker crew do not buy gasoline; they steal it. What if they are caught and pay for what they have taken? Has justice then been satisfied? Not if justice demands that criminal activity be punished. This could be accomplished by either monetary penalties or by restraining the liberty of the individual by sentencing them to a prison term proportional to the severity of their crime. Pure retribution may be seen as unjust revenge.

Instead, the punishment should include rehabilitation to make future unjust behavior less likely.

Plato would not condone Max injuring the wrongdoer, but at least Max makes better choices than those around him. Often the choices that confront us are not black and white, clear self-evident binaries that align neatly with right and wrong. Often we must choose between the lesser of two evils. The people Max usually allies himself with at least exhibit virtuous qualities. They have empathy, warmth, and a sense of justice. Likewise, the people that Max generally opposes lack these qualities. In *Mad Max*, Max may appear vengeful, but he is the only one who can stop the psychotic rampage of the Nightrider and hunt down and prevent Toecutter and his gang from committing further vicious acts. In *The Road Warrior*, Max partners with Pappagallo rather than Humungus, as the latter seeks to obtain access to the refinery not through the toil of hard work, but through fear, intimidation, and murder. In *Thunderdome*, rather than return Max's stolen property, Aunty Entity says she will only do so if Max kills off her political opponent. In *Fury Road*, Max takes the side of Furiosa in resisting the dictatorship of Immortan Joe, who rules not according to principles of justice, but arbitrarily, based only on his control of the access to fresh water. He treats the men as mere extensions of his will, and he treats the women as mere breeders to pass on his genes. Immortan Joe sees clean water only as a commodity to be hoarded to ensure submission to his power. As a result, his people shed no tears at his death, for his rule was oppressive.

Differing from Plato, John Stuart Mill (1806–1873) argues that the only purpose by which power can be exercised over one against their will is to prevent harm to others.[7] If this principle guides our understanding of justice, then Max is justified in using force to stop his opponents. After all, the bikers pose a threat to others and have no qualms about inflicting damage. Mill was thinking of state power, though, something that is absent in most of Max's adventures. In the post-apocalyptic Wasteland of *The Road Warrior*, there is no rule of law whatsoever, no prisons in which to confine lawbreakers. A state of nature has displaced any social contract and anarchy prevails. Here Max is like an Arthurian knight roaming the landscape, one who embodies the law and is free to distribute punishment however he sees fit. The institutions of society have disappeared and all that remains of the Halls of Justice is the imprint that they have left on Max's soul. In the Wasteland, Max rules not only because he knows the principles of justice but because he can enforce them as well. Max is an administrator of street justice.

Real Men Eat Dog Food and Fear the Wasteland

So, what is the takeaway? What lesson does *The Road Warrior* have to offer, other than the obvious, that real men eat dog food? *Mad Max* and its sequels offer a vision of a potential dystopian future. They are like a visit from the Ghost of Christmas Future. One wakes up the next morning thankful it was just a dream, that civilization is still here, but is left with the warning that if we don't change our ways, this vision could become a reality. Instrumental reason is the dominant form of thought pervading industrial society. When instrumental reason guides national thinking, militarism is the result. Each state tries to create bigger and better technology to dominate the other states, much as the small bands in the *Mad Max* films do, with the end result being nuclear destruction. We need to move beyond our nations acting as the individuals do in *The Road Warrior*, amassing more destructive and efficient weapons of war in order to control and subjugate others. We need to recover the elements of the objective rationalist tradition industrial society has forsaken and supplement instrumental reason with a knowledge of proper ends to ensure the survival of life on Earth. The nuclear genie has been let out of the bottle. If we can't put it back, at least we can work toward nuclear disarmament and nonproliferation.

What has doomed civilization in *The Road Warrior* is our addiction to oil. *The Road Warrior* is prophetic—a warning that if we don't wean ourselves off our fossil fuel dependency toward a sustainable future, this is where we are headed. *Mad Max* came out in 1979 and *The Road Warrior* in 1981, when the combined number of U.S. and Soviet nuclear weapons exceeded 30,000.[8] The Persian Gulf War ten years later confirmed the suspicion that control of the Middle East oil supply was something the world might be willing to go to war over. Let's hope our leaders have the prudence and fortitude to make the transition to renewable energy. The cult of the V8 has been diminished by an understanding of the collective environmental damage that hundreds of millions of cars spewing their noxious fumes can do. Every time we burn a gallon of gasoline, we put five and a half pounds of carbon into the atmosphere. The internal combustion engine is slowly warming our planet. Climate change, deforestation, and ocean acidification are now as much a threat to the survival of life on Earth as nuclear war.

Mad Max and *The Road Warrior* confirm Plato's belief that when we are irrational and unjust we not only harm those around us, we harm ourselves as well. The fate of civilization might depend upon this insight. The preservation of all life on Earth, not just human life, is an inherent good. The destruction of the planet doesn't benefit anyone. Max's words, "If you want to get out of here, talk to me," aren't just addressed to Pappagallo. They are also addressed to us. Max shows us a world we don't want to live in. We should fear the possibility of the Wasteland and work together to avoid ending up there.

Notes

1 Plato, *Republic*, trans. Paul Shorey, in Edith Hamilton and Huntington Cairns eds., *The Collected Dialogues of Plato* (New York: Pantheon Books, 1966), 487e–488e.
2 Plato, *Phaedrus*, trans. R. Hackforth, in Edith Hamilton and Huntington Cairns eds., *The Collected Works of Plato* (New York: Pantheon Books, 1966), 246a–246e; Plato, *Republic,* 442c–443e.
3 Plato, *Republic,* 434a–434d.
4 Ibid., 352e–354b.
5 Ibid., 335b.
6 Ibid., 331d–332d.
7 John Stuart Mill, "On Liberty," in Marshall Cohen ed., *The Philosophy of John Stuart Mill* (New York: Modern Library, 1961), 197.
8 Harold A. Feiveson et al., *Unmaking the Bomb* (Cambridge, MA: MIT Press, 2014), 174.

Part IV

MOTHER'S MILK: GENDER AND INTERSECTIONALITY

Homecoming as Homemaking: The Rise of the Matriarchy in *Mad Max: Fury Road*

Daniel Conway

> My formula for greatness in a human being is *amor fati*: that one wants nothing to be different, not forward, not backward, not in all eternity. Not merely bear what is necessary, still less conceal it—all idealism is mendaciousness in the face of what is necessary—but *love* it.
> —Friedrich Nietzsche, *Ecce Homo*

Even to this day, the defining trope of *homecoming* is dominated by the epic poem from which it originated in the West. Owing to the protracted and oft-delayed homecoming of Odysseus, as recounted by Homer and rehearsed in subsequent tragedies and satyr-plays, homecoming is an activity typically reserved for heroic, kingly, male adventurers, whose supposed love of hearth and home is tested by the adrenaline rush of battle and conquest, the pursuit of honor and glory, the allure of exotic travel and discovery, and, in general, the thrill of measuring oneself against (and prevailing over) previously unknown forces, spirits, and adversaries.

Homer's story of the *Nostos* [νόστος] of Odysseus is a textbook tale of patriarchal privilege. A king leaves home to fight someone else's war. He acquits himself as a counselor, tactician, and leader. Along the way, he earns the patronage of Athena, who occasionally intervenes to extract him from the kinds of predicaments into which his heroic character leads him. After ten years of battle in Troy, he begins his trip home. Although he is keen to return to Ithaca, he manages to find

Mad Max and Philosophy: Thinking Through the Wasteland, First Edition.
Edited by Matthew P. Meyer and David Koepsell.
© 2024 John Wiley & Sons, Inc. Published 2024 by John Wiley & Sons, Inc.

various diversions along the way. Thus emerges the double standard that is characteristic of the patriarchy: while *his* obligations to the home and family are both negotiable and subject to indefinite suspension, other (= lesser) members of the household are expected to discharge their homemaking duties without question or delay. Although Odysseus trysted for (as many as) seven years with Calypso, for example, he fully expected his wife, Penelope, to spurn her many suitors for the full duration of his extended absence.

George Miller's *Mad Max: Fury Road* (2015) offers a refreshingly novel take on the enduring trope of homecoming. Most notably, the hero of the story champions the cause of women's liberation. Seizing a propitious opportunity, Imperator Furiosa emancipates the captive "wives" of Immortan Joe and endeavors to transport them to her birthplace, known to her only as "the Green Place," where, she believes, she and the "wives" will be welcomed home by the Vuvalini—that is, the tribe of many mothers, from whom she was abducted years ago by Immortan Joe.

That the Green Place still exists as she remembers it—*à la* the Ithaca from which Odysseus set sail for Troy—is never questioned by Furiosa. As she executes her daring plan, she is focused only on the accursed place she has left behind—the Citadel—and the magical place that lies ahead. (As we shall see, a third option, patently suicidal, occurs to Furiosa in her darkest hour.) While Miller's direction of the film clearly nudges his viewers toward a sympathetic identification with Furiosa and the refugee wives, he also makes it clear that the escape she has staged is both underplanned and reckless. As we discover in due course, the Green Place is no longer green, and it hardly qualifies as the safe haven she has promised herself and the wives. As the etymology of the word *utopia* suggests, in fact, the Green Place is no place at all.[1]

A Stranger Comes to Town ...

Availing himself of a staple of films in the genre of "the Western,"[2] George Miller—himself an unabashed fan of the genre—launches the fourth installment in his wildly successful *Mad Max* franchise. The stranger in question is none other than Max Rockatansky, the eponymous anti-hero and centerpiece of the franchise. As we know from Miller's previous films, the enigmatic Max is a stranger not only to this particular "town"—namely, the Citadel, a militarized fortress governed with an iron fist by the patriarchal sadist Immortan Joe—but also to settled communities more generally. Cursed, or so he believes, to wander the post-apocalyptic Wasteland, Max tries to keep to himself, only to be drawn against his will into the internal politics of the traumatized pop-up communities that dot the new (and pre-ruined) frontier.

In this film, Max is once again subjected to a dizzying series of humiliating, emasculating indignities: taken by surprise in the desert, he is captured, deprived of his car (and the freedom it represents), bound, gagged, tattooed, pressed into service as a "Bloodbag," muzzled, affixed like a figurehead to the prow of an attack vehicle, grazed and wounded in battle, buried in a Biblical-grade sandstorm, pummeled in a fist fight with Furiosa, whose War Rig he attempts and fails to boost, and relegated to the task of minding a gaggle of runaway breeders, who are probably the same age Glory would have been.[3] At the busy hands of his ruthless captors, in other words, Max actually receives (something like) the treatment he believes he deserves for failing to protect his loved ones. As we shall see, the wisdom he derives from these degrading experiences is central to the advance of the film's plot and narrative.

As in most Westerns, the appearance of the stranger causes neither the distress nor the revival of the town he visits. His arrival is but an inflection point, an occasion for the release or activation of forces already rumbling beneath a seemingly placid surface. While it is true that the stranger typically dispatches the worst of the bad actors who threaten the town, his signal contribution is to rouse the townsfolk and awaken in them their dormant resolve. Having settled into the exhausting daily routines of peaceable homemaking,[4] the townsfolk have become disconnected from the drive, the will, and the passion that initially led them to coax the rudiments of civil society from the unforgiving landscape of the Western frontier. The arrival of the stranger not only alerts the alienated townsfolk to their as-yet-unacknowledged peril, but also emboldens them to *come home* to the way of life they had established and subsequently misplaced.[5]

In the case of *Fury Road*, the arrival of the stranger just happens to coincide with an unanticipated eruption of dissatisfaction with the gender inequities on which Immortan Joe's patriarchy trades. Unbeknownst to Joe and his henchmen, the young women whom he has indentured as breeders, including one who carries his child, are no longer willing to endure the demeaning terms of their subjugation. The wives find an improbable champion in Imperator Furiosa, who, no longer fancied by Joe and his youth-crazed followers, has risen through the ranks of the patriarchal hierarchy. Determined to transport the runaway breeders to the Green Place, Furiosa smuggles them aboard her War Rig and goes rogue. Joe and his carnival battle caravan gleefully give chase, amped to a fever pitch by the hot licks of a flame-spouting death-metal combat guitarist. The War Boys, in particular, relish the opportunity to be witnessed for their valor, which, they hope, will land them in Valhalla. Although they would never admit as much, the brazen insubordination of Imperator Furiosa has granted them the opportunity to reap the meaning and purpose that sustains them.

What is true of the devil-may-care War Boys, all shiny and chrome, is true more generally of the patriarchy over which Joe presides. Like the clueless master in Hegel's famous dialectic,[6] Joe is trapped in a cul-de-sac of unacknowledged dependency. He and the supposedly valiant warrior-outlaws who support him are reliant on the women whom they have enslaved for the nourishment they seek—whether in the form of labor, pleasure, milk, heirs, recognition, or vitality. And now they find themselves energized, once again, by their pursuit of a woman who, they believe, holds their fate in her hands. (To be sure, Joe's patriarchy is also dependent on the uncompensated labor and supplication of the dehydrated denizens of the Citadel. But that is a story for another occasion.)

Time for a New Plan

The film's pivotal scene occurs toward the end of its second act, as Furiosa leads the fugitive wives and the surviving members of the Vuvalini tribe on a motorcycle trip across the uncharted salt flats. Rudely divested of her childhood dream of returning to the Green Place, Furiosa wagers her life, and the lives of her companions, on the desperate, insane hope for something better on the other side of the vast Wasteland.

Thus far in the film, we have only known Furiosa to be grimly determined, chillingly competent, and eminently resourceful. Passing for a man in a man's world, she receives none of the disrespect—for example, catcalls, objectifying gazes, patronizing language, passive-aggressive chivalry, and so on—that female strivers typically endure. Even her plan to liberate the wives comes across as businesslike, as if she were simply delivering cargo to an assigned destination on a tight deadline. That Furiosa is *also* frightened, deeply wounded, and tempted by suicidal nihilism should not surprise us, given her circumstances, but it does come as something of a shock when her reckless plan unravels before our eyes. In truth, she knows next to nothing about the Green Place, despite promoting with steely assurance the safe haven it would afford them. As it turns out, in fact, her entire plan is predicated on the wishfully conjectured validity of her gauzy childhood memory of the Green Place, prior to her abduction by Immortan Joe.

What Furiosa needs in her moment of existential despair is not a tacit affirmation of her death wish, nor a mansplained lecture on the proper role and place of women, but a new plan, one firmly rooted in the (admittedly harsh) reality of her situation. The plan proposed by "Mad" Max is as simple as it is daunting: turn the Rig around and reclaim the Citadel. Stop running away and make a new home—a new Green Place—for yourself and your loved ones. Address your childhood trauma by confronting your tormentor. Fight for the opportunity, finally, to *come home*.[7]

How did it happen that Max, feral and barely literate, was able to persuade Furiosa to return to the Citadel? That he had earned her trust is apparent, as is the earthy wisdom of the counsel he so sparingly dispenses. A kindred survivor of trauma, he acknowledges without judgment both the appeal and the folly of a mad, under-provisioned dash across an uncharted Wasteland. In his capacity as the film's designated stranger, moreover, Max sees in Furiosa something that she cannot yet see in herself—namely, that she has something to live for and, if necessary, to fight and die for. (So does he, of course, if only he would forgive himself for his past lapses.) Sealing the deal, Max instinctively homes in on what Furiosa needs most of all: "We might be able to, together, come across some kind of redemption."

The mysterious stranger has spoken. When the stranger comes to town, of course, he leads not with words but with deeds, which Max delivers aplenty on their return to the Citadel.

Nietzsche's Critique of Idealism

The philosophical significance of the plan devised by Max is succinctly conveyed by the influential critique of *idealism* that was advanced by the German-born philosopher Friedrich Nietzsche (1844–1900). In his Preface to *Beyond Good and Evil* (1886), for example, Nietzsche diagnoses idealism as involving (and rationalizing) a cowardly flight from reality.[8] Rather than confront the world as it is—imperfect, flawed, limited, and disappointing—idealists dream of (and tarry with) an alternative, invented world, wherein the meaning, security, and recognition they seek are potentially available to them. As we see in the excerpted passage that serves as the epigraph to this chapter, Nietzsche exposes "all idealism" as "mendaciousness in the face of what is necessary."[9] The opposing position, which reflects a resolute posture of *amor fati* (love of fate), enables its adherents "not merely [to] bear what is necessary, still less conceal it ... but *love* it."[10] Nietzsche's "formula for greatness in a human being" thus favors those who embrace the infrangible necessities that others seek to flee.[11]

The idealism described (and reviled) by Nietzsche appears in *Fury Road* in two manifestations: first, and more obviously, as the conviction on the part of the War Boys that they are awaited in Valhalla; and second, as the blind faith Furiosa invests in the immortality of the Green Place (as she recalls it). In both cases, to be sure, the default recourse to wishful idealism is perfectly understandable, especially given the grim, post-apocalyptic setting of the film. Like Furiosa, the War Boys crave an intensity of meaning and recognition that is not otherwise available to them. After enduring the systemic collapse of civilization, their health ruined and their lifespans halved by the aggressive advance of radiation sickness, the War Boys need to make some sense of their staggering misfortune. Is their anticipation of a repeating cycle of combat-death-rebirth any more outrageous than the beliefs endorsed by other, more familiar religions? And if Furiosa does not dream of the sanctuary that awaits her in the Green Place, what are her prospects for liberation from Immortan Joe's oppressive patriarchy?

Viewers of *Fury Road* are likely to be taken aback by the comic incongruence of (a version of) Norse mythology transplanted into the desert Wasteland of post-apocalyptic Australia. By what trick of the imagination do these emaciated, underdressed War Boys fancy themselves to be welcome in Valhalla? This incongruence is instructive, however, for it primes Miller's audience to attribute a similar intensity of desperation to the seemingly unflappable Furiosa. As it turns out, her fixation on the Green Place is no less idealistic, and no less incongruous, than the War Boys' fantasies of joining the heroes of mythic yore as they prepare for the battle of Ragnarök.[12] Nor should we be surprised by the parallels that obtain between these two manifestations of idealism. Like the War Boys, Furiosa is a victim not only of the calamities that have triggered the collapse of civilization, but also of the authoritarian rule imposed in the aftermath by Immortan Joe.

Although these twin expressions of idealism make useful, saving sense to their respective adherents, they also distract from (and in fact occlude) the possibilities that are consistent with and supported by the situation on the ground. So long as Furiosa and the War Boys restrict their focus to the redemption they seek elsewhere, they will fail to "come home" to the world in which they actually reside. That they might rebel against Immortan Joe, liberate the Citadel, and establish a just form of government, simply never occurs to them. It falls to Max, the stranger in their midst, to forge the missing link between homecoming and homemaking: they must fashion for themselves the home to which they may triumphantly return.

As an alternative (and antidote) to idealism, Nietzsche recommends the position he associates with *realism*,[13] of which the aforementioned posture of *amor fati* is supremely indicative. Like the idealists, the realists set ambitious goals for themselves and others, hoping thereby to elicit what is best within them. Unlike the idealists, who allow naïve wishes and childish beliefs to determine the goals they will pursue, the realists establish goals that are consistent, first, with what is actually known about human nature; and second, with what is actually possible in the situation at hand. Whereas Furiosa wished to find the Green Place magically unchanged and intact, and was willing on that basis to risk her life and the lives of the wives, Max is able to conduct a realistic assessment of the options available to them, as determined by the non-negotiable necessities by which they must abide. As the film's designated stranger, he administers the dose of realism that the others have refused thus far to swallow.

Just as idealism is vulnerable to an overestimation of human potential, so it is that realism can and (often does) result in an underestimation of human potential. As we see in the case of Immortan Joe, for example, realism is a popular position of (dishonest) refuge for those who wish to conjure and/or implement a self-fulfilling prophecy. So long as the wives and wet nurses believe that they are suited by nature to the subservient, second-class existence he imposes upon them, and so long as the half-life War Boys believe that he keeps the gate to Valhalla, he needn't cede or share any of the political authority he has amassed. In perhaps the most egregious instance of his sadism-as-realism, he paternalistically cautions/threatens the denizens of the Citadel not to "become addicted to water," lest they "resent its absence" when he suddenly closes the spigot.

As these examples from the film confirm, both positions—idealism and realism—can lead one astray. Although Nietzsche prefers to align himself with realism, the truth of the matter is that he does not eschew all ideals. He openly calls for a successor to the ascetic ideal,[14] for example, and he goes so far as to propose an alternative ideal, which he associates with "the great health."[15] To be more precise, then, we might refer to his preferred position as that of an educated (or mature) idealist. In the case of *Fury Road*, the parallel maturation of the relevant idealists—Furiosa and Nux—is catalyzed by the flinty realism of the film's designated stranger. As Max consistently models to anyone who pays him the requisite attention, one must place one's own unexamined preferences in temporary abeyance, especially if they evince an unaddressed childhood trauma, precisely so that one's assessment of the situation is not unfairly biased for or against those whose goals (and lives) are at stake. This is why his homecoming plan was received so positively by the others, despite the perils they knew they would encounter. Speaking for the others, Nux remarks that the plan devised (and warranted) by Max "sounds like hope."

Something Like Redemption

In the film's triumphant final scene, the stranger slinks away. After helping Furiosa to reclaim the Citadel, Max returns to the life of nomadic penance that his curse (supposedly) requires of him. He was able to talk Furiosa out of her death wish, steering her toward the concrete, realistic ideal that guided their homecoming, but he cannot (or will not) persuade himself to join her in her efforts to govern and green the Citadel.

As he departs, Max fulfills the (supposed) destiny of the *wounded healer*: despite his success in helping, advising, and rescuing others, earning their trust and affection along the way, he regards himself as well beyond redemption. If anything, or so he believes, his positive contribution to the liberation of the Citadel was a fluke, an anomalous reprieve from a fate that he dared not tempt any further. And although it is likely that he caught an intoxicating whiff of familial conviviality as he led the motley crew homeward, he evidently feared that he would be useless—or worse—to them as a homemaker. Convinced of the toxicity of his love for others, he performs the final, healing gesture of removing himself from their midst. Despite demonstrating that he *can* protect those whom he loves, his failure to protect Glory (and her mother) continues to haunt him. Like Cain, who failed to stand forth as his brother's keeper, Max is condemned to wander the Earth, East of Eden, barred (or so he believes) from the green paradise the Citadel someday might become.

And what of Furiosa? She watches Max slip away and offers no resistance. Although they share a knowing glance while exchanging nods of appreciation, no words—of love, regret, gratitude, care, or concern—pass between them. Perhaps she is distracted by the daunting task that lies ahead, or preoccupied with the innumerable details to which she and her leadership team now must attend. Perhaps she wishes to honor his desire to resume his nomadic existence and thereby restore the normalcy he associates with the burden of guilt he is obliged to bear. Perhaps she suspects that he joined forces with her largely, though not exclusively, to distract himself, ever so briefly, from his defining anguish. Familiar in her own right with the madness to which his *nom de guerre* attests, and the searing guilt that sustains it, she may wish for him to enjoy the limited therapeutic benefits he derives from wandering the desert alone. In any event, she is finally liberated from a lifelong subjection to the needs and whims of men. Although she could make good use of the talents and skills Max has displayed, she does not need him. His blood courses through her veins, and that will suffice.

Carried aloft to a perch once occupied by her former nemesis, Furiosa represents the promise of a matriarchal ruling order. As an immediate down payment on this promise, she authorizes a release of the water that previously had been withheld, cruelly, from the denizens of the Citadel. Their telltale response to her gesture of good will confirms that she is guided by the singular lesson imparted to her by the departed stranger: the goal of one's homecoming, both literally and figuratively, is to return *not* to the home of one's origin, but to the home one has made for oneself. As Furiosa now understands, the labor of homecoming is neither distinct nor separate from the labor of homemaking. Homecoming is in fact the happy outcome of one's renewed commitment to earnest, dedicated, collective homemaking.[16]

Notes

1 From the *Online Etymology Dictionary*: "*Utopia*, literally 'nowhere,' coined by Thomas More (and used as the title of his book, 1516, about an imaginary island enjoying the utmost perfection in legal, social, and political systems), from Greek *ou* 'not' + *topos* 'place'," at https://www.etymonline.com/word/utopia.

2   The films I have in mind include *Shane* (1953), directed by George Stevens; *A Fistful of Dollars* (1964), directed by Sergio Leone; *The Good, the Bad, and the Ugly* (1967), directed by Sergio Leone; *High Plains Drifter* (1973), directed by Clint Eastwood; and *Pale Rider* (1985), directed by Clint Eastwood.

3   I appeal here to the thesis presented by Cathal Gunning in "Why Mad Max Is Haunted by the Little Girl in *Fury Road*—Who Is She?" which appeared in *Screen Rant* on December 3, 2021, at https://screenrant.com/mad-max-fury-road-girl-hallucination-meaning-backstory/. According to Gunning, the "comic backstory" of *Fury Road* identifies the little girl as Glory, whom Max initially saved (along with her mother) from the Buzzards gang prior to the crash that claimed their lives.

4   I take my cue here from Robert Pippin's attention to the dawning of frontier "embourgeoisement," which serves as the backdrop of many films in the genre of "the Western." Robert B. Pippin, *Hollywood Westerns and American Myth: The Importance of Howard Hawks and John Ford for Political Philosophy* (New Haven, CT: Yale University Press, 2010), 20–25, 86–93.

5   The link between *The Odyssey* and the genre of "the Western" was noted by André Bazin, "The Western, or the American Film *par excellence*," in R. J. Cardullo ed. and trans., *André Bazin, The Critic as Thinker: American Cinema from Early Chaplin to the Late 1950s* (Rotterdam: Sense Publishers, 2017), 16–18. See also Pippin, 18–25.

6   G.W.F. Hegel's influential "master-slave" (or "lordship-bondage") dialectic appears in *Hegel's Phenomenology of Spirit*, trans A.V. Miller (Oxford: Oxford University [Clarendon] Press, 1977), 104–119.

7   Max thus emerges as the film's unlikely champion of what Pippin calls the *mythic universality*, to which some directors in the genre—including Miller—aspire. What Pippin has in mind here is "the universality of a common experience of a basic human problem, the political problem" the films in the genre characteristically raise and answer (Pippin, 21).

8   Friedrich Nietzsche, *Beyond Good and Evil: Prelude to a Philosophy of the Future*, trans. Walter Kaufmann (New York: Random House, 1989), 1–3.

9   Friedrich Nietzsche, *On the Genealogy of Morals*, trans. W. Kaufmann and R. J. Hollingdale, and *Ecce Homo*, trans. W. Kaufmann (New York: Random House, 1989), 258.

10 Ibid.

11 Ibid.

12 With respect to the role of meaning-conferring myths and legends in the genre of "the Western," I am indebted to Bazin, 19–24; and Pippin, 21–25, 96–98, 142–147.

13 Friedrich Nietzsche, *Twilight of the Idols*, in *The Portable Nietzsche*, trans. and ed. Walter Kaufmann (New York: Viking Penguin, 1982), 552–556.

14 Nietzsche, *On the Genealogy of Morals*, 145–153.
15 Friedrich Nietzsche, *The Gay Science*, trans. W. Kaufmann (New York: Random House, 1974), 346–347.
16 I am grateful to David Koepsell, Matthew Meyer, and Bill Irwin for their instructive comments on a previous draft of this essay.

15

Liberating Mother's Milk: Imperator Furiosa's Ecofeminist Revolution

Jacob Quick

Women hooked up to milking machines. "Breeders" wearing chastity belts. A masked man telling people not to "become addicted to water." What in the world is going on here? In addition to imprisoning and subjugating women, Immortan Joe also hordes natural resources like water and uses it to control the people. In a post-apocalyptic nightmare, Immortan Joe has cruelly subjugated an entire society and ecosystem to his will. His empire is a patriarchal hellscape ravaged by greed, exploitation, and violence.

Clearly, *Mad Max: Fury Road* presents a world terrorized by misogyny and environmental catastrophe. Indeed, the connection between environmental degradation and misogyny lies at the heart of ecofeminism. According to ecofeminism, both nature and women are oppressed, objectified, and exploited by patriarchal systems, and this overlap of oppression is no mere coincidence. In many modern societies, the oppression of women goes hand-in-hand with the abuse of nature. In other words, patriarchy is not just bad news for women, it's also bad news for the planet.

Ecofeminism is more than a fascinating theory, more than just analysis and criticism. Ecofeminists don't just want to understand the world; they want to change it. Liberation from patriarchy is essential for the flourishing of all people and for the well-being of the natural world. This is where our protagonist, Imperator Furiosa, grabs the wheel. She takes matters into her own hands, a decision that leads to a car chase to end all car chases. What we see unfold over the course

Mad Max and Philosophy: Thinking Through the Wasteland, First Edition.
Edited by Matthew P. Meyer and David Koepsell.
© 2024 John Wiley & Sons, Inc. Published 2024 by John Wiley & Sons, Inc.

of the film is nothing less than an ecofeminist revolution: one that not only liberates women, but also frees nature and its inhabitants from the shackles of patriarchal domination.

The Inhumanity of the Citadel

Needless to say, Immortan Joe's Citadel is no paradise. We are introduced to the Citadel through the experience of Max, who is captured and forced to be a "Bloodbag" for Nux, a War Boy who supports Immortan Joe's reign of terror. Nux is dangerously low on blood, and since Max is a universal donor, Nux seizes on the opportunity to pump Max's blood into his own veins. This introduction to the Citadel has plenty of red flags: no healthy and desirable society has the habit of capturing, torturing, and enslaving people, let alone stealing their blood. But the injustices don't end there.

Eventually, we get a broader perspective on the Citadel, beyond the cavernous walls of Max's prison. Taking a step back, we see that the Citadel is a place of massive inequality. People at the bottom of the Citadel (geographically and socially) are impoverished. But this poverty is not simply about lack of money or income. The people don't have immediate access to the most fundamental of natural resources: water. Immortan Joe keeps water reserves that he rarely, and reluctantly, share with the people, all the while commanding them not to "become addicted" to it.

Immortan Joe's water reserves are located at the top of a cliff, forcing the people to (literally and metaphorically) look up to him and beg for hydration. The inequality of the Citadel, therefore, is captured in its architecture. Power, privilege, and natural resources are located at the heights of the Citadel's cliffs. Not only is water stored hundreds of feet above the ground, but vegetation grows at the top of the cliffs. The Dag (one of the women running away from Joe) explains that the Citadel "has everything you need, as long as you're not afraid of heights." So, looking at the architecture of the Citadel, we have water, growth, nutrition, and abundance at the top, and scarcity and desperation at the bottom. In the Citadel, a privileged few reside "at the top" of society, where they have an excess of resources, while the majority reside "at the bottom" of society, where they have little to no access to necessities. So how do we make sense of this hierarchy?

Some ecofeminists propose that we can better understand oppression and injustice by taking a close look at the concepts of humanity and animality. At first glance, they may seem distinct: humans (*homo sapiens*) belong to one category and animals (in other words, animals that aren't *homo sapiens*) belong to another. But if you think carefully about how the ideas of "human" and "animal" function in society, you will see that they aren't as straightforward and distinct as they initially appear.

We generally believe that humans have basic rights that should be respected, but some humans enjoy luxury and privilege while others are treated "like animals." We may think of animals as creatures that humans can kill and eat, but there are plenty of animals (like pets) that we treat like fellow humans (or, in some cases, even *better* than humans!). In other words, the terms *human* and *animal* aren't simply scientific terms, but also concepts that represent many ideas about value, dignity, and purpose. *Animal* and *human* as concepts intersect and diverge in interesting ways.

Humanized Humans and Animalized Humans

To make sense of these concepts, contemporary philosopher Cary Wolfe introduced the notions of humanized humans and animalized humans.[1] Not long after Wolfe proposed this distinction, contemporary ecofeminist Carol Adams added the categories of animalized women and feminized animals.[2] As we will see, these categories map onto the social hellscape of *Mad Max: Fury Road*, and they help us understand how each character fits into the politics of the Citadel. So what are these concepts? And how do they apply to our characters? We can start by looking at the people at the top of society: humanized humans.

Humanized humans have all the respect and rights that humans should have. They have access to necessities, opportunities to pursue their goals, and a legal system that protects their well-being and interests. In Immortan Joe's Citadel, the humanized humans are Immortan Joe and his sons. Joe and his heirs have plenty of water, food, and technology, as well as slaves who cater to their needs. The entire political structure of the Citadel is organized to support their health, wealth, and happiness.

Animalized humans are humans who are perceived and treated (in one way or another) like animals. Animalized humans suffer various indignities: they are thrown into cages, deprived of resources, enslaved, exploited, and killed. Animalized humans are called *brute savages*, *barbarians*, *pests*, *pigs*, *snakes*, *rats*, *beasts*, and a whole host of other derogatory terms. Animalized humans are dehumanized: they are perceived as subhuman creatures who (for whatever reason) don't deserve to be treated with human dignity.[3] Using derogatory, animal-related language is an effective way to dehumanize people. It's no surprise that historically groups of people are animalized before they become victims of genocide.[4]

The Citadel's Animalized Humans

Unfortunately, there is no shortage of animalized humans in the Citadel. The War Boys are treated like subhumans in that they are forced to devote their lives to violence and war. Brainwashed, they believe that their greatest calling is to die while killing other people, all for the sake of Immortan Joe and his empire. Joe even calls them "my half-life War Boys," indicating their short lifespan. Since the War Boys are taught that the lives of animalized humans (which includes them and their enemies) have no inherent value, they wreak havoc wherever they go, killing without compunction and celebrating their own deaths as mere collateral damage. That is what Immortan Joe wants because he sees the War Boys as nothing other than "kamakrazee" "battle fodder."

The War Pups, the children who are painted in white, are also animalized humans. They are forced to serve Immortan Joe and his heirs, catering to their every whim and following the orders of their superiors. When a War Pup is old enough, he becomes a War Boy. So, War Pups' lives will always revolve around pleasing the humanized humans of the Citadel. It is no surprise, then, that they are called *pups*. After all, they have only subhuman status in the Citadel.

The most prominent animalized human is Max, who describes himself at the beginning of the film as "hunted by scavengers.... A man reduced to a single instinct: survive." And survival is no easy task. After enjoying some fast food (in the form of a two-headed lizard), Max runs for his life from a group of War Boys who eventually capture and cage him.

We then learn the reason why Max was hunted down: they want his blood. The Citadel tattoos Max with "Universal Donor" and tries to brand him with the Citadel symbol. Max is forced to hang upside down while Nux takes his blood. But Nux refuses to stay still for the blood transfusion because the battle drums begin pounding, calling him to wage holy war for Immortan Joe. Creatively, Nux mounts Max onto the front of his car so he can drain his Bloodbag while driving on Fury Road.

Max's introduction is rife with animal imagery. Max (who looks unkempt and wild) is operating solely on the basic animal instinct of survival, so he eats a raw lizard whole without hesitation. Max is then hunted down and captured like a wild animal. After his capture, he is thrown in a cage and shocked with a cattle prod. Forced to wear a mask that resembles a muzzle, he hangs upside down like a bat while his blood is drained from his body. What's more, when Nux proposes mounting Max to his car, another War Boy objects, "It's got a muzzle on it. It's a raging feral!" As if to reinforce Max's subhuman status, he isn't called by a proper name but is simply referred to as "it." Max is not considered a proper human with his own thoughts or feelings. He's just another instrument of war; a feral animal, reduced to his survival instinct, who is valued only for the blood that can be drained from his veins. In other words, Max is an animalized human.

Feminized Animals and Animalized Women

Two examples of feminized animals are cows and chickens. We eat a fair amount of eggs and dairy, or what Adams calls "*feminized protein*, that is, protein that was produced by a female body."[5] Adams notes that there's a particular disadvantage to being a female animal in food production: "Besides the bee's production of honey, the only beings who produce food from their own body while living are females of child-bearing age who produce milk and eggs. Female animals become oppressed by their femaleness and become essentially surrogate wet-nurses. These other animals are oppressed as *Mother* animals."[6] In animal agriculture, female reproductive systems are used to produce products that can be sold for a profit. Cows produce milk to feed their calves, but this process is manipulated and the milk is taken from them for the sake of human consumption.

Fury Road doesn't show us any feminized animals like cows or chickens. There are barely any animals in the barren Wasteland. But Adams's discussion of the dairy and egg industries sheds light on the role of *animalized women* in the Citadel. Animalized women are dehumanized and oppressed through their sexuality. They aren't treated as persons in their own right but are sexually objectified: they have societal value insofar as they can sexually gratify others and reproduce. In the Citadel, there are two categories of animalized women: the women who produce Mother's Milk and the breeders.

The fact that there are no cows in the Citadel doesn't stop Immortan Joe from creating a disturbing dairy industry of his own. He uses animalized women to produce feminized protein: Mother's Milk. Just as humans hook cows up to machines to take their milk, Immortan Joe hooks these women up to milking machines so that he can consume and commodify their milk. The women are oppressed through their lactation. And if this machine milking is not disturbing enough, a close look reveals that the women aren't holding human babies, but toy dolls. They aren't allowed to nurse their own children but are forced to produce milk for the humanized humans of the Citadel.

Joe's enslaved wives are also oppressed through their reproductive systems. As their name suggests, the Citadel values the "breeders" insofar as they can produce healthy heirs for Immortan Joe. They are animalized women who are forced to produce humanized humans. Their subhuman status is indicated by their name: we typically use the term *breeder* for breeding animals, like horses, cattle, and dogs. At one point, someone tells Nux that Imperator Furiosa is helping Joe's "prize breeders" escape. These prize breeders are kept well-dressed and clean, and Immortan Joe speaks of them as if they are well-groomed show animals.

Looking at these various categories of people, we see that the Citadel has a horrific social structure. A few people at the top of society are valued, while everyone else is devalued as subhuman. But the mistreatment of people is not the only cause for concern. The Citadel is also estranged from the natural world.

Immortan Joe's Unnatural Empire

Immortan Joe's society has a bizarre relationship with the land and its natural resources, treating the natural world in an unnatural way. Something is off. We come to realize that *Immortan Joe owns everything*. He owns the land, the water, the greenhouses.... What is going on here?

According to ecofeminists like Val Plumwood (1939–2008), patriarchal ways of thinking present the myth that "real men" conquer and consume "mother nature."[7] Masculinity is associated with a man's ability to dominate his surrounding environment and its inhabitants. Immortan Joe embodies the masculinity that ecofeminism criticizes: he sees all of mother nature (including women) as an object to be conquered, controlled, and consumed. When he looks at nature, he doesn't see an environment to live in and interact with, but an object to be owned.[8] In this way, the Citadel is Immortan Joe's attempt at turning all that he sees into private property; property that he alone owns.

But Immortan Joe doesn't simply own land, water, and resources; he also owns people. Or, put another way, he owns people *because* he owns natural resources. The Dag explains that "because he owns it [water], he owns all of us." When Immortan Joe tries to shoot Furiosa, he refrains from firing the gun because the Splendid Angharad has put her pregnant body in his line of fire. Joe yells, "Splendid! That's my child! That's my property!" As Joe sees it, they are not human women, but animalized women whose bodies and babies belong to him. He even forces them to wear gruesome chastity belts to reserve their sexuality and reproductive systems for himself.

Immortan Joe's unhealthy relationship with nature pervades the Citadel and even influences language. People refer to organic objects using inorganic language, and vice versa. They call bullets "Antiseed" because you "plant one and watch something die," and the Citadel gets its bullets from "the Bullet Farm." A disturbing irony is at play here: bullets are inorganic weapons, but people use organic farming terms to describe them. Instead of encouraging natural agriculture that cultivates life (like planting trees), the Citadel demands violent conquest that causes death (like bullet farming). This violence is dressed up in agricultural terminology.

While inorganic objects are given natural names, natural resources have unnatural names. Max's blood is described as "high-octane" as if it were another form of guzzolene. Even something as basic as water goes by "Aqua Cola." By calling water "Aqua Cola," Immortan Joe is branding water for the same reason he brands people: to claim property. The more people think of water as Aqua Cola, the less they will perceive it as a natural resource that must be shared. To be fair, when Immortan Joe calls his branded Aqua Cola "water," he treats it as a precious commodity. He instructs the people of the Citadel not to "become addicted to water. It will take hold of you, and you will resent its absence." Addicted to water? He talks about hydration like it's a dependence on Coca-Cola. So Immortan Joe hoards the water for himself but speaks as if he is in possession of a rare product that he benevolently provides to the masses.

All of these cruel practices and misguided terms highlight a central fact about the Citadel: the people are alienated from the land. No one is allowed to relate to the world as a healthy human being. They aren't even able to hydrate themselves, never mind grow fruit and vegetables. No wonder Nux doesn't even know what a tree is when he comes across one. The people of the Citadel are trapped in a machine: an oil-fueled, unnatural operation of violence and oppression. But the Citadel is about to face its most formidable foe: Imperator Furiosa.

"We Are Not Things!"

As the engines rev at the beginning of the film, Immortan Joe proudly salutes Imperator Furiosa as the leader of the mission to get more guzzolene and bullets. But Joe doesn't know that Furiosa has hatched an escape plan. She's going to help liberate Joe's "breeders" so that they can be who they truly are: women in their own right.

The women reclaim their own dignity by climbing into Furiosa's War Rig. When Immortan Joe figures out what has happened, he rushes to their former cell where he finds that his wives have left after painting "We Are Not Things" and "Who Destroyed the World?" on the walls. Miss Giddy remains behind to confront Joe, telling him, "They are not your property. You cannot own a human being!" The message is loud and clear: no matter how much Joe claims to own them, they are not his property. They are more than reproductive vessels, more than animalized women. They are human beings, full stop.

Furiosa's plan is to head to the Green Place of Many Mothers, where she grew up as a child until she was kidnapped and brought to the Citadel. The Green Place of Many Mothers is a place where women live in equality with one another, a landscape that is not subject to the tyrannical rule of greedy men like Joe. But when Furiosa and her crew finally arrive there, she learns that the fertile ground of her memories has now soured. One of the Mothers, though, keeps seeds and grows them like potted plants in animal skulls. This small practice shows the resilience of hope in a bleak world. The plants also symbolize feminine fertility and the Mothers' harmony with nature. But the Mothers need more than potted plants to sustain their community. They must plant their hopes in fertile ground, and the Green Place is no longer green. They must move on to more habitable land.

Initially, Furiosa and the others decide to drive in the opposite direction of the Citadel, as far as their fuel can take them, on the off chance that they come across water. But Max intercepts them and convinces Furiosa that their only hope of finding water lies in returning to the Citadel. More important, returning to the Citadel can also bring what Furiosa has been looking for all along: redemption. Furiosa wants to atone for the terrible things she had done for Immortan Joe in the past, and now she has an opportunity to do so. Instead of running away from Joe and the Citadel, she's going to bring the Green Place of Many Mothers right to his doorstep. What was once a daring escape plan has now transformed into a full-scale ecofeminist revolution.

"Who Killed the World?"

As Imperator Furiosa and her crew make their way back to the Citadel, several characters seize the opportunity to redeem themselves. Redemption begins with taking responsibility for their actions and resolving to improve themselves and the world around them. Earlier in the film, the women confront Nux and explain that Joe sees him as nothing other than "Battle Fodder," just as he sees the women as nothing but "Breeding Stock":

CAPABLE:	"You're an old man's Battle Fodder! Killing everyone and everything."
NUX:	"We're not to blame!"
THE SPLENDID ARANGHAD:	"Then who killed the world?"

At this point in the film, Nux refuses to take responsibility for his role in the destruction of the world. He is correct that it is not all his fault: he was already born and raised in terrible conditions. But he's not innocent either. Once Nux stops trying to excuse himself and begins contributing to a worthy cause, he begins to travel his road to redemption.

The redemptive character arcs show that Fury Road is not a film about "women against men," but rather an epic tale of humans reclaiming their dignity in the face of rampant dehumanization. The women in the narrative not only insist that they are subjects in their own right, but they help humanize others by treating them with respect and dignity. Just look at Max and Nux: they were treated like animalized humans and acted accordingly, but their encounter with Furiosa and the other women empowers them to reclaim their humanity.

In a beautiful twist, Nux fulfills his own prophecy that he "will die historic on the Fury Road," but not in the way he initially expected. Instead of dying for Immortan Joe and the Citadel, he dies to liberate the Citadel from Immortan Joe's tyrannical rule. He doesn't give his life for the sake of personal glory or to be "McFeasting with the heroes of all time" in Valhalla. Instead, Nux gives his life to save the ones he truly cares for; those who helped him to become fully human in his own right.

Similarly, Max begins to act like a human after the women treat him like one. Imperator Furiosa empowers Max to take his muzzle off, and once he does so, he stops acting on his survival instinct. Instead, he risks his life to save others. In a moving scene near the end of the film, he gives Imperator Furiosa his own blood to prevent her from dying. While transfusing his blood into her veins, he finally reclaims his own personhood as he declares: "Max. My name is Max. That's my name." The feral, no-named "Bloodbag" who was running for his life at the beginning of the film now reclaims his identity, drives toward danger, and freely gives his blood to save the life of someone else.

At the end of the film, we see the fruit of Furiosa's revolution as she inaugurates a new era. Immortan Joe has been defeated, and the Citadel is under new management. But Furiosa and the women don't simply replace Joe. They liberate the Citadel from oppression and scarcity. As they are elevated on the platform, they take others with them, helping people onto the platform rather than kicking them off. The women who are now liberated from Joe's rule unleash the water for the thirsty land and people to drink. Everyone can find redemption in the land of equality and abundance.

Where Must We Go?

In true ecofeminist fashion, our heroes respond to the call of redemption. As ecofeminists note, the regrettable state of our world is not any single individual's fault, but this doesn't excuse us from accepting the responsibility we have for the ecological crisis. Instead of pointing fingers or deflecting the blame away from ourselves, we must face the facts ... and ourselves.

The movie ends with the question: "Where must we go ... we who wander the Wasteland in search of our better selves?" The answer to that question, in the story arc of *Fury Road*, lies in reclaiming selfhood from those who would diminish it. In a barren and unjust world, we must insist upon the dignity of the earth and the equality of its inhabitants, no matter the personal cost. In the end, *Fury Road* invites us to ponder the dangerous, revolutionary idea that true redemption is not found in simple survival, but in radical solidarity.

Notes

1 Cary Wolfe, *Animal Rites: American Culture, the Discourse of Species, and Posthumanist Theory* (Chicago: University of Chicago Press, 2003), 101.
2 There are other categories as well, such as Wolfe's humanized animals and animalized animals, but these are not as relevant for the Citadel since it doesn't have many animals.
3 I will be using contemporary philosopher David Livingstone Smith's definition of *dehumanization* throughout this chapter, which can be found in David Livingstone Smith, *On Inhumanity: Dehumanization and How to Resist It* (New York: Oxford University Press, 2020). According to Smith, "To dehumanize another person is to conceive of them as a subhuman creature," 19.
4 Ibid., 9–21.
5 Carol J. Adams, *The Sexual Politics of Meat: A Feminist-Vegetarian Critical Theory* (New York: Bloomsbury Academic, 2015), xxxi.
6 Ibid., 62.
7 Val Plumwood, *Feminism and the Mastery of Nature* (London: Routledge, 1993), 106–107.
8 Ibid., 1.

16

Demarginalizing Aunty Entity and Dismantling Thunderdome

Edwardo Pérez and Thanayi Jackson

For all the visionary aspects of George Miller's work, the first two *Mad Max* films failed to consider race and gender in any meaningful way. There are no people of color in Max's dystopia. Women exist, but not in a way that considers their agency beyond wife and mother.[1] Women characters are flat, their brutalization catalyst for the patriarch. In *Mad Max*, the most horrific scenes are men witnessing their women's violation. Max is driven mad not by thermonuclear war, but by his inability to protect his wife and child. *Mad Max* and *The Road Warrior*, for all their harrowing, grotesque visuals, probing critiques of humanity, themes of societal decay, and heroism, depict a *de facto* patriarchal society ruled by (and largely occupied by) white men.[2] And so in *Beyond Thunderdome*, when we see Aunty Entity, a powerful lead character played by Tina Turner—both Black and woman—it's significant. Not just because she's Black and female, but because of the position she occupies in relation to white patriarchy.

Kimberlé Crenshaw, a critical race theorist who coined the term *intersectionality*, maintains that because Black women are both Black and female, their struggle exists within an intersection of race and gender, an intersection that Black men do not find themselves in, and an intersection that white women also do not find themselves in. Because, for all the ways Black men are oppressed by society, at least they're men, and for all the ways white women are oppressed by society, at least they're white. So, Aunty Entity, not just Black and not just woman, becomes the perfect foil for Max in this dystopian (and still

Mad Max and Philosophy: Thinking Through the Wasteland, First Edition.
Edited by Matthew P. Meyer and David Koepsell.
© 2024 John Wiley & Sons, Inc. Published 2024 by John Wiley & Sons, Inc.

patriarchal) world. Throughout the film they vie for power and, by the end of *Thunderdome*, we see Aunty as an equal to Max and possibly "another hero." So, does Tina Turner's Aunty Entity position her to do the work of demarginalizing women of color—or does she reinforce the exoticization of non-white women as commodity under patriarchal white sovereignty?

What's Race Got to Do with It?

Of course, if you are going to introduce the specter of race into the dystopian world of Max, Tina Turner is a powerful selection of crossover genius. The first two films were almost a caricature of what Australian Indigenous feminist Aileen Merle Moreton-Robinson called White Possessive Doctrine, whereby whiteness is uncritically understood as the *de facto* standard. The "possessive logic of patriarchal white sovereignty," Moreton-Robinson argues, "works ideologically to naturalize the nation as a white possession."[3] This suggests that there was no intent to create an all-white world, indeed the *not noticing* is evidence of the theory. So normalized is whiteness that whiteness does not even notice the absence of people of color from the Pacific world. Of course, once there is a conscious decision to add a non-white character to a dystopian movie involving social commentary, how do you do it? Well, you do it big! Can one Black woman take on white possessive doctrine? If it's 1985 and you're Tina Turner, then the answer is a resounding *yes*.[4]

Tina Turner's 1984 album *Private Dancer* was a breakthrough, triumphant return for her and undoubtedly made her a desirable box office choice for the movie. By 1985, when *Mad Max: Beyond Thunderdome* opened, Tina Turner was already a household name with proximity to whiteness in a way few Black artists had. She was one of the few Black musicians to break the MTV color line.[5] She was a woman. She was Black. She was the Queen of Rock! She was an iconic global superstar. And in 1985, Tina Turner was bigger than *Mad Max*, a power that positioned Aunty Entity on equal footing from her first scene.

Aunty? Historically, *aunty* is a moniker used within Black communities for respected elder women, signifying an important provider of crucial emotional labor. "Aunty" was also adopted by some white communities—not to refer to elder white women but to refer to elder Black women, often isolated Black domestic workers working in segregated-white space.[6] Interestingly, this intra/inter-cultural use of the word *aunty* is discussed in both Black America and Aboriginal Australia. Hmmm ... so ... was Aunty Entity written to be Black or Aboriginal? Does it matter? Does "Aunty" make Turner's character more recognizable to an Oz audience? And if so, recognizable as what? ... Colonized access to Black and Brown women's emotional labor? Or, despite intent, does naming her "Aunty" unite Black and Brown women in Crenshaw's margins?

Notably, the only other person of color, Ton Ton Tattoo, Aunty's Asian bard, is played by Singapore-born big-time jazz saxophonist Andrew Oh. Blind and dressed in a sumo-wrestler's loincloth, he is seated alongside Tina Turner's trademark legs (which were insured for $3.2 million in 1994). Ton Ton and Aunty work in the film because both Oh and Turner are already exotically proximal to whiteness—ready for consumption by a global white audience.

"You Can Shovel Shit, Can't You?"

Aunty Entity governs Bartertown which, at first glance, doesn't appear to be much of a town. As the name implies, people trade whatever they scavenge. But as we're shown the town, we realize that it's more civilized than it might seem. Business operates with a scant sense of civility and people seem to be getting along in a system with clearly defined rules. There are brothels, bars, butchers, blacksmiths, and barbers. There is a sense of order rather than chaos. But the town runs on methane harvested from animal waste, specifically "pig shit," making methane production the key to civilization. It is this drive to produce pig shit that gave rise to Master Blaster's brutality. Production ruled all because everybody in the town was dependent on the shit. Aunty wants Master Blaster dead because, from her perspective, Bartertown's successes were her doing. She offered those who came to Bartertown hope, but Master Blaster's control over the means of production has left the town in despair and at his mercy.

In Australia, *entity* is a word used to signify business or corporation. Sooooo ... Aunty Entity? In a society premised on the market, the barter, Aunty Entity does not represent free capitalism but checked capitalism. *Thunderdome* critiques the dystopian reduction of humans to profit, a critique also at the root of Black feminism. Black women's history of commodification—both enslaved and producer of enslaved people—adds dimension to Aunty Entity, a caged Black woman, fighting to regulate the means of production. Anti-Entity?

"Welcome to Another Edition of Thunderdome!"

Turner's Aunty Entity is a strong Black woman occupying a position of power in a white supremacist capitalist patriarchy. Yet, as such, Aunty is sexualized (fetishized?) in her attire.[7] And the cage she lives in, high above Bartertown, seems like a prison, alluding to Maya Angelou's "caged bird," suffering in captivity (and singing on the soundtrack[8]). Her power is a costume, though, since she needs Max to rescue her with brute force. As Master humiliatingly reminds her early in the film, she's not really in charge of Bartertown—he is.

Master Blaster is clearly the villain. They are cruel, beating workers for production and mocking Aunty Entity and the rule of law. They threaten all people of Bartertown. Yet when we see that Blaster is mentally disabled—referred to as a child by Master, who lovingly mourns Blaster's death—his execution, though legal, plays out like an abuse of power. It went too far for a character called "Mad" Max, who coincidentally was a police officer in the before times. Thus, when Max refuses to kill Blaster, his mercy is correct. Blaster's violence becomes irrelevant once he's revealed to be mentally disabled—Master proclaims, "It's not his fault." The intended audience reaction—to the reveal of Blaster's white, youthful face, portraying a childlike, diminished mental capacity—poses questions regarding intersections of race, gender, and ability.

Does it matter that Blaster is white? Would it be easier for Max to kill Blaster if Blaster were a person of color? Does Blaster's disability strip him of villainy and, thus, agency? Why do we have sympathy for the villain? Ton Ton's blindness never evokes sympathy; indeed, his blindness is barely perceptible outside of his exoticism. How *do* race and gender intersect with ability? By the end of the Thunderdome scene, even Master becomes sympathetic once his own fragile post-apocalyptic identity is laid bare. What does it mean that neither Master nor Blaster have the capacity for true patriarchal power despite whiteness and maleness?

Suddenly, after Thunderdome we see Aunty as the new villain! In contrast to Aunty, Max embodies the hypermasculine, patriarchal archetype of the lone wolf hero, who is typically a white man operating with an assumed authority.[9] Max's reaction (by virtue of being a white male endowed with Mel Gibson's piercing glare[10]) *makes* Aunty a villain in that moment. In turn, all of her actions now appear illegitimate and authoritarian (because he's the titular hero, right?). Her *clear* authority appears suspect considered next to his *assumed* authority. Does white possessive doctrine authorize Max? How did the 1980s backlash against the liberation movements of the previous decades affect audience interpretation? Eighties conservatism recast feminism and civil rights as reverse discrimination—an attack on white masculinity by unqualified minorities and women demanding power through government regulation. Aunty Entity does represent regulation, but in 1985 does she, a Black woman, *automatically* evoke regulation? ... the angry Black woman? And, if so, is Aunty's Black womanness part of what makes her authority seem so fraudulent? Does her identity as a Black woman make her authority authoritarian by default?

No matter, Anti-Entity ain't here to play. After she removes Blaster, she sees the opportunity not just to rebuild, but to rethink their way of life in Bartertown. Contrary to her intent, the Thunderdome system did not prevent mass violence. But she still believes that she can build a better way. Even at the end of the film, when Max escapes with Master, Aunty tries to rally the town and shows compassion for the townspeople: "Where are you gonna run? Where are you gonna hide? Listen to me! Bartertown will live! [...] We will rebuild!" Yes, she calls for "no mercy" for those (like Max) who helped free Master—which, if she's following the law, she's in the right to do—but later, she's merciful. "Well ain't we a pair, Raggedy Man," she smiles and laughs as she leaves, but it's Max's smile that telegraphs what we're supposed to feel about Aunty: that she's not a villain after all. If anything, she's a hero, perhaps the most just and honorable hero in Max's world.

"But How the World Turns"

By the end of the movie, we're rooting for Aunty Entity, and a powerful Black woman is a powerful metaphor. Vulnerable to patriarchy in Black space and racism in women's space, Black women symbolize the need for intersectional liberation movements.[11] Crenshaw illustrates this when she reminds us that, "[t]he value of feminist theory to Black women is diminished because it evolves from a white racial context that is seldom acknowledged. Not only are women of color in fact overlooked, but their exclusion is reinforced when *white* women speak for and as *women*." Oh, white possessive doctrine.... Crenshaw continues,

> The authoritative universal voice—usually white male subjectivity masquerading as non-racial, non-gendered objectivity—is merely

transferred to those who, but for gender, share many of the same cultural, economic and social characters. When feminist theory attempts to describe women's experiences through analyzing patriarchy, sexuality, or separate spheres ideology, it often overlooks the role of race. [...] Consequently, feminist theory remains *white*, and its potential to broaden and deepen its analysis by addressing non-privileged women remains unrealized.[12]

We never see Aunty directly interact with Black men or White women in *Thunderdome*. Nevertheless, she remains intersectional, not just because she's a Black woman, but because *we*, watching *from* a Crenshawian world that overlooks Black women, *see* her wield "authoritative universal voice."

While 1980s portrayals of Black women capitalize on the radicalism of the 1960s and 1970s often in a stereotypical blaxploitation kind of way, *Thunderdome*'s Anti-Entity has some qualities that herald Black feminism. In 1977, two years before the first film and seven years before *Thunderdome*, the Combahee River Collective, a self-professed, "collective of Black feminists," mobilized against white supremacist capitalist patriarchy. "The most general statement of our politics at the present time," their founding statement reads, "would be that we are actively committed to struggling against racial, sexual, heterosexual, and class oppression, and see as our particular task the development of integrated analysis and practice based upon the fact that the major systems of oppression are interlocking." In a fan-fiction version that we imagine, there is no Max, and Anti-Entity reads straight from Combahee:

We realize that the liberation of all oppressed peoples necessitates the destruction of the political-economic systems of capitalism and imperialism as well as patriarchy. We are socialists because we believe that work must be organized for the collective benefit of those who do the work and create the products, and not for the profit of the bosses. Material resources must be equally distributed among those who create these resources. We are not convinced, however, that a socialist revolution that is not also a feminist and anti-racist revolution will guarantee our liberation.[13]

Black feminist philosopher Keeanga-Yamahtta Taylor summed it up by saying until Black women are free, none of us will be free.[14] As Aunty recounts to Max: "Do you know who I was? Nobody. Except on the day after, I was still alive. This nobody had a chance to be somebody. So much for history." What does she mean? How do we interpret "nobody" and "somebody"? Is Aunty referring to race? Sex? Class? When thinking about who she was she is crestfallen: "Play something, Ton Ton, something tragic." So, when Aunty says, "So much for history" are we to understand that she is still "nobody"? Or would she be "somebody" but for Master Blaster and his embargos? Or has thermonuclear war killed the old world, made her "somebody," and freed her from history? Looking through a Black feminist lens, is she everybody? After all, once she, a Black woman is somebody, isn't everybody? To quote Combahee, "If Black women were free, it would mean that everyone else would have to be free since our freedom would necessitate the destruction of all the systems of oppression."[15]

Black Dystopia: "So Much for History"

Historical memory, a philosophical archive where all movies eventually reside, has a habit of coopting intent. In the time since *Thunderdome*, Tina Turner's Aunty Entity has become perhaps the most iconic character of the franchise. The initial absence of any characters of color fits with white possessive doctrine. So the addition of Tina Turner seemed like an intentional progressive correction in a 1985 acutely aware of racial representation in film. In retrospect, a single Black lead character may appear to be tokenism but, lest we forget, it was the efforts at racial inclusion of the 1980s that coined the term *tokenism*! And in 1985, one Black leading character was enough to draw a Black audience and spark dialogue about that character's representation of Blackness within larger Black philosophical discourses. In other words, all intent aside, at a time when few mainstream movies included leading roles for Black people period, *Mad Max* became Black culture as soon as Aunty Entity was on the cover of *Jet Magazine* and "We Don't Need Another Hero" was on Black radio.[16]

Since then, Thunderdome, as a dystopian concept, has taken on a life of its own in the Black philosophical imagination, especially through hip-hop. Here, the concept of Thunderdome is informed as much by the song as the film. "We Don't Need Another Hero" acknowledges Thunderdome as another repressive system. Tina philosophizes, "And I wonder when we are ever gonna change, change / Living under the fear'til nothing else remains / We don't need another hero / We don't need to know the way home / All we want is life beyond the Thunderdome." References to Thunderdome rose alongside an ever-growing prison industrial complex wrecking the very Black communities from which hip-hop culture emerged. Thunderdome, a carceral system of order in which the exploited are pitted against one another for survival, resonated with a Black generation coming of age in the wake of civil rights dreams. In the language of hip-hop, the Thunderdome is the system. According to Tina Turner, the only hope is a new way that rejects a society built on patriarchal brute force. "Mm, love and compassion / Their day is coming (coming) / All else are castles built in the air."[17]

Exactly ten years after *Thunderdome*, 2Pac and Dr. Dre released *the* hip-hop anthem, "California Love." In the video, widely played on MTV, Pac and Dre return to Thunderdome ... or, in this particular case, Oakland. In this take, Bartertown becomes synonymous with Oakland—a capitalist wasteland of worker exploitation.[18] Tupac Shakur and Andre Young utilize *Thunderdome* to represent the post–Cold War inner city—a dystopia of racialized law and order. In 1985, inner cities were at the height of a state-sponsored crack epidemic fueled by the military industrial complex of Cold War colonialism. By 1995, the criminalization of crack through crime bills had transformed inner cities into police states. The inner city *was* like Thunderdome.[19]

Indeed, Thunderdome has become a hip-hop trope. In "Gangbangn 101," Snoop Dogg makes sure we know that Thunderdome is synonymous with these streets, "It's the turf by the surf but we don't play in the sand / We just, slip and slide out, we Rip and ride out / Let it C known, nigga welcome to the Thunderdome." In the highest-charting track from Kendrick Lamar's politically poignant *Untitled Unmastered*, "Untitled 02–06.23.2014," Lamar directly reinforces Thunderdome as systemic and dystopic as now. He addresses listeners from within Thunderdome: "World is going brazy / Where did we go wrong? / It's a tidal wave, it's a thunderdome."[20] Similarly, Nipsey Hustle reinforces this concept in "The Weather" (featuring Rick Ross and Cuzzy Capone), a first-person narrative straight from the lost children trapped in a post-apocalyptic white supremacist capitalist patriarchy where brute force is power, and love is invisible—and it's worth considering the full lyrics:

> Reporting live from the land of the hopeless
> Representing for the team that won rings with no coaches

We stay strapped and we cocky so don't approach us
Price Johnson with a big gold chain and Louis Loafers
Been hiding guns in the sofa since toy soldiers
Thunder-domes up in Hyde Park, didn't nobody know us
We took all fades, our introduction was from the shoulders
We was kids, honestly we just needed someone to hold us
Grindin' hard on them corners with cane boulders
Fascinated by the green, all we wanted was Range Rovers
On the block politicking with brain blowers
Real niggas that got love in their hearts but can't show it
We live and die for the fame and the lights glowing
Fox Hills buying Jordans, but still the pain showing
When I die, put me next to the dead poets
Tell 'em God had a plan for me and I didn't know it
Victory[21]

Mm, love and compassion. Their day is coming. All else are castles built in the air. And if this is the message we interpret today, then Aunty Entity has been demarginalized by history. As such, Aunty represents the freedom dream—new ways to protect us from the old failures. Hope. A hope not just that the future will be better than the past, but that we remember what once was and where we came from so that the future can belong to everyone—not just the few who are left, but everyone who can find their way home.

Notes

1   To be fair, some women are shown to be warriors. Yet, even these depictions aren't fully developed in the first two films or in *Thunderdome*, which only shows Savanna Nix to be anything close to a female warrior, besides, of course, Aunty Entity.

2   George Orwell's *1984*, Margaret Atwood's *The Handmaid's Tale*, and Suzanne Collins's *The Hunger Games* all echo this structure, suggesting that the future, despite all the mixing (and browning) of races our contemporary world is witnessing, will be predominantly white, especially when it comes to authority and power.

3   Aileen Moreton-Robinson, "The Possessive Logic of Patriarchal White Sovereignty: The High Court and the YORTA YORTA decision," *Borderlands E-Journal* 3 (2004). Quoted material from abstract. See also Aileen Moreton-Robinson, *The White Possessive: Property, Power, and Indigenous Sovereignty* (Minneapolis: University of Minnesota Press, 2015).

4   And if *Thunderdome* were made today, Beyoncé, Rihanna, or Janel Monáe would make great choices, as would Nicki Minaj, Cardi B, and Megan Thee Stallion.

5   At this time, MTV infamously avoided Black artists. See Gil Kaufman, "Watch David Bowie Call out MTV for Not Playing Black Artists in 1983," January 11, 2016, at http://www.mtv.com/news/2726379/david-bowie-calls-mtv-out-black-artists-diversity/; "Why It Took MTV So Long to Play Black Music Videos," *Jet*, October 9, 2006, quotes Rick James from 1983: "There are no Blacks on MTV's program list except for Tina Turner, and she stopped being Black about 10 years ago."

6   Stacie Evans, "Not Your Auntie," *The Rumpus*, November 1, 2017, at https://therumpus.net/2017/11/01/not-your-auntie/. The intracultural/intercultural usage of this term is not unique to Blacks in the United States. An Australian campaign even produced a handbook advising "outsiders" against referring to Aboriginal elders as "aunty"; see NSW Department of Community Services, *Working with Aboriginal People and Communities: A Practice Resource*, 2009.

7   "White supremacist capitalist patriarchy" is a phrase coined by bell hooks; see *Cultural Criticism & Transformation* (1997). In "Selling Hot Pussy: Representations of Black Female Sexuality in the Cultural Marketplace," hooks argued that Turner's Aunty Entity, a sexualized dominator, exploited stereotypes of Black women for white consumption; see Katie Conboy et al., eds., *Writing on the Body: Female Embodiment and Feminist Theory* (New York: Columbia University Press, 1997), 120.

8   "We Don't Need Another Hero" may be the more memorable track—played over the end credits, its lyrics pine for a better world, representing the hope. Yet it's "One of the Living," played during *Thunderdome*'s opening, that encapsulates a more pessimistic (realistic?) message that we're all caged birds living in a post-apocalyptic, dystopian Australian desert.

9   See John Wayne, Clint Eastwood, Sylvester Stallone, Arnold Schwarzenegger, Bruce Willis, and Mel Gibson, as well as James Bond and Jason Bourne. Indeed, the lone wolf hero takes command, engages in violence, and is portrayed as being in the right, regardless of how questionable or morally compromised his actions might otherwise seem—such as Max hitting Savannah Nix after shooting a rifle at her to scare her. Because it was for her own good, right? Just consider Max's actions in all three films. As Lord Humungus says, "There has been too much violence, too much pain. None here is without sin."

10 See also *Braveheart*, *Lethal Weapon 2*, and *The Patriot* for more examples of Gibson's version of a *Zoolander* "Blue Steel." Also, to be fair, she created the Thunderdome system.

11   Kimberlé Crenshaw, "Demarginalizing the Intersection of Race and Sex: A Black Feminist Critique of Antidiscrimination Doctrine, Feminist Theory and Antiracist Politics," *University of Chicago Legal Forum* (1989), 1(8): 152, at http://chicagounbound.uchicago.edu/uclf/vol1989/iss1/8.

12   Crenshaw, 154.

13   Combahee River Collective, *The Combahee River Collective Statement*, 1977, at blackpast.org.

14   Keeanga-Yamahtta Taylor, "Until Black Women Are Free, None of Us Will Be Free: Barbara Smith and the Black Feminist Visionaries of the Combahee River Collective," *New Yorker* (July 20, 2020); *How We Get Free: Black Feminism and the Combahee River Collective* (Chicago: Haymarket Books, 2017).

15   Combahee River Collective.

16   *Jet*, July 29, 1985. Tina Turner also did the rounds in several issues of *Ebony* in 1985 while promoting *Thunderdome*, but the *Jet* cover is her in full Aunty Entity costume.

17   Tina Turner, "We Don't Need Another Hero," *Mad Max Beyond Thunderdome: Original Motion Picture Soundtrack*, 1985.

18   Tupac Shakur, "California Love," YouTube.com, October 20, 2018.

19   Even the symbolism of Savannah Nix and the lost children is so T.H.U.G. L.I.F.E.—Tupac's acronymic philosophy (The Hate U Give Little Infants Fucks Everybody). Tupac Shakur, "Tupac Explains Thug Life," YouTube.com, June 11, 2007.

20   Snoop Dogg, "Gangbangin' 101," YouTube.com, July 24, 2018; Kendrick Lamar, "Untitled 02 | 06.23.2014," YouTube.com, July 3, 2018.

21   Nipsey Hustle, "The Weather Ft. Rick Ross & Cuzzy Capone (Crenshaw)," YouTube.com, October 8, 2018.

17

Gayboy Berserkers at the Gate: Sex and Gender in the Wasteland

Jacob M. Held

There's a great deal of homoeroticism in *Mad Max: Road Warrior*, or so I've heard. As a child of the 1980s, it was lost on me at the time. Growing up with professional wrestling, where muscled men in tights and Day-Glo frills[1] grapple each other in an oily orgy of double entendre and violence, and a music scene populated by Boy George, Prince, and Peter Burns (Dead or Alive), a few leather-clad barbarians and a pair of assless chaps didn't seem out of place, or exceptional. But I understand the sentiment. The Lord Humungus clan is decked out in BDSM gear, a product of a costume designer who lived near a bondage shop.[2] And Wez does have a romantic connection to the Golden Youth, who is doing an impressive Mick Ronson impersonation. So there is something going on with sex and gender in *Road Warrior*, something that invites investigation.

If *Road Warrior* is interesting for its homoerotic elements, then *Fury Road* is fascinating for its feminist themes. In *Fury Road*, there are wives being enslaved as breeders. Women are milked as a resource. Pregnant women, and their children, are referred to as property. Women scream, "Who killed the world?" and insist that their (male) babies won't be warlords, because, as we know, only men can be violent tyrants. (I guess these women never heard about Aunty Entity and her totalitarian grip on Bartertown.)

The scenarios presented in the *Mad Max* franchise raise interesting issues about sex and gender. Society has crumbled, and you'd hope antiquated notions of gender roles and the oppression associated with them would have crumbled as well. Still, less than half of the population has the potential to incubate: young women. So women are still "breeders," and with this fact comes the potential for oppression; tyrants need their populations. But conventions, like gender roles or the stigmas surrounding same-sex relationships, are confounded in the post-apocalyptic world, as seen with Wez and the Golden Youth. But what would one expect after an apocalypse?[3] Gender roles and social stigma surrounding sexual practices are shown to be superficial when other social pressures, like a cataclysm, come to pass. Yet other factors of human existence, like biology, which are manifest through breeding and the constraints of nature, are reinforced. The viewer is presented with the relationship and the tension between facts of human physiology and the tenuous connection between these facts and social conventions. The *Mad Max* franchise, set in a post-apocalyptic world, provides fertile ground to consider how our conventions might unravel, but also highlights that human nature is not infinitely malleable. We have constraints placed on us by nature, but how we build society around natural facts is a choice—and our choices reflect our values.

We Don't Need Another (S)Hero: Beyond Thunderdome, Beyond Sex and Gender

The basic premise of feminism is that the world is a different place for women than it is for men by virtue of the fact that they are women. Consider a working definition of *feminism*: "a set of ideas that recognize in an explicit way that women are subordinate to men and seek to address imbalances of power between the sexes."[4] This definition recognizes the fact that, historically, women have occupied a subordinate position to men, and that this is a contingent, social construct.[5] In fact, some have noted that what brand of feminism one subscribes to is predicated on how one understands the nature of this problem. Is patriarchy, the subordination of women by men, still a persistent problem? Or has it been mostly eliminated? And if it is still a problem, what is the legitimate scope of the government's power to rectify the situation?[6] Recognizing that women have been historically oppressed, and continue to be discriminated against, makes these issues salient to all members of society. We can begin from the fact that when it comes to women and men, "perhaps [the] differences are superficial, perhaps they are destined to disappear. What is certain is that right now they do most obviously exist."[7]

"One is not born, but rather becomes, a woman."[8] With these nine words Simone de Beauvoir (1908–1986) defined the terms of a conversation we're still having today, a conversation about the origin and meaning of gender. Beauvoir tells us that one is not born a woman. But when Beauvoir discusses being, or becoming, a woman, she is speaking about something different than one's physiology. She is distinguishing between sex and gender and using *woman* to refer to gender. When we use the word *woman* outside of academic contexts, of course, most of us take it to refer to both sex *and* gender. But the two concepts can, and many argue should, be separated. Let's look at that distinction more closely.

Kathleen Jenkins articulates one way to make the distinction: "[S] ex is understood to be the anatomical and biological differences between males and females, and gender is understood to be the social differences between men and women produced by society that attaches significance to sex difference and uses it as the basis for organizing social practices."[9] Sex is biological. Sex denotes primary sex characteristics like the possession of a penis or vagina, testes or ovaries, for example. Gender, on the other hand, is about the meaning a sexed body acquires within society. Gender is about how those who possess vaginas are expected to act. Yet there is no necessary symmetry between sex and gender. Vagina owners can behave in ways consistent with penis possessors, and vice versa.

According to Beauvoir, one becomes a woman through being acculturated to adopt, accept, and emulate gender. The myth of the eternal feminine[10] constructs a "natural" binary between male and female, and those that are female possess an essential nature, one different from men. On the basis of this supposed essence, expectations are set for them, expectations regarding dress, behavior, etiquette, and general comportment.[11] Thus, one's body, one's being female, strongly influences one's cultural possibilities. Gender is a construct that carries with it expectations, expectations that once accepted appear natural as expressions of an intractable essence. As Judith Butler notes, "'[W]oman' is a historical idea and not a natural fact. [Beauvoir] clearly underscores the distinction between sex, as biological facticity, and gender, as the cultural interpretation or signification of that facticity."[12] But gender is a construction that conceals its genesis. Our forgetfulness allows gender to appear as a natural law such that deviations are not new or novel constructions, but flaws in the deviant.

"As an existentialist, Beauvoir was concerned about the tension between freedom and determinism and believed that there is nothing necessary or inevitable about who a person ultimately becomes."[13] Gender, as the reified expectations of society and as a limiting factor on a person's possibilities is thus in tension with their ability to be and become whomever they choose to be or become. Beauvoir's existentialism is about enhancing one's agency. The *Mad Max* franchise plays with this theme frequently.

The apocalypse throws socially constructed expectations into disorder. Hence, we see Aunty Entity. The day before, she was a nobody. Perhaps she was just another young, poor black woman, living in a world where being a woman, specifically a woman of color, presented a particular set of challenges. But the day after, that's another story. After the atomic bombs, after the rioting and the chaos, there was only survival. She was still alive, and she could thrive. The old order was overturned, the expectations about sex, gender, race, and class were no longer relevant. It wasn't about maintaining a patriarchy, or white supremacy, anymore. It was about survival: fuel, power, life, and death. No longer did it matter that she was a "woman." She could be a leader; she could dominate Bartertown through will and cunning. If she could write the law, instill order, and provide security and promise to the people, they wouldn't care about superficialities like sex, gender, or race. Aunty Entity, Furiosa, and the Warrior Woman from *Road Warrior* adopt roles often associated with men: political tyrant, military leader, or general badass, thus demonstrating the disconnect between sex and social expectations. In fact, Furiosa eclipses Max in *Fury Road*, adopting the role of protagonist, while Max is, literally, along for the ride.

Yet when it comes to men and women, as Beauvoir notes, there are some differences that are conventional, but other differences are not superficial. Only women possess uteruses, and only women produce ova, which when fertilized by sperm, contributed by men, leads to fertilization, subsequent incubation, and eventually live birth of a tiny human. This is the biological fact of human reproduction. Thus, women, and only women, insofar as they are fertile uterus possessors, can bear children. This is a nonarbitrary, real difference between men and women. It has profound consequences on women's health and all aspects of their lives. The medical field would be negligent were it not to acknowledge and accommodate this difference and treat women differently than men in light of these differences. Your OB-GYN had better know the difference between boy parts and girl parts.[14] As one scholar notes,

> Sex is appropriately characterized in terms of a cluster of endogenously produced morphological, genetic, and hormonal features. None of them are individually essential for human femaleness or maleness, though possession of some vague number of them is sufficient for it. This view accommodates the many existing disorders and differences of sexual development well, whilst remaining compatible with realism about biological sex. Variation can be, and in fact is, endemic to biology generally, without threatening the existence of natural kinds.[15]

Some may bristle at this definition. Some may have a more inclusive definition. For our present purposes, all we need to recognize is that, unquestionably, Aunty Entity is a woman, and so is Furiosa. Now, we only have various visual cues to go from, unless you have a bootleg XXX version of *Fury Road* or *Beyond Thunderdome* I'm unaware of. But all indications point to these two humans being biological women, and from this we can see that women are able to adopt and dominate roles historically adopted by men. Clearly, there is a disconnect between sex and social expectations.

Even though women and men are biologically different, what we do, socially, with these differences is conventional. If, because women can incubate offspring, we enslave them as breeders,[16] and later milk them like cattle, then we've taken a real, biological difference and used it to reinforce an arbitrary social convention that oppresses women. Because women can "breed," Immortan Joe treats them like property and thereby turns a genetic difference into oppression. Likewise, if we use only men as cannon fodder in wars, we've taken a biological difference and reinforced a social convention: men fight and die, but at least they shall ride all shiny and chrome on the way to Valhalla.

What the *Mad Max* franchise seems to indicate about sex and gender is that sex matters. How humans breed matters, especially when it comes to sustaining the human race in a post-apocalyptic Wasteland. You'd better grasp the basics of the birds and bees if you want to continue to populate this planet. Although this does raise the troubling question of Savannah Nix, matriarch of the Lost Tribe in *Beyond Thunderdome*, and all those little children. But with respect to sex differences, what we do with this biological fact is a choice. Furiosa kicks ass, plain and simple. She kicks Max's ass. Clearly, her vagina isn't getting in the way. Aunty Entity has a grip on Bartertown as strong as any penis-owning dictator could. Sex is not destiny in the Wasteland. Sex is a fact. Our response to that fact, how we wish to understand or impose gendered norms, is a choice. And the women in the Wasteland choose to be what is needed at the time: strong, independent, and tough as nails. *Mad Max* helps us see what is malleable and what is not and how our values shape our world.

One of the philosophically rich elements in the *Mad Max* franchise has to do with how it deals with gender by highlighting that when we boil humanity down to the bare bones, all these identities and distinctions ought not to matter. Aunty Entity isn't going to ruminate on how her experiences as a woman of color affect her reception in Bartertown because she's too busy trying not to be overthrown by Master Blaster. Likewise, Furiosa probably isn't too concerned with how her experiences as a (privileged?) white woman amputee affect her role in Immortan Joe's patriarchy; she's too busy overturning it and not dying. So where does that leave us? We can recognize and take seriously gender-based oppression and discrimination without denying the realities of biological sex. We can do so by seeing how *Mad Max* problematizes ideas around sex, gender, and sexual orientation. On this final note, let's get back to Wez and the Golden Youth.

Everybody's Looking for Something

There are myriad definitions of *sexual orientation*. Some focus on the sex or gender of those attracted to each other, others focus on dispositions or desires, and still others focus on behaviors.[17] Let's begin with a common definition, one most people would accept: "'Sexual Orientation' is the preferred term used when referring to an individual's physical and/or emotional attraction to the same and /or opposite gender."[18] Now clearly there are issues pertaining to how we define gender, acknowledging trans individuals, as well as non-binary folks. Some may say that the preceding definition unduly favors people who identify as heterosexual, and who identify with the gender they were assigned at birth, and it assumes only two genders, which may not be inclusive of trans and queer folks.[19] Attempts to be inclusive should recognize these issues when crafting a definition of *sexual orientation*. For instance, how does such a definition square with the relationship between Wez and the Golden Youth?

Defining *orientation* is about classifying the world, in this case humans, by their tendencies to pair off in various ways. And breaking up the world in this way, between straight, gay, bisexual, pansexual ... is purposeful. We have reasons for wanting to do so. Some reasons may be laudable, to celebrate and recognize the diversity of human experiences and affirm the lives of others and secure for them basic rights, like marriage. Other motivations may not be so praiseworthy. Sometimes we distinguish in order to discriminate.

But nothing could seem more irrelevant in the Wasteland than one's sexual orientation. In a world where people are murdered for a tank of gas, who would care whom you preferred to be involved with sexually or romantically? The inspiration for this chapter was the "homoeroticism" of *Road Warrior*. A cursory glance at the film shows why some might see it as "homoerotic." Wez wears assless chaps, the Golden Youth is an effeminate male, and Lord Humungus's tribe wears bondage gear affiliated with the leather man, gay subculture of the 1970s and 1980s.

But let's begin from a simple proposition: *Road Warrior* is only homoerotic if you begin from heteronormativity. That is, if you didn't assume that romantic pairings should be male/female, then there'd be nothing odd about Wez and the Golden Youth. So it's not homoerotic. Rather, the viewer who claims as much is communicating their internalized norm of heteronormativity, or rather they are communicating their recognition of society's expectation of presumed heterosexuality. We don't call Max and his wife's relationship "heteroerotic." Why? Because it's "normal." Eroticism is by default "hetero." Only outliers, like Wez, need to be categorized, and thereby distinguished from what is normal. So the homoeroticism in *Road Warrior* is interesting, not because there are ostensibly gay characters in the film, but because our highlighting the homoeroticism forces us to face our tendency to highlight a gay relationship as different.

Wez and the Youth are clearly in a relationship, a romantic, sexual relationship. Even Lord Humungus acknowledges this when he remarks to Wez that "we've all lost someone we love." What kind of "love" Wez is capable of as a homicidal lunatic is dubious, but he and the Youth share something. Notice how casually that is handled in the film. It's a non-issue. Are they gay? Bisexual? Pansexual? Does it matter? In the Wasteland you'd be lucky to find another non-hostile human, let alone a companion. You'd be blessed to have a meaningful relationship, and everyone would recognize as much. Do you think antiquated notions like straight or gay are going to matter to those for whom survival is a day-to-day matter? Surely we could categorize Wez if need be, but to what end? Wez surely is not concerned with how he is categorized; he has more important things to worry about, like gas, murder, and Max. Is it relevant at all to Lord Humungus that Wez is "gay" or "bi?" Where he fits in a somewhat arbitrary architectonic of sexual relationships isn't going to affect much, if anything, in the Wasteland. So why does it seem to matter so much to us? Perhaps this is a lesson in Mad Max.

This Ain't One Body's Tell, It's the Tell of Us All

The Wasteland provides a conceptual playground where modern presuppositions can be removed, and society reset to its basic elements. In this way, we can play imaginatively with social structures that appear deep seated and envision a world otherwise. Remove social conventions and structures, divest ourselves of various assumptions, and what is left ... nature, necessity, and humanity.

The Wasteland is a Hobbesian dystopia. As Thomas Hobbes (1588–1679) hypothesizes, in the state of nature, absent the organized monopoly of power and force that is the modern state, humans exist in a constant struggle over sparse resources, "... no Arts; no Letters; no Society; and which is worst of all, continuall feare, and danger of violent death; And the life of man, solitary poore, nasty, brutish, and short."[20] The Wasteland is such a world of scarcity and survival. It is also brutal, which is to be expected when the comforts of modern life are removed—things like law and order, or stability and security. In this world, we can envision a hard reset of how we, as natural, biological, and social animals would choose to organize ourselves. Where would concepts like sex, gender, and orientation fit in such a world?

From what's been said above, a few tentative conclusions can be drawn. Sex is biological. That is what we learn from the scholars noted above, and from simple, empirical reality. Our species is, for the most part, non-arbitrarily bisected into two sexes, male and female.[21] Once we discern how to understand the difference, we also notice various patterns, trends, or tendencies. Males are, on average, stronger, with denser muscle and bones. Males, in general, are faster.[22] Females, in general, are equipped to incubate tiny humans. Nothing about the apocalypse changes this. Human nature, as biological fact, persists. But in a Hobbesian world, what one lacks in strength one can make up for in skill or cunning. Furiosa can climb the military ladder to Imperator by being fast, clever, and a good fighter, even if she is out matched in terms of brute strength. Actually though, it seems Furiosa is probably at least the equal, if not the better, of most biological males when it comes to brute force. Likewise, through guile, charisma, and intelligence Aunty Entity can rule Bartertown. Conversely, Max— strong, cis-gendered, heterosexual white male that he is—can be enslaved as a Bloodbag, manipulated into fighting in Thunderdome, and even presumed to be an aspiring prostitute. Females, like Aunty, can be tyrants. Males, like Max, can be objectified. The Wasteland shows the disconnect between sex and gender, and highlights that sex is not destiny, and gender is not natural. Gender is confounded in the Wasteland. But some differences do remain. Females are the only humans that can bear children. What does this still mean in the Wasteland? Surely it means that for the human race to survive females must bear children, but it does not require that they be enslaved as breeders, milked as cattle, or traded as chattel. Nature will dictate the necessary conditions of our survival, but as rational, social animals, we dictate on what terms.

Notes

1 Of note: Randy "The Macho Man" Savage, Brutus "The Barber" Beefcake, and Jesse "The Body" Ventura.
2 Robin Welch, "Smegma Crazies, Gayboys, and the Golden Youth," at https://theradlands.com/2017/04/04/smegmacrazies-gayboys-goldenyouth/ (accessed January 6, 2022).
3 Veronica Dolginko, "Down Low Down Under: Homoeroticism in Australian Cinema," at https://www.back-row.com/home/2018/6/20/down-low-down-under-homoeroticism-in-australian-cinema (accessed January 6, 2022).
4 June Hannam, *Feminism* (Harlow, UK: Pearson Education, 2007), 3–4.
5 Ibid., 4.
6 Andrew Altman, *Arguing About Law: An Introduction to Legal Philosophy*, 2nd ed. (Ontario: Wadsworth Publishing Company, 2001), 202. Altman classifies feminists into one of four groups: Liberal, Progressive, Radical, or Conservative, depending on responses to the questions posed.
7 Simone de Beauvoir, *The Second Sex* (New York: Vintage Books, 1974), xvii.
8 Ibid., 301.

9   Kathleen Jenkins, "How to Be a Pluralist About Gender Categories," in Raja Halwani, Jacob Held, Natasha McKeever, and Alan Soble eds., *The Philosophy of Sex*, 8th ed. (Lanham, MD: Rowman and Littlefield, 2022), 237.

10   Beauvoir, 285.

11   Ibid., 592.

12   Judith Butler, *Gender Trouble* (New York: Routledge, 2006), 99.

13   Mimi Marinucci, *Feminism Is Queer: The Intimate Connection Between Queer and Feminist Theory* (London: Zed Books, 2010), 69.

14   Recently, we've seen that biological sex can affect how one responds to Covid-19 vaccines. Tom T. Shimabukuro, Matthew Cole, and John R. Su, "Reports of Anaphylaxis After Receipt of mRNA COVID-19 Vaccines in the US—December 14, 2020–January 18, 2021," *Journal of the American Medical Association*, 325 (2021), 1101–1102, at doi:10.1001/jama.2021.1967.

15   Kathleen Stock, "Sexual Orientation: What Is It?" in Raja Halwani, Jacob Held, Natasha McKeever, and Alan Soble eds., *The Philosophy of Sex*, 8th ed. (Lanham, MD: Rowman and Littlefield, 2022), 167.

16   The "forced breeding" aspect of *Fury Road* raises questions about pregnancy, abortion, and reproductive freedom and choice. I won't address this specific issue; however, it should be noted that the biological fact that females are the only humans biologically capable of incubating young does put them in a particular, vulnerable position with respect to society, namely as regards child rearing and the burdens affiliated with the family unit. We ignore or dismiss this biological difference between males and females to the detriment of females, for whom this difference is consequential.

17   For a good discussion of these issues, see Robin Dembroff, "What Is Sexual Orientation?" in *The Philosophy of Sex*, 141–162.

18   Cited in Dembroff, 142.

19   Ibid.

20   Thomas Hobbes, *Leviathan*, rev. student ed., ed. Richard Tuck (Cambridge: Cambridge University Press, 1997), 89.

21   Kathleen Stock, in recognizing the existence of intersex individuals, a fact that is often used to problematize thinking of our species as a sexual dyad, notes that "intersex people in the general population is miniscule: around 0.018 percent." She cites Leonard Sax, "How Common Is Intersex? A Response to Anne Fausto-Sterling," *Journal of Sex Research* 39:3 (2022), 174–178.

22   Recent controversies in sport, specifically regarding transgender women competing in female divisions, have brought this issue to national and international attention. Data is still forthcoming, but suggests that biological advantages are recalcitrant to hormone suppression, so biological sex may be strongly determinative of one's physical capabilities. On

recent controversies, see "NCAA's New Trans Athlete Guidelines Sow Confusion amid Lia Thomas Debate," at nbcnews.com (accessed January 9, 2022). For one recent study, see Emma N. Hilton and Tommy R. Lundberg, "Transgender Women in the Female Category of Sport: Perspectives on Testosterone Suppression and Performance Advantage," *Sports Medicine* 51 (2021), 199–214.

Part V

WASTELAND AESTHETICS: MUSIC, FASHION, AUSTRALIA, AND NATURE

18

Driving Insanity, Chaos, and Emotion: The Music of *Mad Max: Fury Road*

Lance Belluomini

> Where words fail, sounds can often speak.
> —Hans Christian Anderson, *What the Moon Saw*

The opening scene of *Mad Max: Fury Road* is unforgettable. "My name is Max. My world is fire and blood." With these words, we understand the state of Max's existence—he's the living embodiment of this post-apocalyptic world, a broken man traumatized by the loss of his family, haunted by visions of his past. After he's captured by the War Boys, however, we get a sense that Max isn't ready to give up on life altogether. In a voiceover, he lets us know what he has become, "A man reduced to a single instinct: survive." When the War Boys bring Max to the Citadel and tattoo him with the words "O-Negative Universal Donor," it's clear what they want: his blood. Next, the War Boys try to brand Max, but like a caged animal, he fights back to survive. He breaks free, desperately flees through the caverns, and battles War Boys (while having visions of those in his past he couldn't save). He then opens a set of doors on the edge of a high cliff and leaps to a hanging crane hook using the chain between his cuffed hands. But as he swings back, the War Boys take him, the doors shut, and we cut to the title card of the film.

This opening sequence is aesthetically pleasing to us for a variety of reasons. The costume design and makeup are practical, which lends the film a very real, textured feel. It allows the characters, like the cult of War Boys, to visually stand out—ghost white, clean shaven, car

Mad Max and Philosophy: Thinking Through the Wasteland, First Edition.
Edited by Matthew P. Meyer and David Koepsell.
© 2024 John Wiley & Sons, Inc. Published 2024 by John Wiley & Sons, Inc.

greased eyes with lips scarred to look like skeleton teeth. The special effects are well-executed, such as Max's visions which serve to capture Max's crazy state of mind. But more than anything, it's the music composed by Tom Holkenborg (aka Junkie XL) that makes the greatest aesthetic contribution. The music literally drives the scenes.

When Max breaks free from the War Boys, the cue titled "Escape" kicks in with its thunderous drums and frantic string arrangements, intensifying the action on screen while capturing the insanity that roams freely in this world. The loud drumming is the perfect primal sound for this post-apocalyptic world. This is Max's main theme which includes a bending electric guitar string riff, "Na-na-naa-naaa-naaaaa!"—representing Max's psychotic and troubled state of mind. The piece also contains a metallic quality that matches the visuals (the music corresponding with the film's action—which director, George Miller, poetically describes as "visual rock 'n' roll").[1]

But how often do we reflect on the aesthetic value of a film's score? Many of us don't realize how the music in *Mad Max: Fury Road* emotionally affects us, because our attention is typically focused on the insane action. By design, it's a film with hardly any dialogue. Instead, Miller chose to have Holkenborg's multilayered score serve as the dialogue and narration. But the score also arouses emotions, creates moods, captures what the characters are thinking and feeling, and plenty more. This essay looks at how Holkenborg's music accomplishes these things and how the music enhances our aesthetic appreciation of the film.

"High-Octane Crazy Blood Fillin' Me Up"

While Holkenborg's score plays a variety of functions, it's often assumed that the most important role of a film's score is as a signifier of emotion. Clearly, the music of *Mad Max: Fury Road* imitates the emotional states of certain characters, conveys the prevailing mood in each scene, and evokes the appropriate emotional responses in us. But what is the value in music imitating emotion? How does the music arouse emotional responses in us? And how could the arousal of "negative emotions" benefit us?

The ancient Greeks included music in education because they believed it plays a part in perfecting our soul and rationality. In fact, Aristotle (384–322 B.C.E.) discusses the importance of this in the eighth book of his *Politics*. According to Aristotle, learning to govern our emotions is crucial to perfecting our soul and rationality: "Rhythm and melody supply imitations of anger and gentleness, and also of courage and temperance, and of the other qualities of character, which hardly fall short of the actual affections, as we know from our own experience, for in listening to such strains our souls undergo a change."[2]

Consider when Nux convinces his fellow War Boy, Slit, that instead of dying soft, he deserves the chance to "die historic on the fury road" in an effort to stop Furiosa—the heroic figure of the film who's gone rogue and betrayed Immortan Joe by stealing his top wives. Nux passionately shouts, "We take my Bloodbag and strap him to the lancer's perch!" After he says, "High-octane crazy blood fillin' me up," the cue titled "Bloodbag" begins as we cut to Immortan Joe's armada of wild vehicles in pursuit of Furiosa's war rig.

The music begins with a set of loud drumbeat rhythms. Visually, we witness the crazy drummers behind the pounding drumbeats aboard the Doof Wagon (the massive speaker-laden truck). The thunderous drum rhythms build momentum, oscillating from super loud to really quiet, then back to super loud. There's a massive dramatic quality to the loud and high velocity drumming, containing an energetic quality. The cue then evolves from a set of alarming drum rhythms to an over-the-top rock opera piece featuring loud electric guitar riffs by the Doof Warrior—the flame-throwing guitarist charging up the fleet.

Aristotle would say this music imitates the negative emotions that Immortan Joe and the War Boys are experiencing (anger, betrayal, and fear), thus strengthening our ability to govern and control our emotions. The music also emphasizes this chaotic, aggressive, toxic, and brutal society. Holkenborg underscores this: "I wanted to emphasize the fact that all these people are chasing each other in cars with rough rusty metal, and I wanted to make sure the drive, aggression, and humanity [were] coming through in the score."[3] Holkenborg accomplishes this with "Bloodbag" through his brutal mixing approach—with its randomized drumbeats and electric guitar riffs blended with metallic sound effects.[4]

Notice that the cue also arouses our emotions. In particular, the music makes us tense and uneasy; it even strikes fear into us. But how? According to contemporary philosopher Jenefer Robinson, "People respond emotionally to music because of the associations they have to it; different sorts of music have associations that are widespread in the culture."[5] In fact, the loud pulse-pounding drumbeat rhythms and guitar riffs in "Bloodbag" are musical elements that are culturally associated with military music on the battlefield—which we automatically connect with anger, fear, anxiety, and tension.[6] Essentially, the drummers and Doof Warrior aboard the wagon are heavy-metal buglers in a war party. It's no wonder that the cue (centered on a road war) evokes these negative feelings in us and gets our hearts palpitating.

But why do we enjoy listening to film music that expresses negative emotional states? Some philosophers have suggested that we can't understand the music we're engaging with unless we understand everything it expresses, which includes the negative emotions.[7] The idea is that there's a payoff to engaging with the musical piece in question that is eliciting negative emotions. The "Bloodbag" cue expresses fear and panic, but it's the price we pay to understand the musical score and engage with the positive emotional responses that the other pieces evoke.

Aristotle, however, offers a different yet more appealing suggestion: his theory of catharsis. According to this view, our negative emotional responses to music result in a positive psychological purification of the negative emotions.[8] By arousing these negative emotions of anger, fear, and anxiety while listening to *Mad Max: Fury Road*, we're able to safely release these repressed emotions and purify our soul. Indeed, for Aristotle, experiencing these negative emotions is key to regulating our emotions in the real world.

"Oh, What a Day! What a Lovely Day!"

Our admiration for a film is elevated when we evaluate the music as beautiful and well-crafted. Robinson mentions that music arouses certain emotions when we're moved by the sheer beauty of a melody or harmony.[9] Contemporary philosophers refer to these types of emotions as "emotions of appreciation"—such as awe, amazement, and excitement.[10]

Recall the "Storm Is Coming" cue that accompanies the chase sequence where Furiosa creates a roadblock for Immortan Joe's pursuing armada by getting them to follow her into a massive dust storm. Here we learn that Immortan Joe's cult of War Boys are committed to toxic honor and prepared to reach true glory and entry into Valhalla by sacrificing themselves in their quest to stop Furiosa. This is why the War Boys utter, "Witness me" before their sacrifice, inspiring others to die in a blaze of battle too.

As they enter the tornado storm, the six-minute orchestral cue expresses triumphant and heroic feelings, resembling a patriotic power anthem. Yet we also experience this feeling of amazement over the elegance and artistry to the ascending harmonic chord progressions, the dramatic melody carried by brass and string instruments. The orchestra soars—full of hope, victory, and majesty as we witness the explosive destruction of vehicles and sacrificial War Boys being sucked up, disintegrating in the topsy-turvy energy of the storm's tornado. After Nux witnesses this carnage and sacrifice, he unforgettably says, "Oh, what a day! What a lovely day!"

We even take pleasure in the beauty of the cue's percussion—there's a gracefulness to the drum beat rhythm (as opposed to brute force) that plays when Nux releases the gasoline in his vehicle. Nux shouts to Max, "I am the man ... who grabs the sun ... riding to Valhalla! Witness me, Bloodbag!" But when Max punches through the back window to stop Nux, who has positioned his vehicle in front of Furiosa's rig, we experience more pleasure in the beauty of the woodwinds, strings, and drumbeat rhythm. Our feeling of amazement over the music continues as Nux lights the flare and says with glory, "I live. I die. I live again!"

We also experience emotions of appreciation during the fantastic cue titled "Brothers in Arms." Remember the scene where Furiosa decides to trust and team up with Max while approaching the rocky mountain canyon. Furiosa has a deal in place with the bikers who rule the canyon: safe passage through their rocky terrain in exchange for the fuel pod attached to her rig. However, because Furiosa hasn't lived up to her end of the deal concerning how many vehicles would be in her pursuit, the deal goes bad. As the tension rises, the three war parties arrive. When Furiosa signals Max to start driving, the "Brothers in Arms" cue begins with electronic bleeps and squirts over a catchy drum rhythm.

Next, we're treated to one of the best action sequences in the history of cinema—Furiosa and Max working together (like brothers in arms) to repel the attacking biker gang determined to stop them and retrieve their promised fuel. When the bikers catch up to the rig, the cue evolves into a wonderfully dynamic and engaging piece—the rhythm of the melody mirroring the energy, drive, and feverish pace of the action on screen which features insane bikers flying over the rig, dropping small explosive balls onto it, causing damage to the engine. But Furiosa and Max strike back. Trusting one another, they pass guns to one another and take out the attacking bikers.

What stands out and captures our attention is Holkenborg's propulsive music. At times, the powerful rhythm of the melody plays with hardly any percussion, allowing us to hear the strings and brass of the orchestra playing these ascending and descending chord progressions which dramatically sway back and forth. In effect, the music places us in a cheerful mood as well as expressing hope, perseverance, and determination. We also recognize that it's the beauty of the music that aesthetically enhances these scenes, arousing "emotions of appreciation" in us—amazement and excitement.

Interestingly, Holkenborg composed these musical compositions to both supply additional energy to these action sequences and describe what the characters are feeling. And because these pieces are meant to be heard in the context of these scenes, it's challenging for us to disassociate the music from them. But does the merit and emotional impact of these cues depend on witnessing these action sequences? No, these musical cues stand on their own. For instance, we don't need to watch Furiosa and Max working together to defeat the biker gang in order to feel the heroism and triumph that the music conveys.

"You Want That Thing off Your Face?"

In addition to arousing our emotions, the music of *Mad Max: Fury Road* also telegraphs important narrative information and serves to characterize the heroic figures in the film. By performing these functions, the music thus deepens our aesthetic admiration for the film.

Max's memorable motif that surfaces throughout the movie is a case in point. It's a simple yet effective musical statement that consists of a repeated cello note. We first hear the motif at the start of the film after Max utters, "Survive." There it's heard with three repeated cello notes: "Dah-Dah-DAH!" It's more prominently featured during the tense scene in the war rig cabin between Furiosa and Max after she convinces Max to let her drive. Because Max desperately wants to be free of the face mask that the War Boys placed on him, Furiosa decides to hit Max's freedom instinct: "You want that thing off your face?" Immediately following this line, we hear Max's motif as he looks at Furiosa. The note plays two times: "Dah-DAH!" Playing the note twice feels stable and grounded. The two notes communicate what Max is experiencing and thinking—that he feels comfortable enough to let Furiosa and the five wives into the rig. But in the very next moment when Furiosa enters the cabin, the motif plays with only one note: "DAH!" The one note instantly transmits to us that Max is still in a state of panic inside. The one uneven note also sounds unstable—characterizing Max's state of mind. As he grabs a chisel tool from Furiosa and furiously starts to work at removing his mask while aiming a gun at her, the theme plays the note three times: "Dah-Dah-DAH!" The three notes communicate several things. First, they express that Max feels unsure, scared, and still driven by that one instinct: survival. Second, they express uncertainty: Is Max going to shoot them? Is he going to explode? Finally, the three notes reveal how Max is making Furiosa and the wives feel—threatened and unsafe.

Next, when Max begins to look for anything dangerous, discovering multiple guns in the cabin, we hear two notes: "Dah-DAH!" This is because Max feels confident and safe after collecting them. After he secures more guns, we hear three notes while the wives start conjecturing about Max's dark motives. One of the wives says, "He's not going to hurt us. He needs us." Another replies, "Oh, he'll hurt us, all right." Yet another exclaims, "He's a crazy smeg who eats schlanger!" This line is followed by one note, then three notes. Again, the uneven notes denote danger, signaling to us that the wives are unsure about Max: Is he dangerous?

But then we hear two notes right before the group learns that Immortan Joe has rallied other cities to the chase. The two notes narratively function to let us know that Max, Furiosa, and the wives are about to collaborate and work together. Max even helps by unlocking the dragging fuel pod slowing the rig down.

Max's cello motif advances the film's narrative, characterizes Max by revealing bits of his identity (given his lack of dialogue), and conveys what he and those around him are feeling. Moreover, it allows us to experience tense feelings. Think of John Williams's iconic shark motif in *Jaws*. The repeating low staccato notes reliably signal the presence of the shark and convey that something bad is about to happen. Consequently, we have negative emotional responses to the shark motif, primarily fear. Holkenborg does the same thing with Max's motif. We feel uneasy, tense, wary, and fearful whenever we hear one or three notes played, telegraphing to us that something bad could occur. Conversely, when two notes play, we feel a bit calmer, more relaxed. Because this simple motif moves the narrative, describes what Max and the others are feeling, and prompts a range of emotions in us—there's no doubt this motif plays a significant role in our appreciation of the film's artistry.

"I Can't Wait for Them to See It ... Home ... the Green Place"

Surprisingly, the score doesn't just reflect the insanity and accelerating chaos of Max's world. At times, Holkenborg delivers soft and warm themes, capturing what's left of humanity.

Consider the music for Furiosa. Early in the film, whenever we see Furiosa, she's musically represented with just a soft repeating pulse sound. But her main theme surfaces in the cue titled "Many Mothers"—a gorgeous piece that not only expresses and arouses painful feelings of loss but also evokes a mood of sadness. This is a prime example of how certain musical themes can go beyond just expressing and arousing emotions. Rather, they can also induce pleasant or unpleasant moods. But how do moods differ from emotions? According to Robinson, "Moods differ from emotions in that they are not directed at anything in particular but pervade experience as a whole."[11] As we'll soon see, the sad mood created by Furiosa's theme induces sad feeling states and global thoughts, in general, about this post-apocalyptic world.

Before we witness Furiosa's theme in the film, her backstory is revealed when Max asks her how she knows the Green Place even exists. Showing vulnerability, she opens up to Max, telling him she was born there, stolen as a child, her mother killed, and that her motivation ever since has been redemption—the driving theme in the film. When she reunites with the "many mothers" of her clan, she says, "I can't wait for them to see it ... Home ... the Green Place." But they tell her that she already passed it, describing the poisoned bog with all the creepy crows. Devastated, she realizes her home is gone.

This is when Furiosa's sad theme begins. It starts as a simple melody played by a viola, lending a silky yet sorrowful quality to the piece. We then hear more violas blended with a powerful cello base, the sounds of the high cello notes providing the theme with a thicker yet somber quality. The music conveys Furiosa's sadness, hopelessness, grief, and painful loss. In despair, Furiosa wanders off into the desert, drops her prosthetic arm, falls to her knees, and screams out into the wind in agony while Max looks on. In these moments, the music becomes fully orchestral—the harmonic chords of the melody dramatically carried by sweeping strings, woodwinds, and brass. All of this facilitates our emotional involvement with Furiosa, eliciting a range of emotions in us such as compassion and anguish.

Yet Furiosa's theme also evokes a mood of sadness, creating this sorrowful atmosphere.[12] We relate to Furiosa's devastation over her childhood home becoming a place corrupted by the decay and death of this horrible Wasteland. When this theme plays, we are placed into a sad mood about the tragedy in this post-apocalyptic world. The story-appropriate music underscores the loss of something vital in one's life. What Furiosa was hoping for (everything she fought for and dreamt of) is no longer there: her home—the Green Place. Furthermore, the theme makes us think of what has happened on a global scale. Because the world fell, there is no rule of law. Instead, there are wars for water and oil, food is scare, the air is poison, civilization is a memory, and cities (like the Green Place) have been erased. The music projects a mood of sadness, directing us toward these global thoughts and to the realization that there isn't much humanity left in a world that's gone mad.

"If You Can't Fix What's Broken, You'll Uh ... You'll Go Insane"

Her home destroyed and efforts in vain, Furiosa decides to flee across the salt flats. But Max gives some advice against what she's doing: "You know, hope is a mistake. If you can't fix what's broken, you'll uh ... you'll go insane." This is one of the most powerful quotes in the movie, packing multiple meanings. For instance, it speaks to how broken Max is—his loss and hopelessness over not being able to bring back the dead. In fact, the next morning, when he watches Furiosa and the women take off, he's hit with a vision of a girl who says, "Where are you, Max? ... You promised to help us. Come on, pa. Let's go."

Immediately after these lines, we hear the melody in the cue titled "Claw Trucks"—a dynamic piece containing hopeful and energetic qualities that exhilarate us. Max's morning vision has planted a hopeful seed in his mind. This is when he realizes he was wrong in what he said to Furiosa: hope isn't a mistake and there is a way to fix what's broken. He races over to them, points to the Citadel on a map, telling Furiosa, "This is your way home." Max is right. After all, it's a place where green, water, and life are—the very things that they've been chasing after. And it's now undefended. They just have to travel back through the canyon and block the archway pass. Nux endorses the plan: "Yeah. It feels like hope."

Through his vision, Max has learned a lesson: there are some things you can't run from on your own. He knows that if they defeat Immortan Joe's armada and reach the Citadel, they can all find the one thing Furiosa is looking for. He says to her, "At least that way, you know, we might be able to ... together ... come across some kind of redemption." He then holds his hand out to Furiosa and she shakes his hand, confiding in him as the uplifting rumblings of the "Claw Trucks" melody kicks in, expressing the hopeful and redemptive nature of this scene. Philosopher Arthur Schopenhauer (1788–1860) aptly captures this point: "When music suitable to any scene, action, event, or environment is played, it seems to disclose to us its most secret meaning and appears to be the most accurate and distinct commentary on it."[13]

This is precisely what Holkenborg gives us with "Claw Trucks." It's the most suitable music for both this scene and the subsequent harrowing action sequences where our heroes furiously road-battle Immortan Joe's armada. The cue's melody consists of a drumbeat and cello rhythm along with frenetic strings and brass, the piece alternating back and forth from soft to loud—producing cheerful feelings. There's a relentless climbing drive to this cue which fits with the action on screen. But the music also functions to capture the perseverance of our heroes along with highlighting their moments of victory. Despite facing danger from every direction, suffering injuries and loss, our heroes help one another and triumph.

Given all this, Schopenhauer would correctly say the music provides us with the most accurate commentary on this scene, expressing the hope and redemption our heroes are striving for.[14] By doing so, it thus furthers our aesthetic respect for the film.

"Max. My Name Is Max ... That's My Name"

Consider the music when Max delivers these words, revealing his name to Furiosa. The appropriately titled cue "My Name Is Max" is a soft, slow, emotive piece played by strings. The music reflects Max's heroism—saving Furiosa's life with his own blood and getting everyone home. The music produces other feelings as well. We feel the hope for humanity and the will to survive in a world that can do better. All of this matters, just like Max's name matters because he matters to someone: Furiosa. And she matters to him, too. For us, it's the music that matters, injecting additional emotion into this heartfelt scene.

Unquestionably, Holkenborg's score plays a number of functions. There's value in the music imitating emotions, allowing us to govern our own emotions. We take delight in listening to the musical compositions and benefit even when they imitate negative emotions. But we've also seen how the music serves a variety of other purposes. It arouses emotions through cultural associations and through the beauty of the music itself; fosters emotional involvement; reveals the psychological and emotional states of different characters; conveys how intense Furiosa's grief is over her loss; projects story-appropriate moods; telegraphs narrative information; and provides accurate commentary on each scene—such as the film's memorable ending where Furiosa and Max share a look of understanding and appreciation. Likewise, we share that same look with respect to the music of *Mad Max: Fury Road*.[15]

Notes

1 During *The Madness of Max* documentary (2015), Miller aptly describes *Mad Max* as a car action film and mentions, "I often call it visual rock 'n' roll or visual music."
2 Aristotle, *Politics*, trans. C.D.C. Reeve (Hackett, 2017), ch. 5, 1340a23; b18–19.
3 "*Mad Max: Fury Road* Official Soundtrack, Behind the Music, Tom Holkenborg (Junkie XL), WaterTower," at https://www.youtube.com/watch?v=xESFyIxito0&t=112s.
4 Incidentally, given the lack of dialogue, this piece also serves as the voice of Immortan Joe and the War Boys.
5 Jenefer Robinson, "Emotional Responses to Music: What Are They? How Do They Work? And Are They Relevant to Aesthetic Appreciation?" in Peter Goldie ed., *The Oxford Handbook of Philosophy of Emotion* (Oxford: Oxford University Press, 2010), 654–655.
6 The music also motivates the War Boys to passionately fight with courage and bravery. This is something Plato highlights in *The Republic* where Socrates says the Guardians of his ideal city should be exposed to certain tunes and rhythms that imitate brave men engaged in warfare. For more, see Plato, *The Republic*, trans. Benjamin Jowett (New York: Vintage, 2012), Book III, 398c–400e.
7 For more on this suggestion, see Jenefer Robinson, *Deeper Than Reason: Emotion and Its Role in Literature, Music, and Art* (Oxford: Oxford University Press, 2005), 348–378.
8 Aristotle, *Poetics*, trans. Stephen Halliwell (London: Duckworth, 1987), ch. 6, 1449b21–1450b20.

9   Jenefer Robinson, "Music and Emotions," *Journal of Literary Theory* 1 (2007), 411–412.
10 To learn more about "emotions of appreciation," see Peter Kivy, *Music Alone: Philosophical Reflections on the Purely Musical Experience* (Ithaca, NY: Cornell University Press, 1990).
11 Robinson (2010), 661.
12 For more on how music evokes moods, see Noël Carroll, "Art and Mood: Preliminary Notes and Conjectures," *The Monist* 86 (2003), 521–555.
13 Arthur Schopenhauer, *The World as Will and Representation*, vol. 1, trans. Judith Norman and Alistair Welchman (Cambridge: Cambridge University Press, 2011), 262.
14 Schopenhauer claimed that the true inner nature of everything is a blind instinct or force, which he referred to as *the Will*. He considered music the greatest of all art forms because it's not a representation of a higher truth. Rather, it's a direct manifestation of the Will itself. When we listen to music, we're instantly connected with the highest truth. Consequently, we're able to lose track of ourselves, and in doing so, we become free from the struggles of our daily lives.
15 I would like to thank Matt Meyer for his helpful comments on previous drafts of this chapter.

19

Carapaces and Prosthetics: What Humans Wear in *Mad Max: Fury Road*

Laura T. Di Summa

Mad Max: Fury Road is a movie about costumes and about what costumes can do, about how they make a character come alive and convey the mood of a film. It is a movie that uses costumes to better understand the body and our relationship to technology.

There are two main insights to be gained by observing costumes in the film. The first is the co-dependency between machines and humans. The second is that the costumes reveal the inherent vulnerability of our bodies. But more than just speaking to bodies, the costumes also have something to say about ableism—the normative preference for fully functioning bodies. To foster these insights, let's zoom in on the characters' costumes and see how those costumes inform the relationships they have with other characters.

Guzzolene and Aqua Cola: Bodies, Machines, and Survival

Fury Road costume designer Jenny Beavan specializes in period films and costume dramas. And yet what she did with Lesley Vanderwalt, head of hair and make-up, is quite astounding (as recognized by an Academy Award). Beavan and Vanderwalt created a look dense with cultural references and social commentary that goes beyond expectations for sci-fi and apocalypse-based movies. The costume designer "strives for reality to sell a fantasy," and that's the

Mad Max and Philosophy: Thinking Through the Wasteland, First Edition.
Edited by Matthew P. Meyer and David Koepsell.

case here.[1] It does not matter how wild the costumes are: they are credible and they are the costumes you would wear if you were to live in the world of Mad Max.

The costumes constitute a statement about our connection and dependence on technology, and about how technology has altered our nature and bodies. Martin Heidegger (1889–1976) warned us about the ways technology filters our encounter with what surrounds us.[2] Technology effectively transforms nature into a resource, something we can use. Utilizing technology is thus a way of conquering nature that provides us with power. Heidegger saw this as dangerous, since it allows human beings to shape the world on their terms, as opposed to nature shaping itself. Regardless of whether we agree with Heidegger on this point, one thing is clear: we are dependent on technology. The costumes in *Fury Road* show this very well. Picture Immortan Joe, the tyrannical sovereign of the Citadel. In a world characterized by environmental catastrophe and shortage of basic needs, Immortan Joe exercises his power by keeping the water ("Aqua Cola") for himself, by using angelic women as breeders (the wives) and by surrounding himself with devoted "War Boys"–as ready to fight as they are prepared to die. He's a rather unpleasant character, and his unpleasantness is made visible through his attire.

What first strikes us is decay. Immortan Joe, as Vanderwalt remarks, "[had] become quite putrid really, from all the toxic waste and years of battles"; a life spent living and depending on machines has taken any semblance of life and living away from him. He wears a mouthpiece of teeth glued to an oxygen tank; a carapace protects blistering, scarred, and wrinkled skin. Joe barely walks or moves; his vehicles carry him everywhere. Machines allow him to survive, and yet his true desires are deeply human, distant from the machines on which he depends, distant from the world in which he reigns. What matters to Immortan Joe is water and the possibility of human life. His hope is with the sons he tries to conceive with the wives, who are the victims of his abuse and aesthetically the furthest thing from him we can imagine. Thus, in Immortan Joe's inhuman carapace, we see the strong desire to survive and have progeny—an ultimately human drive.

The attire of the wives tells another story. We first see them after Furiosa manages to evade the War Boys, for the moment. Dressed only in muslin cloth, they wash by the truck in the middle of the desert (using the highly coveted Aqua Cola); they are stunning, a mirage. One of them, the Splendid Angharad, Immortan's favorite, is visibly pregnant and will use her body as a shield. It's armor; it's life.

It is the radical opposite of Immortan Joe's carapace, but just as powerful. Whereas the artificial shield of Immortan Joe reminds us of decay and death, the soft fabrics and glowing skin of the wives reminds us of life and light.

But there is a dark side to the wife characters as well, the fact that they are being used as incubators. We can sense immediately the wrongness of using human beings as technology. In addition to the wives being used as incubators, we see women immobile and hooked up to horrifying breast pumps for producing mother's milk.

The War Boys, in their uniform look and their interchangeability (sadly, like any army), could also be seen as a technology—or as deeply intertwined with the technologies they employ. The War Boys act in a group, moving like reptiles in a somewhat jittery way: they are a bit too fast, a bit too flexible. They do not have an individual identity or distinctive character features. Their skin is pale and made paler by some whitish powder with which they cover themselves. The only exception is a streak of black on their eyes (guess: oil grease): the black and white contrast is striking and a reminder that the only two states allowed are life and death or, better, fight or die. The War Boys remind us of their dual nature: machine and human. When joining the battle, invoking Valhalla, they spray chrome paint on their mouth and teeth, a color we usually see on cars. And yet, despite their almost symbiotic relationship with machines—from their look to their fantastic and reckless physical abilities—the War Boys are, like Immortan Joe, deeply in need of anything human. We see it in Nux—a soldier who grows weary of his cause.

The first hint at Nux's need to be human is his (fairly brutal) treatment of Max. Nux is running out of "juice"—clean, non-radioactive blood. (And yes, the cinematography makes him look even paler than when we first see him). To join the battle, he must chain Max (a real human!) to the front of his vehicle, a drip of Max's blood connecting the two and keeping him alive as he drives and fights. Max is his Bloodbag—now he too is forced into becoming technology. It is thanks to Max—the Bloodbag—that Nux will capture Furiosa and her precious cargo. But he'll turn against Immortan Joe in the end. Nux's change of mind has to do with his reliance on the truly human: he falls in love with Capable, one of the wives. It's childish love, tender and awkward. But it's not machine-like, and that's what matters.

Nux's look is based on two colors: black and white. However, the little streak of red connecting him to Max is meaningful, and not just because it is better to be alive than dead. Rather, the red reminds us of how difficult it is to be alive: we need machines; we need technology. But we also need each other—in flesh and blood.

Immortan Joe and Nux are far from the folks you meet on your commute to work. And yet they make sense to us. Their costumes are stellar not just because they contribute to character development and to the narrative unfolding of the film. Costumes in *Fury Road* are meaningful because they tell us something about a collective identity we happen to share. They tell us something about ourselves and our own dependence on machines.

While I may not wear a carapace hooked to an oxygen tank, I rarely leave home without a phone. And all the apps I have on my phone are tech tools I need, if not to survive, at least to live according to standards I find almost necessary. There's one to monitor my child when he's in daycare, one for the dogwalker, one for grocery shopping, one to find parking, one to find my phone if I lose it—because losing it would be an absolute disaster. It does not matter that I have aged better than Immortan Joe. I know we have something in common, and I know it because I have seen what he's wearing. I have seen what his body needs, and I realize that I also have needs: that being human in the kind of society in which I live requires a series of technological appendices—portable machines for survival. But more than just exposing our reliance on technology, *Fury Road* reminds us of our shared vulnerability.

Staring at Furiosa

It is inevitable; we stare. Staring is one of the ways we have to explore the world around us and, in particular, bodies around us. Contemporary philosopher Rosemarie Garland-Thomson thinks of staring as a form of "social choreography."[3] Staring is an interpersonal practice where we learn about others and ourselves through encounter and confrontation. Staring is the "most intense form of looking"; it comes in different forms. There's a frozen stare, and there's fleeing a stare—looking away the moment we realize we have looked at someone for a second too long. There's also a loving stare, the one we direct at dear ones. Staring can lead to personal transformation. It is possible to stare at something that we might at first dislike, at something odd, maybe uncomfortable. And yet we can move from discomfort to appreciation; we can learn to stare lovingly at something we initially felt foreign, different from us. Staring, to use a term from Sherri Irvin, another contemporary philosopher, is a form of aesthetic exploration.[4] Irvin focuses specifically on body aesthetics: on the importance we give to how a body looks, for better or worse, and on the inevitable connection between bodies and identities. When staring at bodies, we explore: we engage with how they look and as a result we assess ourselves and how we understand what surrounds us, for exploring a body through staring can lead to the consideration of social and cultural issues. It can be the beginning of conversations on race, gender, ableism, and their intersectional connections.

Movies can be the vehicles for such explorations. Movies allow us to stare. Furiosa and Max attract our stare. Their bodies capture our attention and the costumes they wear emphasize and clarify their bodily identity—and what it means to think of identity through the body. Staring at Furiosa and Max is a way of initiating a process of aesthetic exploration.

Imperator Furiosa is the only woman, and the most respected figure, in Immortan Joe's army. Her truck carries water, mother's milk, and up to 3,000 gallons of guzzolene. Only she can drive the vehicle—she put kill switches on it. Soon after meeting her, we learn of her intent to disobey Immortan Joe and carry out a different plan. Furiosa smears oil grease on her eyes; her head is shaven; her costume makes her appear as an Amazon. She is a warrior: androgynous with more than a bit of elegance.

She's also an amputee, we realize. As the War Rig stops to let the wives out for a moment of rest, we see her from the back, but there is something different: she left her prosthetic arm by the driver's seat; her stump is left uncovered. The lack of the prosthetic arm, an essential component of her costume, augments her strength. Furiosa is no less beautiful than the wives, no less courageous than any of the warriors, no less relevant to the plot structure than any of the characters. Her missing arm does not make her a victim; its absence is acknowledged and respected, making our gaze transition. It is a process of aesthetic exploration. We first hesitate; a second later, we embrace her. She allows us to engage and identify. Max, we are bound to find out, shares our feelings.

In *Fury Road*, disability is a thing for heroes, as Furiosa shows. To this extent, *Fury Road* accomplishes what contemporary philosopher Tobin Siebers has advocated in his work at the intersection of disability studies and philosophical aesthetics. Siebers criticizes the typical representation of the disabled body as one that is deficient, "other." Instead, he looks at the arts as a vehicle for the appreciation of disability.[5] When discussing the role of disability in art history, Siebers notes how we would not have a conception of the beautiful in art if we had not taken into consideration the disabled body. The famous statue the *Venus de Milo* would not be the same were she to have both arms. In the same vein, Furiosa would not be the same without her prosthetic arm and her ability, and willingness, to remove it.

Fashion and costumes have the potential to expand the conversation on bodies, vulnerability, and even, as in the case of Furiosa, disability. In part, the advantage is that film costumes and fashion are made to be stared at. We cannot (and don't want to) divert our gaze. Watching Furiosa, observing her costume, her look, allows us to see disability in context, to see beauty in it. Returning to Siebers' point: her beauty is a function of her disability—the two working together. A similar process of recognition and embrace occurs as part of the camera's gaze as well. Max, the other main character in the film, also "transitions" his gaze and comes to appreciate Furiosa. Starting as enemies, the movie shows them becoming allies: they become equal; they affirm themselves individually while taking care of each other. They learn to stare. Let's turn to Max.

Reflecting on Max

Max Rockatansky is haunted by visions of the past and is burdened by it. As he announces in his opening monologue, chewing a lizard: "Haunted by those I could not protect. So I exist in this Wasteland. A man reduced to a single instinct: Survive."

Unlike most characters in the film, Max is not a machine or machine hybrid. As the medical chart tattooed on his back by the War Boys indicates, he's distinctively human. He's a universal donor. Hallucinations aside, he's in good health, which is something very few can claim in *Fury Road*. One thing about his costume, call it an accessory, invites our reflection: the chain securing him to the front of Nux's vehicle. Weaved into the chain is a drip transferring Max's blood to Nux. It is a brilliant idea, conjoining the two as antagonists but also as two lives at risk, as two lives that depend on each other—and will continue to until the end of the film. Blood, which builds the connection, is a human component. It runs in our bodies, and, in many ways, makes our bodies alike. For blood is something we can transfer, share, donate. Later in the movie, the same drip will again remind us of a kinship that is quintessentially human: love (or at minimum, respect).

Furiosa and Max find themselves side by side, fighting for freedom. Furiosa is badly injured. This time around, Max will voluntarily donate his blood to her, using the same drip. As he helps her, Max finally tells her his name, which he had so far concealed ("Does it matter?"—he used to say). And a name is yet another sign of humanity—the first mark of identity.

Furiosa and Max are heroes in a world that has lost hope. But as heroes, they are also vulnerable; a prosthetic arm and a drip remind us of such vulnerability, and, in turn, they signal some kind of profoundly human strength. It is an attachment to the bodies they have, to their being in the world. To see their bodies on screen, to follow them, is very close to what Sherri Irvin means by initiating a process of aesthetic exploration. In Furiosa, we are confronted with disability: we stare at it and embrace it. There is something beautiful in it; she is no less a hero, no less a fighter. Max's blood is, we learn in the beginning, his strength and what he's valued for. It is what makes a body work, and pumping blood is what a body does: better than superpowers.

Good art, and film is indeed an art, incorporates disability, weakness, and vulnerability and gives them the dignity they deserve. Good art has "eyes for the outside"—it provokes a reflection on our society while often challenging accepted values. It can be uncomfortable. Good art incorporates people, bodies, and experiences that are bound to make us reflect on ourselves, leading to a conversation on identity: a situated, multifaceted, and performative identity. *Fury Road* is good art.

In Closing: Thinking About the Body in *Mad Max*

Costumes in *Fury Road* highlight the importance of the body. It is essential to see it in the world, moving and participating in our society's systems of values and beliefs; it is essential to appreciate it, for it is a carrier of identity, just like our thoughts, wishes, and plans. Identity is constructed through physicality. Whether in our world or in the *Fury Road* universe, we cannot leave our bodies behind.

Film allows us to see bodies, to see them in motion. The costume choices made in a film are thus the beginning of a reflection on bodily identity and on the ways in which it promotes social and cultural reflection. In *Mad Max*, costumes are both a reminder of the relationship—and co-dependence—of bodies and machines and an invitation to engage in the aesthetic exploration of the body, bringing us past imposed standards of fitness and arriving at the appreciation of differently able bodies.

Notes

1 Booth Moore, "Unfashioning Costume Design," in Deborah Nadoolman Landis ed., *Hollywood Costume* (London: Victoria and Albert Museum, 2012), 150–157.
2 Martin Heidegger, *The Question Concerning Technology, and Other Essays*, trans. William Lovitt (New York: Harper & Row, 1977).
3 Rosemarie Garland-Thomson, "Ways of Staring," *Journal of Visual Culture 5* (2006), 173–192; and Rosemarie Garland-Thomson, "Disability and Representation," *PMLA* 120 (2005), 522–527.
4 Sherri Irvin, *Body Aesthetics* (Oxford: Oxford University Press, 2016); and Sherri Irvin, "Resisting Body Oppression: An Aesthetic Approach," *Feminist Philosophy Quarterly* 3 (2017), 1–26.
5 Tobin Siebers, "Disability Aesthetics," *Journal for Cultural and Religious Theory* 7 (2006), 63–73.

Does It Matter How Australian the Apocalypse Is?

Greg Littmann

As an Australian, I've always had a special place in my heart for the *Mad Max* saga. This apocalypse is *my* apocalypse, the one that happened in my own backyard or, at least, within a couple of thousand kilometers. It was *my* society that had fallen apart. In *Mad Max*, the cops and crooks alike spoke with Australian accents and drove through familiar Australian landscapes. The dusty town Toecutter and his gang terrorize looks like a real Australian small town, complete with an old-fashioned milk bar and a general shop advertising cans of fizzy, lemon-flavored Solo. It should look real, of course—it's Clunes, Victoria. In later films, bands of men with Aussie accents, wearing bondage gear and sporting mohawks, drive in speeding convoys through red Australian deserts, laying waste to everything in their path.

Despite the distinctly Australian flavor of the *Mad Max* franchise, each film in the series so far has been less distinctly Australian than the film before it. Partly, this is inevitable given that society collapses after the first film. *Mad Max* was set in an Australia very like the real one, with cultural and social institutions still in place, though starting to break down. Civilization disappears before *Mad Max 2* begins, and the sequels show us only scattered groups of survivors preyed on by flamboyant automotive bandits.

Partly, though, the films have grown less distinctly Australian because of the inclusion of characters with non-Australian accents in prominent roles. In *Mad Max 3*, American singer Tina Turner plays Max's main antagonist, the boss of Bartertown's surface, Aunty Entity.

Mad Max and Philosophy: Thinking Through the Wasteland, First Edition.
Edited by Matthew P. Meyer and David Koepsell.
© 2024 John Wiley & Sons, Inc. Published 2024 by John Wiley & Sons, Inc.

Turner uses her normal accent, down to the Tennessee twang. In *Fury Road*, Furiosa is more the protagonist than Max is. South African and American actress Charlize Theron plays Furiosa with a Midwestern American accent, the most common accent in film and the one widely regarded as most broadly appealing to American audiences. English actor Tom Hardy makes an effort at some kind of accent as Max, but he sounds more English than Australian. The scenery, too, has changed for *Fury Road*. In place of the scrubby plains of New South Wales and South Australia, the car gangs rocket past the majestic, weathered rocks of the Namibian desert. The deserts of Namibia are spectacular but look like nowhere in Australia.

Does it matter whether *Mad Max* films have an Australian feel to them? I admit that I'm biased. I like *Mad Max* films to feel Australian. But biased or not, I'm going to try to take an objective look at the question. More is at stake than just Australianness in *Mad Max* films. What we say in the case of Max and Australia will have implications for other franchises, nations, and cultures.

Importantly, I'm *not* addressing the question of whether Australian actors should be hired to play Australian characters. In fact, I think the *Mad Max* saga has benefited from foreigners in Aussie roles. Imagine *Mad Max II* without Englishman Michael Preston as the stoic Pappagallo, leader of the oil refinery tribe, and New Zealander Bruce Spence as the manic gyrocopter pilot! I'm concerned only with the feel of the films, not how they're produced.

What Is It for a Film to Feel Australian?

Before we can ask whether the *Mad Max* films should feel Australian, we need some idea of what that means. Must Max appear in shorts and a blue singlet, drinking a tinnie of Foster's Lager as he drives by in a Holden utility vehicle, blasting Midnight Oil? Perhaps at the end of *Mad Max*, when he incinerates Johnny the Boy, he could make a quip about throwing another prawn on the barbie. Of course, I'm being ridiculous, but I have a serious point, which is that making every character a stereotype would just turn the film into a parody.

Perhaps there's something more subtle that could be captured in the characterization, something that we might call "the Australian character." In school, I had to write several essays on the nature of the Australian character, and I regurgitated what I thought the teachers wanted to read. Aussies are tough, hard-working, unpretentious, brave, and just. They love freedom, sports, and the bush. But is there such a thing as "the Australian character"? There are, no doubt, traits that are more common in Australia than elsewhere, like wanting a Foster's, but there are no traits that all Australians have in common, so there are no specific traits a fictional character must have to be realistically Australian. An Aussie character walking up to a bar might order anything. There isn't even any personality that is found only in Australia. Goose from *Mad Max* falls neatly into the traditional stereotype of the Aussie "larrikin"—laid back, mischievous, and cheeky. But the same character could appear, more or less, as someone of any nationality. There are happy-go-lucky Germans, impish Iranians, and easy going, roguish Kenyans.

Perhaps Australian national character is something too subtle to be captured by strict requirements as to what each Aussie is like. Maybe it could be examined through a character study of a cross-section of Aussies. But deep attention to character isn't what the action-packed *Mad Max* saga is about. None of the characters are given much depth and most fall into simple roles—cop, civilian, berserker, survivor, and so forth. Director George Miller says of Max, "He's a timeless character, and he's no different really than a Japanese wandering Ronin, or the classic American western gunslinger, or a Scandinavian Viking warrior ... it's a common archetype."[1] In short, then, if we're looking for an Australian feel to a *Mad Max* film, I don't think we can find it in distinctly Aussie characters.

On the other hand, locations can definitely feel Australian or non-Australian, at least to those who know the difference, and here, the first three films feel more Australian than *Fury Road*. *Mad Max* was filmed around Melbourne, Victoria; *Mad Max 2* in the desert near Broken Hill, New South Wales; and *Mad Max 3*, the desert near Coober Pedy, South Australia. *Fury Road* was filmed in Africa, in Dorob National Park, Namibia, and in Cape Town, South Africa. The Furiosa prequel, to my delight, will be filmed in regional New South Wales.

Even more than Australian locations, Australian accents make a film feel Australian. If you've seen any of the *Mad Max* films dubbed with American accents to make them more accessible to Americans, you know what I mean. At that point, the film may as well be set in Texas, for all the Aussie feel it has.

Even in the case of accents, though, it isn't clear what should count as Australian. What we call "the Australian accent" has many influences, the most important of which are the accents of convicts and settlers from Britain, the source of the majority of immigrants from 1788 to the end of World War II. Even the famous Aussie greeting "g'day" is a contraction of the British greeting "good day." But Australia is home to many accents. Indigenous Australians predate the British by about 50,000 years and have numerous dialects, and since World War II, Australia has accepted immigrants from many nations. If Australian citizens speak with Aboriginal accents, and Greek accents, and Chinese accents, then aren't these accents all Australian accents? Of particular relevance here, some Australian citizens come from America or England and speak with American or English accents. Don't these American and English accents also count as genuine Australian accents then?

For the sake of convenience, I'm going to refer to the familiar "Australian accent," the one that's most common in Australia and almost only found there, as "the Australian accent." But that's a simplification to keep the discussion manageable, and it may turn out that what ends up as an "Australian feel" in terms of majority-Australian culture may leave out a lot of other Australian cultures. That noted, why might we think that it matters whether the *Mad Max* saga feels Australian?

Does the *Mad Max* Franchise Owe Something to Australians?

We might think that Australian flavor matters in the saga because of something owed to Australians. It might be argued that to the degree that the franchise is a product of Australian culture, Australians have a special claim to being served by it. After all, no work of art is ever the pure invention of the artist. Rather, the artist draws from the culture around them. The Australia we see in *Mad Max* is a more violent and chaotic version of the real Australia of 1979. The desensitization to violence it exhibits is an exaggeration of the desensitization to violence that Miller saw in contemporary Australian culture. The obsession with cars and dangerous driving we see throughout the film series is drawn from his experiences growing up. He states,

> [T]here's no question that *Mad Max* (1979) was influenced by my childhood in rural Queensland ... with a very intense car culture. I mean the main street of town and Saturday night were just the kids in the cars. By the time we were out of our teens, several of our peers had

already been killed or badly injured in car accidents. And there was just those long flat roads where there was no speed limit and people would just go.[2]

Prior to *Mad Max* in 1979, the "road movie," in which we follow travelers from location to location, was already a staple of Australian cinema, and the country had already produced two notable road movies about violent gangs in Peter Weir's *The Cars That Ate Paris* (1974) and Sandy Harbutt's *Stone* (1974). It might even be argued that the mobile gangs that ravage Max's world are drawn in part from the roving Australian "bushranger" gangs of the nineteenth century. Criminals led by the likes of John "Bold Jack" Donohoe (1806–1830), Frederick "Captain Thunderbolt" Ward (1835–1870), and the armor-clad Ned Kelly (1854–1880) would raid settlements and disappear back into the wilderness. Their deeds were recounted in popular literature, as in Thomas Alexander Browne's classic 1888 novel, *Robbery Under Arms*.

The view that a culture has a claim on franchises to which it has contributed ideas is most plausible in cases where, as in the case of the *Mad Max* saga, copyright law restricts people from using franchise characters or settings to tell their own stories. Aussies can't just go and make their own *Mad Max* films, not as commercial enterprises anyway. To be fair to Warner Bros., owner of the franchise, they've never discouraged fan films, and you'll find some short beauties on YouTube, such as *Renegade* (2012), *BBQ Roadkill* (2015) and *GoKart Paintball War* (2015). But fan films can't legally charge for their work, putting great limits on budgets. Any Aussie who wants to stage their own epic about Max having a rematch with Humungus, complete with professional grade acting and hordes of mohawked extras in buggies, has Buckley's chance, or as the Americans say, is shit out of luck. Philosophers such as P. J. Proudhon and Ruth Grant have argued that copyright is unjust because ideas are always drawn, at least in part, from the culture in which they arose.

One obvious problem for claiming the *Mad Max* franchise on behalf of Australian culture is that the saga owes such a debt to non-Australian culture. Miller was and is a lover of cinema from a variety of nations, with his work being particularly influenced by American film. Action cinema has been popular since the silent era. James Bond alone had already appeared in ten films by 1979. Automotive action films had been popular since the 1960s, with successful entries like *Bullitt* (1968), *Death Race 2000* (1975), and *Smokey and the Bandit*

(1977). Dark, gritty, violent films were already in vogue in the 1970s, exemplified by the likes of *The Wild Bunch* (1969), *Dirty Harry* (1971), and *The Texas Chainsaw Massacre* (1976). Even films about criminal motorcycle gangs had been a popular subgenre since the 1950s, ever since László Benedek's seminal *The Wild One* (1953). And, of course, films have been taking us to the apocalypse since the 1950s, in films like *War of the Worlds* (1953), *The Day of the Triffids* (1962), and *Planet of the Apes* (1968).

In making *Mad Max*, Miller saw himself as applying techniques developed by American filmmakers of the silent era. He states,

> So with the first *Mad Max* (1979) I basically wanted to make a silent movie. With sound.... And I was particularly struck by the films of Buster Keaton and Harold Lloyd and those—and those kind of very kinetic action montage movies that they made. And basically I saw the action movie, particularly the car action movie, as an extension of that.[3]

If we do decide that Aussies have a claim on the *Mad Max* franchise because of their cultural contribution, and that this claim implies that the *Mad Max* films should have an Aussie feel, then this has implications for other cultures and franchises. For instance, Marvel used Scandinavian mythology as inspiration for their superhero Thor, so perhaps Thor should clearly be culturally Scandinavian, maybe speaking with a Norwegian accent and loving soccer and black metal. Likewise, Marvel used African culture as inspiration for their fictional nation of Wakanda, so perhaps it's important that Wakandans be genuinely culturally African, rather than being culturally American with African window-dressing.

Is It Important for Australians to See Themselves Represented?

It's widely believed that it's important that people of diverse genders and ethnicities see prominent characters of their gender and ethnicity in film. Many think, for instance, that it's important that alongside films about white male heroes like Max, Luke Skywalker, and Harry Potter, there be films about female heroes like Furiosa, Rey Skywalker, and Wonder Woman, and about heroes of color like Black Panther, Blade, and Ms. Marvel. Comcast, the world's largest media company, prominently presents adequate representation of people of color as being a moral duty.[4] The Walt Disney Company, the second largest, takes a similarly prominent stand regarding representation of people of color and women.[5]

If it really is important that media portray characters of diverse genders and ethnicities, then perhaps it's also important that media portray characters of diverse cultures and nationalities. If so, maybe it matters how many prominent characters in major films are culturally Australian, or at least, have an Australian accent. All *Mad Max* films feature prominent characters with Aussie accents, but Aunty Entity, Furiosa, and Tom Hardy's Max are missed opportunities for more.

If it's important for Australians to see culturally Australian characters prominently featured in major films, then the same must be true for people of other nationalities. The three most populous nations, India at 1.429 billion, China at 1.426 billion, and the United States at 330 million, are served by thriving local film industries that heavily represent people of their nationality. But that only covers 40 percent of the world's population. The needs of 26 million Australians pales before the needs of 274 million Indonesians, 221 million Pakistanis, 213 million Brazilians, and the rest of the 8 billion humans on Earth. Just to complicate matters, even nations that are major film producers are, for the most part, culturally and ethnically diverse. This is certainly true of India, China and the United States! If it's important for people who are culturally Australian to see themselves prominently represented in film, what about the Zhuang Chinese, a cultural minority 18 million strong, or the 204 million Muslims living in majority-Hindu India?

Making Sense in a World Gone Mad

Perhaps it improves the *Mad Max* films as art for them to have an Australian feel. One reason we might think that it improves them as art is that it makes them more consistent. It makes sense for Australians to speak with Australian accents and for Australian locations to look like Australian locations.

Our earliest written philosophy of art comes from ancient Greece. The philosopher Aristotle (384–322 B.C.E.), in his book *Poetics*, describes what he thinks makes for good tragic theater. Since Greek theater was limited to comedy and tragedy, tragic theater is the closest they had to non-comic films, like the *Mad Max* saga. Aristotle stresses that characters and events in tragedy must be realistic. He writes,

> As in the structure of the plot, so too in the portraiture of character, the poet should always aim either at the necessary or the probable. Thus a person of a given character should speak or act in a given way, by the rule either of necessity or of probability; just as this event should follow that by necessary or probable sequence.[6]

In other words, events should unfold, and characters act, as they would have to in real life, or at least, as they probably would in real life. For example, when Bubba shoots Max in the knee with a shotgun in *Mad Max*, Max must, as a matter of necessity, suffer a wound and fall over. It would make no sense for him to just shrug it off, so it would make the film worse if he did. If Max were to suddenly decide to join a gang of highway predators, that wouldn't violate what's possible, but it would be so unlikely that it would make the film worse.

Applying this to the real films, it's impossible for Max to visit a place that looks like the Namibian desert, where we find him in *Fury Road*. On the other hand, it isn't impossible for Aunty Entity and Furiosa to have American accents and Max to have an English one. But is it improbable? Aunty Entity might have emigrated to Australia before the collapse and retained her American accent ever since. But Furiosa's American accent is very unlikely, since it's established that she grew up in the Green Place, in driving distance of Immortan Joe's citadel. Tom Hardy's English accent as Max is least pronounced, but highly improbable. This is the same bloke who used to be a cop on the highways of Victoria, chasing the "glory-roaders" in the days before the world fell apart.

It might be tempting to think that realism doesn't matter once a film series has begun to work by action-film logic. The original *Mad Max* wasn't a particularly realistic film, with villains tending toward the cartoonish, and each successive sequel has been more outlandish than the last. *Mad Max 2* saw warriors like Wez flip their way into battle, while the "feral kid" dispatched enemy adults with his sharp metal boomerang. In *Beyond Thunderdome*, Max could defeat multiple opponents at once, and by *Fury Road*, he was having to fend off acrobatic assailants on poles mounted on speeding cars. But Aristotle explicitly acknowledges that wondrous, improbable events, like divine prophecies, may rightly be included in a tragedy if they give the story more emotional power. These are still faults, since the story makes less sense because of them, but the cost of implausibility might be worth it. So Aristotle is in a position to acknowledge the importance of unlikely but thrilling action scenes, such as the speeding pole fights of *Fury Road*, while still insisting that the films should be as realistic as possible when doing so doesn't get in the way of the thrills.

Shouldn't Films Come in All Flavors?

Maybe it's artistically important for the *Mad Max* films to feel Australian even if it doesn't make them better as art. Perhaps it's important for *Mad Max* films to feel Australian just because it makes the films less like the majority of popular cinema. Many of my favorite films are set in the United States, but it's a joy to visit different locations, whether they be other times and nations, like the nineteenth-century China of Ang Lee's *Crouching Tiger, Hidden Dragon* (2000); other planets, as in the *Star Wars* saga (1977–); or other universes, as in Peter Jackson's *Lord of the Rings* films (2001–2003). If it's good for films to come in all flavors, wouldn't it be good for the *Mad Max* saga to have an Aussie flavor, tasting of the gritty red dust of an out-back highway?

Maybe, but judging by performance at the box office, the *Mad Max* saga's appeal hasn't been lessened by any decline in Australian feel. *Fury Road* grossed more internationally than any other installment and is the second-highest grossing Australian film of all time, after Peter Faiman's 1986 comedy *Crocodile Dundee*. Next highest grossing of the *Mad Max* films is *Mad Max*, followed by *Beyond Thunderdome*, with *The Road Warrior* in last place.[7]

Perhaps introducing more American elements has made the films more accessible to a wider audience! Surely it's a good thing, in itself, to make art more accessible. It's good for young American filmgoers to get to enjoy the thrill of a fine *Mad Max* film, watching characters like Max and Furiosa struggle for their humanity against a backdrop of flaming trucks and flying bodies. Perhaps the desire for more variety in film is just selfishness from old farts like me who have seen so many films that we yearn for something different.

I think that if we're going to insist that there's artistic value in diversity, we're going to either have to adopt a notion of artistic value that isn't grounded in appeal to audiences, or we're going to have to give special importance to lasting appeal. Sticking to a popular formula might be the best way to reliably please the largest audience, but it also makes films more forgettable, blurring into other films.

The more time that passes, the more entertainment there will be that the *Mad Max* films are competing with for our attention. When a film first hits the silver screen, it's mostly competing with other new releases. So, for example, when *Fury Road* was released to theaters, its top competition was from *Jurassic World*, *Star Wars: The Force Awakens*, and *Avengers: Age of Ultron*. In the long run, though, *Fury Road* will be competing with every film and TV show ever made. In that context, it's going to be a lot harder to stand out from the crowd.

Mad Max was released in 1979. Not many films from that long ago still have any cultural presence, but the *Mad Max* franchise has never been healthier. There are many things that make the *Mad Max* films stand out from the competition, but one of the things that has made them distinctive is their Australian feel. It may be that this distinct Australianness has been part of their long-term appeal. Only time will tell.

Everyone Should Have an Aussie Hero

Maybe it's good for the people of the world to see characters who feel Australian, to remind them that Australians are just as real as they are. Maybe it's a little harder to go to war with a people, and a little easier to sympathize with them in times of trouble, if you have practiced thinking about them as human individuals. If people identify with Aussies as their heroes, so much the better. Perhaps a non-Australian who identifies with Max and has walked down the scorching highway a few miles in his dusty boots will find it easier to put themselves in the shoes of other Aussies.

If you're an American, ask yourself honestly if it would have more emotional impact on you to hear of the deaths of 100,000 English people than it would to hear of the deaths of 100,000 Bangladeshis or Nigerians. If the deaths of English people would have more impact, might part of the explanation be that you are used to seeing and identifying with English characters in films like the James Bond films or TV shows like *Black Mirror* and *Doctor Who*? For that matter, if the deaths of 100,000 Australians would have more impact than the deaths of 100,000 Bangladeshis or Nigerians, might it have anything to do with Australians being more familiar to you through *Mad Max* films and other media?

To be fair, Aunty Entity, Furiosa, and Tom Hardy's Max are all Australian. (I don't know what Aunty Entity' passport says, but she's a permanent immigrant whether she intended to be or not.) They count as Australian characters who non-Australians might sympathize with. Maybe it's even easier for non-Australians to sympathize with them precisely because they don't have those funny Aussie accents! But maybe it's important that everyone is exposed to Aussies with all their idiosyncrasies and strange ways. Human differences are traditionally a barrier to sympathy, and people tend to side with those who are like them.

If it's good for the world's cinemagoers to see Australians so that they sympathize with Australians, then the same must go for peoples of all nations and cultures. And once again, the good of 26 million Aussies pales compared to the good of the 8 billion other humans on the planet. When was the last time you watched a film with a lead character who was clearly African? How about South American? Or from the Middle East? There are 195 nations in the world, and only 19 of them use English as their primary language, so unless you are watching a lot of dubbed or subtitled films, you probably aren't seeing much of a cross-section of humanity![8]

Where does this leave us? Not with a clear answer to the question of how important an Australian feel is to *Mad Max* films. But I've raised some issues to help you think the matter through for yourself. *Does* a *Mad Max* film need an Aussie feel? Or as long as the cars keep roaring down the tarmac, exploding into flames, does it not matter if the films have all the true-blue, fair dinkum, dinky-di Aussie authenticity of a toy koala manufactured in Taiwan? And if it does matter whether the *Mad Max* films feel Australian, what does that imply about how all the other cultures of the world should be represented on film?

Notes

1   Erin Free and Gill Pringle, "Rewind: The Making of *Mad Max: Fury Road*," *Filmink*, February 17, 2022, at https://www.filmink.com.au/rewind-the-making-of-mad-max-fury-road/.

2   "George Miller: Mad Max's Influences," National Film and Sound Archive of Australia (2006), at https://www.nfsa.gov.au/collection/curated/george-miller-mad-maxs-influences.

3   Ibid.

4 Comcast, "Our Commitment to Diversity and Inclusion," at https://cor
   porate.comcast.com/values/diversity-inclusion/ourcommitment (accessed
   July 4, 2022).
5 The Walt Disney Company, "World of Belonging," at https://impact.
   disney.com/diversity-inclusion/ (accessed July 4, 2022).
6 Aristotle, *Poetics*, (H.S Butcher, Trans.), ch. 15, at https://www.gutenberg.
   org/files/1974/1974-h/1974-h.htm#link2H_4_0017
7 "Box Office History for *Mad Max* Movies," *The Numbers*, at https://
   www.the-numbers.com/movies/franchise/Mad-Max#tab=summary
   (accessed July 4, 2022).
8 University of Sheffield, "List of Majority Native English Speaking
   Countries," at https://www.sheffield.ac.uk/international/english-speaking-
   countries (accessed July 4, 2022).

The Moral Aesthetics of Nature: Bioconservativism in *Mad Max*

David Koepsell

In the modern philosophy of technology, there is a sharp divide between those who believe that there is some inherent moral value to "nature" and those who think that no such moral value exists. The former are often called *bioconservatives* and the latter include many of those who consider themselves *transhumanists*.[1] Transhumanists include those who think that we can alter our bodies and nature as we please, and that either there is no moral reason to hold that which is "natural" in greater esteem than that which is artificial. We can modify ourselves, both individually and as a species, any way we please. Bioconservatives, for the most part, think that it is wrong to alter ourselves or other creatures. Nature has designed life for the best, and trying to change nature is a wrong in itself. The *Mad Max* movies focus largely on a world that has fallen apart due to human technology. Humans have destroyed nature, live among the ruins of their failed technologies, and scramble for mere existence often at the expense of humanity. The movies depict numerous characters who have altered their bodies, in many cases employing devices and prosthetics and mangling or altering their and others' bodies. The movies ultimately embrace bioconservatism as will be argued throughout this essay.

Man Versus Machine

In the very first scene of *Mad Max*, the Nightrider sets the stage, describing himself as a "fuel injected suicide-machine," "born with a steering wheel in his hand," as he escapes from the highway patrol in

Mad Max and Philosophy: Thinking Through the Wasteland, First Edition.
Edited by Matthew P. Meyer and David Koepsell.
© 2024 John Wiley & Sons, Inc. Published 2024 by John Wiley & Sons, Inc.

a stolen V8 Pursuit Special. He is announcing his "code 3" madness to someone named "Toecutter," who represents throughout the film the anarchic, motor-fueled evil that threatens society. The name speaks of mutilation of the human body. Cars roar and clutter the screen with the rolling Australian landscape, still green before the wars that set the backdrop for the other three *Mad Max* movies. The streets are littered already with the detritus of highway warfare between the Bronze and Toecutter's minions. The police operate out of a dilapidated hulking factory-like building, where the chief waters some incongruous, delicate plants among the concrete doom. The Nightrider dies in a horrific metal explosion, the victim of his embrace of machine over man, shortly after lamenting that "it's all gone." Max, who chased him to his death, is then seen with his family, tranquil, by the sea, amid vegetation and with his baby son and his wife, Jessie. The juxtaposition is clear: machines make madness, where nature provides peace of mind.

Meanwhile, in the bowels of the brick and concrete Halls of Justice, the chief has had constructed the last of the V8s to seduce Max to stay on the force. Max's embrace of his V8 Pursuit Special, as opposed to the life of wife, child, and rolling green seascape whom he was contemplating leaving the force to be nearer to, will prove the downfall of all he cares about, even as technology is set to wipe out human civilization. The choice is dichotomous. Either we embrace the rustic, the natural, the serene and undefiled world, or we embrace technology. Once synonymous with civilization, in the *Mad Max* films, technology is portrayed as the problem: the root of the apocalypse. This dichotomy is debated even now among philosophers in the context of advances in genetic engineering, nuclear power, nanotechnology, and space exploration, along with other technological advances that offer us greater control and dominance over nature. Bioconservatives, noting the availability and advance of technologies that can alter nature, argue that nature knows better. Attempts to improve on nature are misguided or even unethical. Most embrace modern medical technology to a point, but draw lines against the use of technology for human "enhancement," often citing "dignity" as the primary value that opposes too much interference by man with nature.

Even the modern medical technology that saves Goose in *Mad Max* is a potential threat to dignity. Burned beyond all recognition by Johnny the Boy, Goose is kept alive by a ventilator in a hospital bed, entirely technological in a sparse and sanitized hospital room. Max sees him and says, "That thing in there, that's not Goose," setting the tone for Miller's view of technology, prosthetics, and enhancements throughout the series. Where humanity becomes altered by machines and changes its nature, it ceases to be fully human. Philosophers like Nick Bostrom urge us to embrace a future where human and machine can better merge, where we are improved and made happier, more fit, and adaptable, even better than human (transhuman) through technologies. "Transhumanists, by contrast, see human and posthuman dignity as compatible and complementary. They insist that dignity, in its modern sense, consists in what we are and what we have the potential to become, not in our pedigree or our causal origin."[2] "Dignity" lies at the center of the debates between transhumanists and bioconservatives and derives from Immanuel Kant's view that "dignity" is at the heart of all ethical value and is something inherent and inviolable for all humans. In the bioconservatism of George Miller's *Mad Max* films, altering nature undermines dignity and takes away from our humanity.

An idyllic retreat to the farm up north, while Max considers leaving the force before he becomes a "terminal crazy" like the scags, underlines the allure and goodness of nature, until once again Toecutter's forces invade on their motorbikes, assault Jessie, and kill his son. Jessie is kept barely alive in the hospital, like Goose who "was not Goose" after his debilitating injuries. Max is spurred into a vengeful rage that will culminate in his own injury; shot in the kneecap by Johnny the Boy, he will be forever altered, his nature changed in a tangible way. For the rest of the series, driven mad by the collapse of his family and civilization, he will limp through the following three movies with a prosthesis. The leg brace he adopts, first as a wrench wrapped around his leg with a medical bandage, then as a metal brace that wraps around most of his left leg, symbolizes his fall. His humanity, his dignity, is forever altered. In consummating the chase with the murder of Johnny the Boy in a metallic explosion of machinery, Max denied dignity, he reaps the apocalyptic future where nature is rejected, destroyed. When next we see him in *The Road Warrior*, full leg brace in view, the narration explains that, to understand Max, we must go back to the time "when the world was powered by the black fuel, and the deserts sprouted great cities of pipe and steel." It's clear that *Mad Max* is forged by technology and its destruction of nature.

Broken Bodies in the Wasteland

By the time of *The Road Warrior*, nuclear war and environmental collapse have left Australia a vast Wasteland. The landscape is barren and the people are broken. Like Max, many have been ravaged by ongoing combat for resources, radioactive fallout, and the absence of any social infrastructure. The scags are outfitted with prosthetic weapons and armor, and the mechanic in the oil refinery community is disabled, hoisted by an engine lift to perform his work. Max walks among those who, broken by the wars and the Wasteland, are enhanced by machinery. Bodies are a patchwork, lives are expendable, and bits and pieces of humanity are lopped off and switched out for mechanical replacements. He rides into the compound in a semi-tractor truck labeled "Earth" to help save the refinery dwellers. In this community, a final bastion of civilization, people lead natural and healthy lives. They are strong and well-nourished, a stark contrast to the desperate struggle beyond their borders. Outside, the world is fraught with hardships and conflicts, as those less fortunate try to disrupt the peace of the community, to shatter their lives, and to seize their resources. They covet the community's aspirations of a better place under the sun—the Sunshine Coast. This dream destination is envisioned as a mythical beach, radiating an ethereal blue, teeming with life and promise. It is to this sanctuary they hope to flee, away from the chaos and toward a brighter future. This theme will echo through the series: vibrant green and blue life versus mechanical, broken, patchwork bodies and burnished chrome symbolizing death. In the Wasteland, enhancement means barely surviving—cheating death—as opposed to becoming better than human. The world of *Mad Max* is posthuman, as humanity is on its last, braced legs, and not the sort of utopian transhumanism imagined by some philosophers.

Transhumanists view the merging of technology and nature as morally good, and perhaps even necessary. Nick Bostrom argues against the bioconservative claims that enhancement undermines human dignity. Bostrom describes the role, rightly, of dignity in bioethics as deriving from Kant and playing a central role in the emergence of bioethics in the twentieth century by way of the Nuremburg Code, the result of the Doctors' Trial against Nazi brutality in medical experiments by people like Josef Mengele. He notes that the notion of Kantian dignity means something inherent in the nature of humankind and that it is used in different senses throughout debates about human enhancement and bioethics. Specifically, he views dignity as a form of excellence or as a superior attribute. Unsullied, untarnished, unmodified nature may have the same quality; the dignity of the Earth before humans and their machines (whom the refinery tribe described themselves as fleeing) is lost as the Wasteland expands.

Bostrom defines *enhancement* as "an intervention that improves the functioning of some subsystem of an organism beyond its reference state; or that creates an entirely new functioning or subsystem that the organism previously lacked."[3] He lists some elements of human dignity, including "composure, distinctness, being inaccessible to destructive or corruptive or subversive interference, self-contained serenity."[4] Finally, he notes that some enhancement can improve our dignity, while others may undermine it. In other words, not all enhancement is bad, and presumably not all nature is good. We use enhancements ethically when we, for instance, alter our bodies to improve some broken subsystem and return it to its original state, or for the disabled, to enable them to achieve better than nature (or life circumstances) afforded them.

Nature and Dignity in *Mad Max*

All of the *Mad Max* films have some special, untouched, natural place in which life thrives; the greens offset the stark, barren Wasteland; and technology is forgotten or irrelevant. In *Mad Max*, Max and Jessie flee to a relative's farm where greenery and forests abound along with the blue of the ocean. In *The Road Warrior*, the Sunshine Coast beckons the community at the refinery that Max helps out. The narrator at the end, a resident of that community, says they made it there and lived happily ever after. In *Beyond Thunderdome*, the Crack in the Earth, otherwise called *Planet Earth*, is inhabited by children who live with only the memory of technology in a green oasis in a canyon, with fresh water and abundant food and life. In *Fury Road*, the Green Place lives on in Furiosa's memory and hopes as she seeks to return to where she was taken from, a place that is alive, green with plants, better than the Wasteland, and free, unlike the Citadel.

These green places are all reminders of the world not only before the apocalypse, but before technology. Whereas the Wasteland is dominated by technology, it lacks life. Cars roar, and pig-shit electrical plants, Geiger counters, and mechanized, modified, and prosthetic-wearing broken humans abound. What the Wasteland

lacks is green, life, blue water ... the idyllic Eden from which humankind fell. The descriptions of the green places toward which many of
those who Max saves gravitate harken back to the biblical land of
milk and honey, the greenest place ever from which humans long
ago fell and to which they cannot return. It is also an ideal that lies
behind much of the theory of bioconservatives who reject people's
overmodification of bodies and land, who appeal to some inherent
dignity present in nature itself, and who view humans as harming
nature by changing it.

In 2008, Leon Kass, as a member of the President's Council on
Bioethics, warned:

> A new field of "transhumanist" science is rallying thought and research
> for wholesale redesign of human nature, employing genetic and neuro-
> logical engineering and man-machine hybrids, en route to what has
> been blithely called a "posthuman future." Neither the familiar princi-
> ples of contemporary bioethics—respect for persons, beneficence (or
> "non-maleficence"), and justice—nor our habitual concerns for safety,
> efficacy, autonomy, and equal access will enable us to assess the true
> promise and peril of the biotechnology revolution. Our hopes for self-
> improvement and our disquiet about a "posthuman" future are much
> more profound.[5]

Kass's argument takes an explicitly religious turn. After rejecting even
the Kantian view of dignity as being too narrowly focused on rights
and "personhood" (which he calls an *erroneous dualism*, because
humans and nature are monistic—literally one and the same), he
refers to the state of nature reclaimed by the Judeo-Christian God in
the Flood: "The Flood washes out human life in its natural (that is,
uncivilized) state, the remedy for which not nature but only reason
and law can provide. Immediately after the Flood, primordial law and
justice are instituted, and nascent civil society is founded."[6]

The nature upon which Kass's God founds humanity is coincident
with justice and the law. The primordial, green, and flourishing natural world that Noah and the ark alight upon is washed clean of the
civilization that displeased God, which was full of sin and human
hubris. The unspoiled natural world left after the Flood, fresh for
habitation and civilization anew, is good and just as well, unlike the
Wasteland that God flushed out. Bioconservatism and various types
of environmentalism tend to share a belief in the primacy of nature
and the corrupting role of humans' technologies in undermining both
human dignity and the dignity of nature itself.

In *Beyond Thunderdome*, the last of the world's greenery seems to be gone. Unlike in *The Road Warrior*, not even scrub seems to survive. The landscape is barren. Max, still hobbled by his kneecapping in *Mad Max*, no longer wears a full brace. Machinery, technology, and prosthetics enhancing broken bodies abound, however, in the nascent civilization of Bartertown. A saxophonist is blind; "The Collector" wears glasses with loupes; and most notably, Master Blaster is two people working together to enhance each other's shortcomings. Master is a dwarf who is smart enough to understand and run the electricity generation facility (running on pig shit) in Bartertown. Blaster is mentally challenged but enormous and strong; together they are intimidating enough to claim to run Bartertown, controlling the technologically necessary electricity for the town through their combined intelligence and strength. They are held together by a mechanical contraption that elevates Master above Blaster's head, while Blaster's face (which when later revealed shows he has Down syndrome) is covered by a metal helmet.

Bartertown's laws are harsh, the environment fully human-made, and its denizens posthuman amalgams of metal, leather, technology, and disease. In contrast, when Max is exiled from Bartertown (for refusing to kill Blaster as part of a deal with Aunty Entity) through the random justice of the Wheel, he lands unconscious in a lifeless desert, only to awaken in a virtual Eden. The verdant "Crack in the Earth" is inhabited by children who survived an airplane wreck sometime after the "pox-eclipse" as they call it in their "tell," their origin story about their literal fall in a QANTAS 747. They rescue Max in the hopes that he is their fabled and missing "Captain Walker," presumably the dead pilot of the plane that the children crash-landed in. The Crack in the Earth is also called simply "Planet Earth." Recall too the semi-trailer cab that was to be the salvation of the refinery tribe: labeled "Earth."

The children of Planet Earth want Max to take them to Tomorrow-Morrow Land, depicted in a postcard of pre-apocalypse Sydney, but Max tries to convince them that the world outside their oasis is dying, ruined, barren, and dangerous. It's much better to stay in their living shelter, green and fruitful, safe and secure. Nature is better than civilization. Bartertown, with its pig-shit electricity and commerce, still draws the kids, alerted now to its existence by Max's sudden appearance, and a group of them set out to explore it, thinking it to be the Tomorrow-Morrow Land of their tell. Naturally, Max follows to save them from the death and disappointment that awaits.

Leaving the oasis behind, the children journey across the barren Wasteland, drawn toward the illuminating lights of Bartertown. This radiant city appears as the Tomorrow-Morrow Land of their dreams. Led by Max, they undertake a mission to rescue Master, leading to a thrilling chase through the Wasteland. They ride a locomotive, with Max at the helm of a car adorned like a cow, as they are pursued by Aunty Entity's forces.

Beyond Thunderdome's closure follows the children's escape, aided by the aviator/gyro-pilot from *The Road Warrior* and, naturally, with Max's assistance. They take flight toward Tomorrow-Morrow Land, eventually settling in the abandoned skyscrapers of a bombed-out Sydney. Here, they share stories of their past experiences on Planet Earth.

But this new home is a far cry from paradise. They've left their innocence and the remnants of nature behind, trading them for the decaying signs of a once-thriving civilization. No longer in Bartertown, they find themselves in a place that's hardly better: fires raging in the deserted ruins of Sydney's cityscape with no greenery in sight.

The conditions in *Fury Road* show no improvement. Nature has further receded, leaving human bodies to bear the brunt of the Wasteland's harsh conditions. These bodies are crudely patched up using the remnants of deteriorating technology, a stark reminder of the bleak and technologically dominated landscape they now inhabit.

Each of Us in Our Own Way Was Broken

The world of *Fury Road*, including the Citadel, Bullet Town, and Gas Town, is inhabited by the broken. The only greenery is held high up in the Citadel, kept alive by human machines, slaves, War Boys, and Immortan Joe's tyrannical rule making children into cogs in a machine. It is a perversion of nature, its conquest by the mechanical. Somewhere over the horizon is a mythical "Green Place," a memory of a lush, verdant, livable Eden that inspires Furiosa's attempt to escape with Joe's five wives. Of all the *Mad Max* films, the dichotomy between natural bodies and broken, technologically enhanced or fixed bodies is starkest in *Fury Road*. The very first scene has Max once again with his V8 Pursuit Special, his leg brace still on him, the only animal a two-headed lizard that becomes his quick snack. Max is a shell of a man, held together with technology; he is quickly thrust into another nightmare when he is attacked by Joe's War Boys and taken prisoner.

We will see almost nothing "natural" in *Fury Road*. Instead, we witness the dehumanizing, unnatural use of humans as machine parts, interchangeable, degrading, and falling apart. Half-life War Boys whose skin is littered with symbols and tattoos, like machine parts, spray chrome onto their faces as they envision themselves going to Valhalla all shiny and chrome. Water is to be avoided and rationed, lest people become "addicted" to it. Almost everyone, except the wives at the Citadel, is somehow altered, wearing some prosthesis. This includes Immortan Joe and his mutant sons, who appear unable to even live without their prosthetics. In contrast, the five wives are decked in pure white and appear to be perfect physical specimens, not requiring special machinery, appurtenances, or prosthetics. Like Max, Furiosa wears a prosthetic. Hers is an arm, apparently robotic, as capable as any natural body part. But she dreams of returning to the Green Place of Many Mothers, apparently an unspoiled oasis like the Crack in the Earth, where she and the rest of her clan, the Vuvalini, lived free before she was apparently taken by Joe and turned into his Imperator.

Joe wears elaborate breathing gear and armor, apparently to protect his decaying body and enable him to breathe. His allies, the Bullet Farmer and the People Eater of Gas Town, are similarly broken and "enhanced." The People Eater wears a prosthetic nose and suffers from grotesque swelling of his feet, and the Bullet Farmer, bedecked in bullets and with bullets for teeth, wearing binocular goggles, and pursuing Furiosa, will go blind in the process before Max kills him. Max himself becomes a sort of prosthetic, a "Bloodbag" for Nux, one of Joe's half-life War Boys. The only greenery in the film is seen in the Citadel's vertical farm, mechanized, unnatural, isolated from whatever remains of nature. The Wasteland has never been more barren, and the attempt to find the Green Place is a failure. It no longer exists. In *Fury Road*, only the five wives, whom Max finds removing their chastity belts, bathing in their clean white dresses in apparently pure water as Furiosa attempts to break them free from Joe's grips, to take them back to the Green Place, embody nature in its unspoiled form. One is even pregnant, fertile, promising life.

Max and Furiosa's broken, modified, mechanized, and patched-together bodies stand in stark contrast to the wives whom they are trying to save. Nature, in the Wasteland, as represented by mechanized, unnatural, altered human bodies, is in full retreat in *Fury Road*. Nux has no clue even as to what a dead tree is; it is utterly foreign. The posthuman future is not an enhanced utopia of superhumans, but a world of broken, decaying bodies patched together with the remnants of a technological age that broke the world in the first place.

No Nature, No Dignity

Miller's films exhibit a form of bioconservatism, marked from the very start of the series by fear and the rejection of technology. Nature in some pristine state, green, untouched, and living is exalted, while machines are painted as the source and sign of humans' decay. Nature withers away throughout the four movies in the series so far. Human bodies become more and more altered, "enhanced," and appended to; prosthetics abound; and natural bodies become more scarce. The tension between bioconservatives like Kass and transhumanists like Bostrom is played out in the contrasts between protagonists and villains in *Mad Max*. Max, an antihero, is himself aided by machines and roams the Wasteland like the scags, motorized and driven by "guzzalene." The people he saves, however, exhibit few modifications and display healthy intact bodies unaided, generally, by mechanization. These protagonists live in green oases or seek them out; they are unbroken despite the pox-eclipse.

Nature is dignified. Altering nature diminishes dignity. But in the world of *Mad Max*, there is no going back. Antiheroes like Max and Furiosa must embrace their posthumanism, but transhumanism is a myth. Humanity will not be bettered, enhanced, or improved through the same means that the world was broken. Nature will not be reclaimed. This is the bioconservative lesson of *Mad Max*. Humanity's embrace of technology, their machines and enhancements, their attempts to reclaim civilization, are for naught. The Earth and humanity, spoiled permanently by oil, atomics, and machines, are lost in a Wasteland:

> Here is no water but only rock
> Rock and no water and the sandy road
> The road winding above among the mountains
> Which are mountains of rock without water
> —T. S. Eliot, *The Waste Land*[7]

It's a trope of fiction that villains and antiheroes are injured, modified, and enhanced by technology, whereas protagonists are healthy, fully-formed, and "natural." Ahab with his whale-bone leg in *Moby Dick*,

Lex Luthor in his robotic suit in *Superman*, Dennis Hopper's one-eyed Deacon in *Waterworld*, Jaws in the James Bond films *The Spy Who Loved Me* and *Moonraker*. This list is endless. We may well ask, as Bostrom rightly does: What entitles us to view some enhancement as acceptable, medically necessary, and not undermining dignity? Are our glasses unnatural? Hearing aids? Wheelchairs? Do they diminish us? Does the bioconservative rejection of enhancement imply that there is something wrong with the differently-abled?

Ultimately, it is the surviving, deformed son of Joe who lowers the bridge to open the Citadel to the masses, welcoming a new age of Vuvalini rule and the end of Joe's tyranny. Master too flees with the children of the Lost Tribe to help them when he escapes Bartertown. Max and Furiosa too are damaged bodily, depending on devices and prostheses to survive the Wasteland. While Miller seems bent toward the bioconservatism of Kass and his ilk, there is room for and redemption of those who commit themselves to saving what they can of nature even while they themselves are no longer fully natural. Survival in the Wasteland is barely possible, and posthumanity will only make it with a bit of a boost, some leather and metal, and a bit of guzzolene.

Notes

1 For the purposes of this chapter, Leon Kass and Nick Bostrom will be referenced as exemplars of each point of view. Leon Kass was the former head of the President's Council on Bioethics and is the author of such books as *Life, Liberty, and the Defense of Dignity: The Challenge for Bioethics* (New York: Encounter Books, 2002), and Nick Bostrom is a well-known defender of transhumanism, Oxford professor, and author of books and articles such as "In Defense of Posthuman Dignity," *Bioethics* 19.3 (2005), 202–214.

2 Bostrom, 213.

3 Leon R. Kass, "Defending Human Dignity," *Human Dignity and Bioethics* (2008), 180.

4 Ibid., 179.

5 Ibid., 302.

6 Ibid., 322–323.

7 T. S. Eliot, *The Waste Land* (New York: Harcourt, Brace, and World, 1964), 64.

Index

Mad Max and Philosophy: Thinking Through the Wasteland, First Edition.
Edited by Matthew P. Meyer and David Koepsell.
© 2024 John Wiley & Sons, Inc. Published 2024 by John Wiley & Sons, Inc.